EXCHANGE SYSTEMS IN PREHISTORY

STUDIES IN ARCHEOLOGY

Consulting Editor: Stuart Struever

Department of Anthropology
Northwestern University
Evanston, Illinois

EXCHANGE SYSTEMS IN PREHISTORY

EDITED BY

TIMOTHY K. EARLE

Department of Anthropology
University of California
Los Angeles, California

JONATHON E. ERICSON

Department of Anthropology and
Institute of Geophysics
   and Planetary Physics
University of California
Los Angeles, California

ACADEMIC PRESS   New York   San Francisco   London

A Subsidiary of Harcourt Brace Jovanovich, Publishers

ACADEMIC PRESS, INC.
111 Fifth Avenue, New York, New York 10003

United Kingdom Edition published by
ACADEMIC PRESS, INC. (LONDON) LTD.
24/28 Oval Road, London NW1

Library of Congress Cataloging in Publication Data

Main entry under title:

Exchange systems in prehistory.

    (Studies in archeology)
    Includes bibliographical references.
    1.   Commerce, Prehistoric—Addresses, essays,
lectures.   I.   Earle, Timothy.   II.   Ericson,
Jonathon.
GN799.C45E95   380.1'09'01   76-13933
ISBN 0—12—227650—7

Dedicated to our parents and friends

ELEANOR AND OSBORNE EARLE
ERL ERICSON, LAURA AND FRANK BURKE

CONTENTS

Chapter 7   Modeling Economic Exchange   127

Fred Plog

Chapter 8   A Network Model for the Analysis of Prehistoric Trade   141

Cynthia Irwin-Williams

Chapter 9   Identification of Prehistoric Intrasettlement Exchange   153

Glen D. DeGarmo

Chapter 10   Quarry Analysis at Bodie Hills, Mono County, California: A Case Study   171

Clay A. Singer and Jonathon E. Ericson

PART IV   THE USE OF ETHNOGRAPHY AND ETHNOHISTORY

Chapter 11   Aboriginal Economies in Stateless Societies   191

George Dalton

Chapter 12   A Reappraisal of Redistribution: Complex Hawaiian Chiefdoms   213

Timothy K. Earle

PART V   SYSTEMIC MODELS OF EXCHANGE

Chapter 13   The Simulation of a Linear Exchange System under Equilibrium Conditions   233

Henry Wright and Melinda Zeder

Chapter 14   The Ecological Evolution of Culture: The State as Predator in Succession Theory   255

Patricia L. Gall and Arthur A. Saxe

LIST OF CONTRIBUTORS

Numbers in parentheses indicate the pages on which the authors' contributions begin.

STUART AGRELL (35), Department of Mineralogy and Petrology, University of Cambridge, Cambridge, England

ARNOLD ASPINALL (35), School of Archaeological Sciences, University of Bradford, W. Yorkshire, England

GEORGE DALTON (191), Departments of Anthropology and Economics, Northwestern University, Evanston, Illinois

GLEN D. DEGARMO (153), Institute of Archaeology, University of California, Los Angeles, Los Angeles, California

TIMOTHY K. EARLE (3, 213), Department of Anthropology, University of California, Los Angeles, Los Angeles, California

JONATHON E. ERICSON* (3, 109, 171), Department of Anthropology and Institute of Geophysics and Planetary Physics, University of California, Los Angeles, Los Angeles, California

STUART FEATHER (35), School of Archaeological Sciences, University of Bradford, W. Yorkshire, England

PATRICIA L. GALL (255), 27 Banmoor Bld., Scarborough, Ontario, Canada

TREVOR GAZARD (35), ICI Management Services, Wilmslow, Cheshire, England

* Current address: Conservation Center, Los Angeles County Museum of Art, Los Angeles, California.

NORMAN HAMMOND (35), School of Archaeological Sciences, University of Bradford, W. Yorkshire, England

GARMAN HARBOTTLE (15), Department of Chemistry, Brookhaven National Laboratory, Upton, New York

JOHN HAZELDEN† (35), Soil Survey of England and Wales, England

FRED PLOG (127), Department of Anthropology, Arizona State University, Tempe, Arizona

COLIN RENFREW (71), Department of Archaeology, University of Southampton, Southampton, Hampshire, England

EDWARD V. SAYRE (15), Department of Chemistry, Brookhaven National Laboratory, Upton, New York

ARTHUR A. SAXE (255), Department of Sociology and Anthropology, Ohio University, Athens, Ohio

RAYMOND SIDRYS (91), Department of Anthropology, University of California, Los Angeles, Los Angeles, California

CLAY A. SINGER (171), Department of Anthropology, University of California, Los Angeles, Los Angeles, California

PHIL C. WEIGAND (15), Department of Anthropology, State University of New York at Stony Brook, Stony Brook, New York

CYNTHIA IRWIN-WILLIAMS (141), Department of Anthropology, Eastern New Mexico University, Portales, New Mexico

HENRY WRIGHT (233), Museum of Anthropology, University of Michigan, Ann Arbor, Michigan

MELINDA ZEDER (233), Museum of Anthropology, University of Michigan, Ann Arbor, Michigan

† Current address: 16 The Closes, High Street, Kidlington, Oxford, England.

ACKNOWLEDGMENTS

Preliminary versions of most of the papers in this volume were presented at two symposia on prehistoric exchange that were organized by Jonathon E. Ericson. The first symposium, entitled ''Prehistoric Raw Material Trade and Archaeo-economic Processes,'' was held at the 38th Annual Meeting of the Society for American Archaeology in San Francisco on May 3, 1973. Its chairman was Clement Meighan. The participants included Judith Connor and William Rathje; Jonathon E. Ericson; James Griffin; Clifford Hickey; Cynthia Irwin-Williams; Robert Jack; Raymond Sidrys; Phil C. Weigand, Garman Harbottle, and Edward K. Sayre. The symposium examined research strategies and techniques employed in studies of prehistoric exchange.

The second symposium entitled ''Archaeoeconomics—Part I: Goals, Theories, and Models'' was held at the 40th Annual Meeting of the Society for American Archaeology in Dallas, Texas on May 9, 1975. Its chairman was Timothy K. Earle. The participants included George Dalton, Timothy K. Earle, Jonathon E. Ericson, Patricia L. Gall, Norman Hammond, Fred Plog, Colin Renfrew, and Arthur A. Saxe. The symposium goal was to specify theories and models for studying prehistoric exchange.

The papers by Glen D. DeGarmo; Clay A. Singer and Jonathon E. Ericson; and Henry Wright and Melinda Zeder were added to treat those aspects of prehistoric exchange not considered in the original symposia. The introductory paper, ''Exchange Systems in Archaeological Perspective,'' was written by the editors especially for this volume.

The editors would like to thank the participants, contributors, and members of the Society for American Archaeology for their support in this undertaking. We would especially like to thank Jerome Kimberlin for taping of the first symposium and George Dalton for editorial advice.

Part I

Introduction

Chapter 1

EXCHANGE SYSTEMS
IN ARCHAEOLOGICAL PERSPECTIVE

TIMOTHY K. EARLE AND JONATHON E. ERICSON

I. INTRODUCTION

This volume suggests new methodological and theoretical perspectives on prehistoric exchange. As recent publications indicate (e.g., Sabloff and Lamberg-Karlovsky 1975; Wright 1974; Hodder 1974; Wilmsen 1972), exchange transactions have become the focus of extensive archaeological research (cf. Webb 1974). This interest in prehistoric exchange stems from two factors: (1) a recognition of exchange as central to maintenance and change in cultural systems, and (2) the technological innovations permitting detailed quantitative studies of exchange.

Anthropological studies of exchange have concentrated research on the interrelationships between material transactions and social organizations. Karl Polanyi (1957) was largely responsible for introducing to American anthropology a functionalist perspective that viewed exchange as the material base for society and as an organization "imbedded" in society's institutions. Polanyi's "substantivist" economics have been reinterpreted in an evolutionary framework by the "Michigan School" of ethnologists (Service

3

1962; Sahlins 1972) and archaeologists (Flannery 1972; Wilmsen 1972; Wright 1969; Webb 1974).

In addition to this interest in the social and evolutionary significance of exchange, archaeological methods have become increasingly sophisticated with the adoption of quantitative techniques to assess the evidence for prehistoric trade. In this volume, contributors draw on analytical chemistry, locational geography, ethnography and ethnohistory, computer simulation, and general systems theory. The intent of the papers is to provide a more accurate description of prehistoric exchange and a more thorough investigation of the importance of exchange in prehistory.

Four aspects of archaeological research on prehistoric exchange are covered here: (1) chemical characterization, (2) descriptive modeling, (3) application of ethnographic and ethnohistorical research, and (4) systemic modeling.

II. CHEMICAL CHARACTERIZATION OF RAW MATERIALS

With the diffusionist interests of early archaeologists, the aim of research on exchange was to document contact between two culture areas. The qualitative nature of this research resulted from the methods that relied on gross cultural, biological, and geological differences. For example, by first showing that a pottery style was "intrusive" to a site, it was often suggested that the pottery had been traded in from another area where it was "indigenous"; however, on stylistic criteria alone, it was hard to distinguish between "trade pieces" and "local copies." Additionally, the presence of faunal and botanical remains of species coming from remote areas or the presence of nonlocal raw materials were taken as evidence for exchange. Although such evidence is still employed, quantitative research based on the chemical characterization of raw materials is rapidly becoming the primary approach used to identify prehistoric exchange.

The recent developments in quantitative research have been made possible by scientific and technological innovations in the description of raw materials. Beginning with the work of Shepard (1956), who used petrographic analysis of ceramic tempers to distinguish different ceramic types, the chemical characterization of artifacts has rapidly expanded (cf. Hester and Heizer 1973). Several characterization techniques adopted from analytical chemistry include X-ray fluorescence, instrumental neutron activation, and optical spectroscopy. Each has selective advantages and disadvantages, which depend on cost, accuracy, precision, sample destruction, and radiation dangers. In addition, the development of sensitive solid state detectors, magnetic tape recorders, and high-speed computers has permitted the semiautomation of data collection and the analysis of the massive data set generated by such studies. Problems of resolving different sources remain, however, depending on the degree of homogeneity of the original raw material or on the alterations to the material done by the prehistoric craftsmen. Two general solutions that have been explored are (1) increasing the number of elements analyzed by using both short and long half-life nuclides in instrumental neutron activation analysis, and (2) using several multivariate statistical analyses in a stepwise procedure including use of the Mahalanobis distance, cluster analysis, and stepwise discriminate analysis.

In chemical characterization of any raw material, the basic procedures are ideally the same, regardless of the specific analytical techniques employed.

(1) A raw material and a region are selected for research.

(2) A geological survey is made of possible sources for the material and samples are taken from each source.

(3) The samples are chemically analyzed by neutron activation or other techniques and the resulting data is then statistically analyzed to determine the homogeneity (variance) and grouping (means) of sources. The goal of this procedure, "fingerprinting," is to isolate the characteristic element composition for each source.

(4) Artifactual material is collected from archaeological sites. Sampling procedure is critical here to ensure representativeness for the sites chosen within the region and for the collections within the sites.

(5) Finally, the artifactual material is chemically analyzed and the results are used to identify the specific sources for the artifacts.

Characterization studies are designed to yield information on the distribution of raw materials from identifiable sources. For each site analyzed, these procedures produce a typology of raw materials: so much from source A, so much from source B, etc.

The papers by Weigand, Harbottle, and Sayre (Chapter 2) and by Hammond et al. (Chapter 3) discuss two extensive characterization projects exemplifying these procedures. Weigand, Harbottle, and Sayre describe the many steps required in the sampling and resolution of turquoise sources and artifacts from Mesoamerica and the American Southwest, while the research by Hammond et al. on the characterization of Mesoamerican jade shows the problems involved in characterizing a material that in its finished artifact form is usually too precious for sampling or destructive analysis. Although the procedures of chemical characterization are seemingly routine, these two chapters illustrate the difficulties involved, especially when the individual sources themselves are heterogeneous.

III. DESCRIPTIVE MODELS OF EXCHANGE

Data derived from chemical characterizations are of two sorts: (1) the absolute or relative abundance of a source-specific material at each site, and

(2) the distribution of these sites through space and time. These data then form the basis for descriptive models of prehistoric exchange systems and their temporal development. There are four approaches to modeling presented in this volume: (1) two-dimensional, graphic analysis, (2) three-dimensional, synagraphic map analysis, (3) network analysis, and (4) nodal (site-specific) analysis. The procedures particularly applicable to archaeological data will now be summarized.

A. Graphic Analysis

The most direct way to model exchange is to represent the abundance of a raw material at a site as a function of the distance to the material's source. The general hypothesis is that the amount of interaction between a source and site is determined by the cost of transporting the raw material. Interaction is calculated as an absolute or relative measure of abundance of a source material at a site:

(1) *Absolute abundance*

$$I_{ij} = W_{ij}/N_i \tag{1}$$

where I_{ij} is the interaction between site i and source j, W_{ij} is the weight of raw material from source j estimated to be present at site i, and N_i is the population estimate for site i.

(2) *Relative abundance*

(a) $$I_{ij} = P_{ij} \tag{2}$$

where P_{ij} is the percentage either by weight or artifact count of raw material from source j in the total raw material class from site i.

(b) $$I_{ij} = R_{ij} \tag{3}$$

where R_{ij} is the ratio either by weight or artifact count of raw material from source j at site i to a second artifact class like pottery, which is produced commonly at the site. Additional measures are discussed by Hodder (1974). For any study, the choice between measures of interactions will be influenced by the purpose of the research and the quality of the available data (cf. Sidrys, Chapter 5; Ericson, Chapter 6). Since these measures are *not* comparable, a single format must be used consistently throughout a study.

Transportation cost for raw materials is most often measured by the straight-line distance from source to site. Other measures of transportation cost include estimates of work along probable transport routes, intermediary population, and social distance (cf. Ericson, Chapter 6).

In cases where sources of raw material are either very few or closely clustered in space, it may be sufficient to assume that material at a site came from the nearest source. This simplifying, conservative assumption allows the calculation of interaction and transportation costs *without* expensive characterization procedures (cf. Sidrys, Chapter 5). When making this assumption, however, certain types of information will necessarily be obscured, so the researcher must carefully weigh the effects.

The next step, following the calculation of interaction and transport cost, is to represent these two variables in a graphic format with the y-axis equal to interaction and the x-axis equal to transport cost (usually distance) (see Renfrew, Chapter 4; Sidrys, Chapter 5). Regression analysis of interaction against cost is then used to find the equation that best predicts the data array (Hodder 1974; Renfrew, Chapter 4). As Hodder (1974) shows, there are several families of curves that may be used to model the exchange system and compare it to the observed distribution of raw materials. Renfrew (Chapter 4) suggests that variability between regression curves is determined by variation in factors such as trade item (utilitarian versus primitive valuable), transportation type, and competitive resources. For example, Sidrys (Chapter 5) suggests that a change in the regression curves for obsidian from Classic to Postclassic Maya was a result of a change from land to sea transportation. Ideally, different types of exchange should be represented by different regression curves; however, Renfrew (Chapter 4) is careful to emphasize the many difficulties in recognizing such diacritic patterns.

All these regression curves may be classed within a general fall-off pattern. This is what Renfrew (Chapter 4) proposes as his Law of Monotonic Decrement—raw materials from a source become increasingly scarce as one moves away from the source. Deviations in this general "law" may then be used to identify the interaction of other critical variables. For example, Sidrys (Chapter 5) and Renfrew (Chapter 4) discuss how anomalies, unusually high densities of a raw material, may be used to identify central places or general hierarchical structure in settlement.

B. Synagraphic Map Analysis

Synagraphic map analysis is a means to represent a prehistoric exchange system as a contour map in two-dimensional space. For a region, the distribution of sites presents a data array such that, at each site, the abundance of a raw material from a given source is the operational measure of interaction between the site and source. This data array, when analyzed by the computer program SYMAP, produces a contour map showing the changes in a material's abundance through space.

Regionally, a simple fall-off model would produce a series of concentric bands surrounding a source, with each band having successively less of a given source's material as a function of distance from the source. By using synagraphic mapping, Ericson (Chapter 6) is able to demonstrate the existence of such banding in the distribution of obsidian within the exchange systems in California. However, this observed pattern does not correspond to the pattern of *circular* rings predicted by an ideal fall-off model. Rather, spatial irregularities in the patterns indicate the importance of other factors, including alternative raw materials, location of trails, and perhaps social boundaries. Synagraphic mapping is a simple and efficient technique to construct a first order approximation of spatial patterning of exchange based entirely on published data. Additionally, it may be used together with characterization studies to isolate specific exchange systems and to analyze anomalies.

C. Network Analysis

Network analysis is a descriptive technique used extensively by geographers and sociologists to analyze patterns of interaction. The papers by Plog (Chapter 7) and Irwin-Williams (Chapter 8) discuss the possible applications of network analysis to archaeological research on exchange. In this approach, sites are the nodes of the network and exchange linkages are the interactions. Of the analytical approaches discussed in this volume, network analysis is the most detailed and requires the most specific archaeological data. A primary difficulty is to demonstrate exchange interactions between sites rather than just between sites and sources. If it is possible to quantify interactions, network analysis becomes a powerful tool for analyzing exchange at various levels (see Irwin-Williams, Chapter 8). Plog (Chapter 7) shows the possibilities for studying many characteristics of exchange, such as symmetry and centrality, which have correlates in prehistoric social organization. Although the difficulties of a network approach should not be underestimated, the types of information produced are invaluable for detailed processual studies of prehistoric economies and societies.

D. Nodal Analysis

Most archaeological studies of exchange focus on measuring interaction between sites on either an interregional or regional scale. The possibilities of quantitative research on exchange in the context of single site analysis has received little attention, with two notable exceptions being the work of Wright (1972) and Cobean et al. (1971). Here, the papers by DeGarmo (Chapter 9) and Singer and Ericson (Chapter 10) propose interesting methodologies for analyzing exchange at the site level. DeGarmo, who is studying exchange within a small pueblo settlement, uses a three-step approach: (1) identification of intrasettlement groups, (2) analysis of production activities within each group, and (3) documentation of possible intergroup exchange. DeGarmo's procedures offer a means of studying the internal organization of a prehistoric community, but he is careful to emphasize the many difficulties of such small-scale analysis.

In a different vein, the paper by Singer and Ericson (Chapter 10) analyzes exchange by focusing on prehistoric production at a source. Where most researchers have concentrated on the distribution of raw materials through residential sites, Singer and Ericson suggest that, by analyzing production at a quarry site, it is possible to measure the total output produced for an exchange system. In this way, a diachronic study of quarry production is used to investigate fluctuations in the production of an exchange item through time.

IV. ETHNOGRAPHIC AND ETHNOHISTORICAL RESEARCH

Archaeologists read economic anthropology to learn about the material aspects of culture. Because British social anthropology and American substantivist economic anthropology emphasize the systematic relationships between social and economic organizations, the possibility of reconstructing social organization from the material remains of economic activities has great appeal to archaeologists. Numerous ethnographies contain detailed information on the types of goods exchanged and on the social context of exchange, such as trade partnerships, ceremonial exchange, and redistributive hierarchies.

The archaeologist, however, must be cautious in his use of ethnographic analogy. Because of rapid changes in economic organization following contact, traditional systems of exchange are now virtually extinct following colonialization and postcolonial development. As a result of imposed peace, decreased transportation cost, and the introduction of cash economies, the economic organizations now investigated by ethnographers are radically altered from the aboriginal forms. But there is a large body of early ethnographic descriptions and ethnohistorical data awaiting thorough analysis. The papers by Dalton (Chapter 11) and Earle (Chapter 12) illustrate the use of these data sources to investigate the functional and evolutionary significance of aboriginal exchange.

In this present volume, a distinction is drawn between nonhierarchical (egalitarian) societies and hierarchical (ranked and stratified) societies. Dalton's paper (Chapter 11) on nonhierarchical societies emphasizes the multiple "political," "social," and "economic" functions of exchange systems. He argues convincingly that in precolonial stateless societies, exchanges were *regional* and *interregional* networks critical for individual and group survival. These social networks were important for security in time of natural disaster and warfare and as a direct "economic" mechanism for obtaining localized raw materials or locally manufactured goods.

Dalton makes a distinction between primitive valuables and subsistence goods. It is the primitive valuables that are particularly important for the maintenance of the regional social networks. One of the most striking aspects of exchange in stateless society is its common ceremonial context (Webb 1974; Ford 1972). Ceremonial cycles are a social mechanism that acts to regularize and stabilize regional networks.

In hierarchical societies (Earle, Chapter 12), the dominant form of regional organization is the redistributive hierarchy, which may be understood as functioning in a manner very similar to the regional interpersonal networks and ceremonialism in nonhierarchical societies. The redistributive hierarchy functions as a security mechanism against natural and social disasters like droughts and warfare, and, to a lesser extent, it functions as a means of distributing raw materials and craft goods. Earle, however, argues that the primary function of redistribution in hierarchical societies is to mobilize goods to finance the elites. An evolutionary explanation of redistribution is, therefore, not related to simple environmental conditions but is intricately bound to the evolution of social stratification (cf. Gall and Saxe, Chapter 14).

Owing to the differences in interests and data between archaeologists and ethnographers, the archaeologist's search for ethnographic analogies is not a simple task. With a primary interest in social relations, ethnographers have focused their research on exchange events in which the rights and obligations of a social structure are given material form. To the archaeologist, however, these exchange events are in themselves almost transparent. Since exchange is the simple transfer of goods, it lacks the waste byproducts analyzable by archaeological methods (cf. Ericson, Chapter 6). Only the facilities associated with exchange, such as ceremonial areas and market places, are directly observable by the archaeologists, and such facilities are difficult to link to exchange or use to measure exchange quantitatively (large ceremonial areas, for example, cannot be equated necessarily with large exchange volume). Because archaeology analyzes the waste products of production and consumption, ethnographic descriptions of exchange events are often of limited use as explanatory models; therefore, the archaeologist, with his specific data requirements, is becoming increasingly involved in ethnographic reanalysis and ethnohistorical research.

V. SYSTEMIC MODELS OF EXCHANGE

Although still in its infancy, systemic modeling of exchange permits an examination of the dynamic properties of exchange systems. Two related questions are addressed by such models: (1) How do systems operate or function? and (2) Why do systems change or evolve? Wright and Zeder (Chapter 13) use computer simulations to investigate the regulatory mechanisms in decentralized, egalitarian exchange, while Gall and Saxe (Chapter

14) employ general systems theory from biological ecology to examine cultural change (evolution) as it relates to exchange.

Most ethnographers have concentrated on interpersonal and ceremonial aspects of exchange while ignoring the system-wide characteristics. Because ethnographic research is usually performed *within* a community, the regional and interregional organization has received little systematic comment (a notable exception being Malinowski 1922); therefore, the archaeologist, whose primary interests are in the broader spatial integration of exchange, finds most ethnography poorly suited to his needs. An alternative approach suggested by the Wright and Zeder paper (Chapter 13) is computer simulation. Working from ethnographic descriptions, these researchers have constructed a systemic model of the operation (dynamics) of egalitarian exchange and have studied the homeostatic properties of this model through simulation. Such models may then be tested with the archaeological data. At this point, archaeology ceases to be a simple, passive recipient from ethnography; rather, archaeology can take the lead in research on the regional and interregional operation of traditional exchange.

Regarding exchange from a different, evolutionary perspective, Gall and Saxe (Chapter 14) consider the evolution of exchange in the context of cultural adaptation to the ecosystem. Their intent is to build a general theory of change in complex, living systems that will permit an explanation of specific evolutionary changes in cultural systems. Again, this diachronic approach cannot rely on ethnographic analogies. The solution suggested by Gall and Saxe is the formulation of an overarching theory/model of change that can be operationalized for testing in the archaeological record.

VI. CONCLUSIONS

The papers in this volume discuss methods and theories designed to describe, analyze, and explain archaeological data on prehistoric exchange. Among the many approaches presented here, there emerge the outlines of an integrated research strategy for studies of prehistoric exchange that will include multiple stages from the accurate collection and analysis of data to cultural interpretations and hypothesis testing. This volume hopefully anticipates future research on prehistoric exchange that will yield further insight into the organization and evolution of social systems.

Acknowledgments

We would like to acknowledge the many ideas that we have gained from the contributors to this volume. We would especially like to thank George Dalton for his editorial comments on this introductory chapter.

References

Cobean, R., M. Coe, E. Perry, K. Turekian, and D. Kharkar
  1971   Obsidian trade at San Lorenzo Tenochtitlan, Mexico. *Science* **174**:666–671.
Flannery, K. V.
  1972   Evolutionary trends in social exchange and interaction. In *Social exchange and interaction*, edited by E. Wilmsen. *Museum of Anthropology, University of Michigan Anthropological Papers* **46**:129–135.
Ford, R. I.
  1972   Barter, gift, or violence: an analysis of Tewa intertribal exchange. In *Social exchange and interaction*, edited by E. Wilmsen. *Museum of Anthropology, University of Michigan Anthropological Papers* **46**:21–45.
Hester, R. T., and R. F. Heizer
  1973   *Bibliography of archaeology I: experimental, lithic technology and petrography*. Reading, Massachusetts: Addison-Wesley.
Hodder, I.
  1974   Regression analysis of some trade and marketing patterns. *World Archaeology* **6**:172–189.
Malinowski, B.
  1922   *Argonauts of the western Pacific*. London: Routledge.
Polanyi, K.
  1957   The economy as instituted process. In *Trade and market in the early empires*, edited by K. Polanyi, C. Arensberg, and H. Pearson. New York: Free Press.
Sabloff, J. A., and C. C. Lamberg-Karlovsky
  1975   *Ancient civilization and trade*. Albuquerque: University of New Mexico Press.
Sahlins, M. D.
  1972   *Stone age economics*. Chicago: Aldine.
Service, E. R.
  1962   *Primitive social organization: an evolutionary perspective*. New York: Random House.
Shepard, A. O.
  1956   *Ceramics for the archaeologist*. Washington, D.C.: Carnegie Institution.
Webb, M. C.
  1974   Exchange networks: prehistory. *Reviews in Anthropology*, pp. 357–383. Palo Alto, California: Annual Reviews.
Wilmsen, E. N.
  1972   Social exchange and interaction. *Museum of Anthropology, University of Michigan Anthropological Papers* **46**.
Wright, G. A.
  1969   Obsidian analysis and prehistoric Near Eastern trade: 7500–3500 B.C. *Museum of Anthropology, University of Michigan Anthropological Papers* **37**.
  1974   *Archaeology and trade*. Reading, Massachusetts: Addison-Wesley.
Wright, H. T.
  1972   A consideration of interregional exchange in greater Mesopotamia: 4000–3000 B.C. In *Social exchange and interaction*, edited by E. Wilmsen. *Museum of Anthropology, University of Michigan Anthropological Papers* **46**:95–105.

Part II

Chemical Characterization of Raw Material

Chapter 2

TURQUOISE SOURCES
AND SOURCE ANALYSIS:
MESOAMERICA AND
THE SOUTHWESTERN U.S.A.

PHIL C. WEIGAND, GARMAN HARBOTTLE,
AND EDWARD V. SAYRE

I. INTRODUCTION

As civilizations expand, the demand for rare resources becomes more systematized. Systematic demands are concomitant with systematic acquisition techniques. Mesoamerica, viewed as an ancient world system, certainly had such demands, and sections of the system must have become heavy consumers of exotic produce. Rare resource source areas eventually became so heavily exploited by Mesoamericans that province formation and/or colonization was finally reached in some cases. There were many types of rare resources for the Mesoamericans: important rare resources (those items necessary for primary exploitation of the environment) such as obsidian, and, later but of less importance, copper; and luxury rare resources (those items culturally identified as status markers) such as jade, "turquoises," gold, silver, feathers, etc. Rare resource provinces are those areas where these items, either important or luxury, in any combinations, are found naturally. We chose "turquoise" for analysis for several reasons: There were already many archaeological conclusions about turquoise trade that we could

15

test with the aid of a new analytical procedure; "turquoise" artifacts are relatively abundant in greater Mesoamerica; the location of "turquoise" sources was thought to have been well known; and "turquoise" was thought to be well understood chemically.

The term "turquoise" is used in two quite different manners: the narrow definition, which is a chemical one; and a broader designation, a cultural term embracing a whole range of blue and blue-green stones. The cultural term would include chemical turquoise but also certain types of malachites, azurites, chrysocollas, a green garnet, plus several other copper-bearing minerals not yet fully identified. The comparisons that are made, to be more fully explored below, are between source specimens and artifacts of good provenience. Matches between the trace element chemistry of a source sample and an artifact suggest trade between the source areas and the artifact find site. Matrix analysis could become an adjunct to artifact and mineral analysis as workshop scrap could thus be brought into the analytical picture. While we can infer trade of "turquoise" from source area to area of consumption, we cannot by this method date the objects or trace the exact routes over which the materials traveled. Another complication is that many objects described as "turquoise" in the archaeological literature are not analyzed in any further detail. This has required a great deal of work in museums and collections in order to validate the materials before any analysis can be considered.

As an analytical procedure we adopted neutron activation. We had already gained considerable experience in applying this technique to archaeological ceramics, ancient glass, and precious metals, and felt that we could most efficiently carry out multielement analyses in this way. In the course of these studies we also carried out a number of X-ray diffraction measurements leading to more positive identification of the various minerals investigated.

II. ARCHAEOLOGICAL BACKGROUND AND SOURCES[1]

Cultural use of turquoise begins to be extensive in the Classic Period of Mesoamerica, around 100 to 900 A.D. Although Vaillant (1935) reports one piece of "turquoise" during the Formative at El Arbolillo, systematic exploitation of "turquoises" does not appear to have equaled that of jade, for which early acquisition patterns are well documented, especially for the Olmec (Bernal 1969). Perhaps because of a developing appreciation of the minerals' qualities during the Formative, demand and exploitation of "turquoises" became systematized with the ascent of Teotihuacan in the Central Valley of Mexico (see Figure 1). The growth of the urban polity at

[1] Figure 1 presents a map of the source sites.

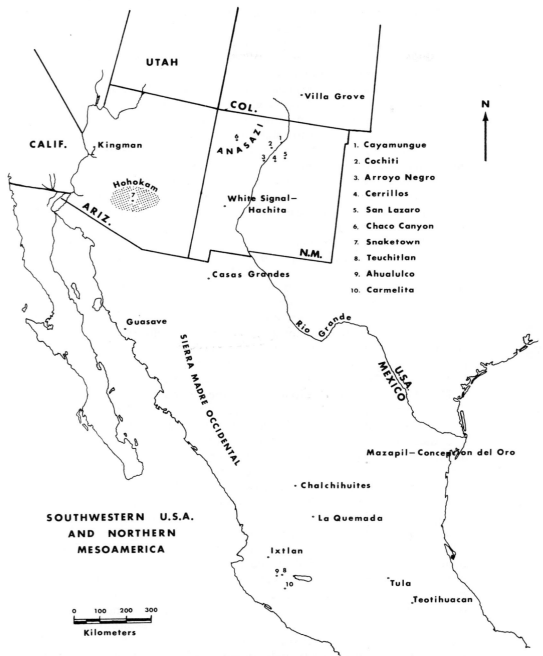

UTAH

·Villa Grove

COL.

CALIF.

Kingman

ANASAZI

6   1
2
3 4 5

1. Cayamungue
2. Cochiti
3. Arroyo Negro
4. Cerrillos
5. San Lazaro
6. Chaco Canyon
7. Snaketown
8. Teuchitlan
9. Ahualulco
10. Carmelita

N

Hohokam
7

ARIZ.

White Signal—
Hachita

N.M.

·Casas Grandes

Guasave

SIERRA MADRE OCCIDENTAL

Rio Grande

MEXICO

U.S.A.

Mazapil—Concepcion del Oro

·Chalchihuites

·La Quemada

SOUTHWESTERN   U.S.A.
AND   NORTHERN
MESOAMERICA

Ixtlan

9 8
10

·Tula

·Teotihuacan

0   100   200   300

Kilometers

Figure 1 Source sample localities and archaeological sites of Mesoamerica and the American Southwest. (Map by Emil Veakis.)

Teotihuacan and its numerous workshop zones for materials like obsidian (Millon 1973) suggest that this area might also have become a major consumer of "turquoises" and the intermediary in its exchange further south. As Teotihuacan became more complex, colonies apparently were established for the acquisition of rare resources. Institutional control over rare resource acquisition on a dependable basis may partially explain the political and economic success of Teotihuacan. Teotihuacan also became the manufacturing and redistribution center of its rare resource monopolies. The polity apparently was able to establish control over one important rare resource (obsidian) for much of Central Mexico and control over two luxury rare resources, cinnabar and "turquoise." These latter two commodities, as status markers, were also valuable for long distance trade.

Obsidian exploitation became a mainstay at Teotihuacan. The major quarry areas were located near Pachuca and Otumba (Spence 1967). Direct Teotihuacan control over these resource zones is strongly implied. The ability of Teotihuacan to exploit so thoroughly this important rare resource is seen as part of its economic predominance and physical growth during the Early Classic. Cinnabar (Secretaría del Patrimonio Nacional 1970) is another resource that was exploited in quantity by the polity at Teotihuacan. The major mines are in the Sierra de Queretaro. These are chambered, complex mines with adits and tunnels that extend hundreds of meters. This was such an extensive extractive complex that highly centralized control, in effect colonization, must have occurred. Cinnabar was processed for use as red paint, which decorated the pyramids and elegant residences at Teotihuacan, and hence can be viewed as a luxury rare resource.

The "turquoises" appear to have been the second Teotihuacan luxury rare resource enterprise. Colonization in the natural zones for these minerals began rather early in the Classic, though two discernible patterns for control over these resources are apparent. One pattern, that of colonial exploitation, appears to be present with the direct colonization by Teotihuacan into the Chalchihuites zone of Zacatecas. A complex culture, the Canutillo, was already in existence in this area before the period of Teotihuacan expansion occurred (Kelley 1971). This must indicate that Teotihuacan was trading for "turquoises" before that polity attempted to control the rare resource province more directly. About 350 A.D., with the onset of the Alta Vista phase at Chalchihuites, large scale mining operations began (Weigand 1968). Ceremonial elaboration, especially through the lavish use of sacrifice (Kelley, personal communication), occurs at this time. Since the Chalchihuites area is only marginally productive in terms of agriculture, such a concerted and dynamic Mesoamerican pattern so far removed from the Central Valley must be explained in terms of colonization. While the mines are definitely multipurpose (i.e., cinnabar, rhyolite, chert, weathered chert, red and yellow ochre), the major commodity undoubtedly was a range of blue-green mineral stones. The mines have combined shaft and adit entrances, often with air holes, and underground they can run for several kilometers. They were dug into semisorted alluvial gravels that became semiconsolidated in thick deposits along the hillocks flanking the mountains and overlooking small streams. Exploitation of these deposits was dangerous, but the millions of tons of spoil still visible today attest to the largest yet reported mining operation carried out in antiquity within the confines of Mesoamerica. Hammerstones and stone picks appear to be the main tools for loosening sections of the deposits of gravels, which then were pounded until freed from the binding sands and caliche. Preliminary sorting for the minerals was accomplished below the surface, and abandoned rooms were filled with the refuse. Final sorting was performed on the spoil piles outside. The ratio of recovery for minerals by this method must have been low (Weigand 1968). It was a pattern of labor-intensive mining that required a well organized system of direction and social control.

The Chalchihuites district, however, also served as an important staging area for mineral acquisition from other lands still further distant from the centers of consumption in Central Mesoamerica. The second pattern of acquisition, that of expeditionary exploitation, appears to be dominated also by Teotihuacan but only through the intermediary of the Chalchihuites outpost. Beginning about 350 A.D., chemical turquoise appears at Alta Vista phase sites in considerable quantities. Two areas serve as suppliers, each having particular characteristics. The bulk of the material may well be coming from Cerrillos, New Mexico (see below) when this area was still organized within the relatively simple forms of Basketmaker society. Since no complex society was in or very near the Cerrillos zone at this time, it is possible that expeditions formed in Mesoamerica were responsible for the early patterns of exploitation of chemical turquoise from that region. This observation is important, because it argues for a Mesoamerican exploitative presence in the American Southwest before the Pueblo cultural patterns emerge. As Kelley (1966) points out, expansion of Chalchihuites motifs occurs into the Hohokam of Southern Arizona (Gila Butte phase) beginning about 500 A.D. Expeditionary exploitation for rare resources into the Southwest, we believe, became a progressively stronger theme in the Post Classic, even to the point of colonization. At Cerrillos, no definite quarrying activity from this earliest period has yet been located (Helene Warren, personal communication). Weigand's survey of the Cerrillos area suggests that the more contemporary search for turquoise probably has obliterated almost all evidence of aboriginal activity except the most prominent, later mines such as Mount Chalchihuitl.

The second area that appears to have had an early expeditionary exploitative pattern, probably based upon Chalchihuites, is the Mazapil–Santa Rosa area near Concepción del Oro at the Coahuila–Zacatecas border within Mexico. First reported by the French in the 1860s (Di Peso, personal communication), then by Pogue (1915), the area has never been thoroughly examined despite the growing popularity of turquoise from this zone. In the early 1970s, Weigand examined areas where small, natural outcrops had been reported. He discovered many small quarries, some no larger than animal burrows, dug into the outcrops with crude hammerstones and picks. Aboriginal sherds were also located. As mentioned, this turquoise appears in small quantities in the artifact samples at Chalchihuites and, therefore, the exploitation must have begun in the Classic Period. The overt archaeological manifestations of culture in this zone were probably no more complex than those reported by MacNeish (1958) for the Sierra de Tamaulipas. The more subtle manifestations strongly suggest a Mesoamerican presence in this area never before considered as within the Mesoamerican world system, except as a reservoir of barbarians. Since, contrary to the Anasazi area of the American Southwest, this area has almost no agricultural potential, there were no groups capable of being Mesoamericanized. Exploitation had to remain expeditionary and thus fairly expensive over the long run. The minerals exploited besides chemical turquoise include an unusual green form of calcium aluminum garnet very similar to grossularite. High grade copper is also found within this area.

With the collapse of Teotihuacan sometime in the seventh or eighth century A.D., the particulars of all rare resource trade, including the "turquoises," must have been affected. The "turquoises" by then had been culturally implanted to such a degree that, as a desirable commodity, they outlasted the collapse of any one particular procurer. With the new carbon-14 dates from Alta Vista (Kelley, personal communication), it appears that the Chalchihuites zone may have maintained production for new markets to the south. With the growth and progressive Mesoamerican elaboration of the Hohokam, especially seen at Snaketown, turquoise from the American Southwest appears to have remained available for trade. Sigleo's work suggests that some of the chemical turquoise used by the Hohokam at Snaketown came from the Himalaya mine near Halloron springs (see Sigleo 1975, and our comments, below). Cerrillos, perhaps Kingman, Arizona (Johnston 1966), and other localities in the Southwest might also be viewed as probable quarrying sites during this period. Analysis of the artifacts from Cerro de Moctezuma, a fortified site that has a late component in the Chalchihuites sequence, suggests that the Cerrillos area remained in production. Great centers of consumption continued to flourish in Central Mexico, Cholula being a prime example; and turquoise may have begun to reach the Mayan area, where the trade was surely well established by the early Postclassic. While demand levels, routes, processing and manufacturing centers must have altered, the minerals themselves, plus the mineralogical provinces, continued to be exploited.

In addition, a new area appears to be gaining importance during the Late Classic within the Mesoamerican system. West Mexico is now regarded as the focus for the inception of copper working within Mesoamerica. There remains a question as to whether the techniques were imported from Peru (Mountjoy 1969) or whether they were indeed native. One zone in Western Mexico in particular, Ameca, abounds in native copper and copper ores, including malachites, azurites, and chrysocollas. Since worked native copper appears in some of the late shaft tombs (around 350–500 A.D.), it seems probable that the copper working techniques originated in this region. Along with the interest in native copper, "turquoises" began to be systematically exploited. As the large and complex centers of Ahualulco and Teuchitlán (Weigand 1974a, 1976) flourished, so did apparently the trade in these commodities. Weigand has surveyed the Sierra de Ameca for aboriginal quarrying activities. At the area near the Calabacillas mine, he discovered many quarry pits with associated hammerstones. Sherds suggest a Late Classic start for this mining tradition, but much activity appears to be Postclassic as well. Also, the question remains as to what exactly was being mined, though the spoil talus of the quarries suggest that exploitation was for the full range of blue-green stones (minus chemical turquoise) plus native copper. The Teuchitlán site is truly enormous, but the exotic ceremonial architecture suggests that it was only a strong regional complex. Hence, it is possible that long-distance trade for the commodities from this zone did not occur.

With the inception of the Postclassic period (around 900 A.D.) and the rise of the Toltec empire, demand for "turquoises" enters a new phase in the sense of both quantity and intensity of exploitation. Areas formerly exploited through expeditions now appear to be exploited more formally. The best-documented cases appear to be the Casas Grandes area of Chihuahua (Di Peso 1974) and the Chaco Canyon complex in New Mexico (Judd 1954). Casas Grandes appears to have been a successful competitor with the Hohokam, gradually replacing it as the emporium of the desert river valleys below the Mogollon Rim. The center appears to have had a composite and coastal orientation, and, with the appearance of a modified Puebla–Mixteca artistic style, the markets for the northern produce it handled probably were the west coast, Western Mesoamerica, and Mesoamerica south of the areas of Toltec control. Turquoise is found along the west coast at sites such as Guasave, Sinaloa (Ekholm 1942), and at centers of high culture, as in the case of the beautiful mosaics found at Zaachila, Oaxaca (which probably date from the Late Postclassic). Casas Grandes handled a range of commodities for trade into the Southwest (feathers and copper artifacts being prime examples) and from the Southwest down the coast into Mesoamerica (turquoise, cotton, and perhaps copper ores).

Chaco Canyon, on the other hand, appears to have had a different nature. The great pueblos of the canyon appear rather suddenly, with little forewarning in the relatively simple Pueblo II complex that preceded them. It is as if a population and cultural implosion had taken place. It seems no coincidence that the implosion occurred at the very time of the expansion of the Toltecs and the elaboration of a great fortification, supported by a road system to outlying villages, at La Quemada, Zacatecas. La Quemada lies on the route from the Central Valley of Mexico to the Chalchihuites zone, and hence is a probable southern emporium for an inland trade route that stretched into the Southwest. The architecture at La Quemada is strongly reminiscent of that of Chaco Canyon. Indeed, it appears that the two zones are connected in some fashion both culturally and economically. While Chaco Canyon does not have a turquoise source, it is relatively near several in the southwestern United States, Cerrillos, New Mexico being the most prominent. Processing appears to have been the major function of the artisans at Chaco Canyon, and tens of thousands of turquoise artifacts have been found in all stages of manufacture at Chaco Canyon settlements. If this was a manufacturing center for Mesoamerican trade, then it must have been directly involved in complex mineral extraction as well. Perhaps the great underground pit at Mount Chalchihuitl was begun during this period (Blake 1858). Hammerstones and fire appear to be the tools by which turquoise was forced from its hard rock deposits. The pueblos at Chaco Canyon seem too large to have been a simple response to internal conditions of growth. Indeed, some 200 miles of roadways built to surrounding village areas (Robert Lister, personal communication) appear to have functioned to help provision the canyon. Viewed in the composite, the pueblos give the appearance of a primitive city, imploded for extraction and manufacturing purposes for the Mesoamerican market. Whether this required the presence of Mesoamericans themselves, specifically Toltecs, is an old and heated argument; but if Chaco Canyon is viewed as a rare resource provincial participant in an ancient world system, the possibility of a direct Mesoamerican presence increases (Weigand 1974b). Hardly coincidentally, when the Toltec empire fell in the mid-twelfth century A.D., Chaco Canyon was abandoned by its original builders. Slightly later, it was abandoned altogether. For a brief period, the Anasazi appear to have participated very directly, as a rare resource province perhaps within the Toltec economic system, serving as an extraction and manufacturing base for turquoise along an inland trade route for the demands of the Mesoamerican civilization. Perhaps the fact that Casas Grandes survived the Toltec collapse indicates that it served more as a generalized emporium and was less specialized, hence less dependent, on a particular market than was Chaco Canyon. La Quemada also appears to have collapsed sometime during this period following the Toltec decline. The sub-Mesoamericans immediately to the west appear to have sacked the site (Weigand, in press).

During the late Postclassic, the Aztecs also were major ''turquoise'' consumers, and their art of inlay in stone, skulls, shields, etc., is relatively well known (cf. Carmichael 1970). The Aztecs, however, appear to have been blocked from direct access to the turquoise sources far north (the American Southwest in particular) by the rise of the Tarascans, a highly aggressive western neighbor based in Michoacan. Turquoise obviously continues to be traded south even after the dramatic collapse of Casas Grandes around 1350

A.D. (Di Peso 1974). With major Anasazi settlement now focused in the Rio Grande Valley of New Mexico, access to Cerrillos turquoise must have been relatively easy. Perhaps after the collapse of Casas Grandes, the Anasazi, along with their less organized southern neighbors, took the initiative in supplying turquoise to Mesoamerica. The Concepción del Oro region also appears to have been exploited during this period and even earlier in the Postclassic as the occurrence of Huastecan sherds attests.

Of course, many of the particulars of the summary presented above may need to be modified. Our basic model is that of a world system in which the rare resource provinces play an active role side by side with the more complex centers of civilization and consumption. In this view, cultures in rare resource areas have an economic/political interrelationship with zones that trade for their produce. Since economics and politics are seldom separable, there is an implicit direction required for such relationships—cultural influences from centers of consumption into rare resource zones and an ecological network of systematized demand, exploitation, trade, manufacture, distribution, and increased demand. It is our hope that by documenting the trade network for a high-demand status maker, we may shed light upon the dynamics of the economic systems of an early civilization.

We have mentioned source areas that display positive signs of aboriginal exploitation—Chalchihuites, Concepción del Oro (Santa Rosa, Cabrestante, Mazapil), Ameca (Calabacillas and Santa Clara), Cerrillos (Cerrillos Nos. 1, 2, and 3; Mount Chalchihuitl; Grand Central district; Tiro mine; and Ironstone), and Kingman being our best examples to date. Other samples come from general areas in which aboriginal exploitation has been mentioned, especially in southern Arizona, southern New Mexico, and the Californias. Still other samples come from outcrops at which, to date, no aboriginal activity has been suggested. We have analyzed these two latter categories of sources in order to establish as firm a control as possible over the chemistry of "turquoises," in order to understand the natural chemical ranges of the elements involved. To this end we have sampled Morenci, Gleason, Castle Dome, Los Caballeros, Copper Queen, Mineral Park, and Bisbee (Arizona); O'Neill, Cash Mine, Orogrande, Tyrone, Azure, and White Signal (New Mexico); Lone Mountain, Fox, Mine No. 8, Tonopah, and Searchlight (Nevada); Salida, King Mine, Cripple Creek, and Villa Grove (Colorado); Cananea (Sonora); Puente de Santa Rosa, Cerro de Frijolar, El Tempisque, Amparo, Laureles, Patahua, Arroyo Pozillos, Santa Catalina, Pueblo Viejo, Cristo Rey, and San Cristobal (Jalisco); Evans Mine (California); and La Bufa and Los Dolores (Zacatecas). Finally, for our general information, we included distant sources like Katanga (Africa), Timna (Israel), the Sinai Peninsula, Afghanistan, northeastern Iran, China, and northern Australia.

Many turquoise artifacts from sites, especially those from New Mexico and southern Arizona, are in the process of being analyzed, along with Caddoan materials. Materials from about 125 sites within the United States are to be examined. Mesoamerican sites to date are less numerous but include Potrero de Calichal, Potrero Abajo, Cerro de Moctezuma, El Vesuvio, La Quemada, and Potrero Nuevo (Zacatecas); Tula (Hidalgo), Ixtlán del Rio (Nayarit); Etzatlan, Teuchitlán, El Grillo, and Carmelita (Jalisco); Guasave (Sinaba); Zaachila and Tuxpan (Oaxaca); and Casas Grandes (Chihauhua). As the project begins to shift from source to more artifact analysis, Mesoamerican sites will be stressed.

In the section that follows we will outline our experimental and data-handling procedures and, in the final section, the results to date and our tentative conclusions. The work is still actively in progress, and we estimate that at least another two to three years will be required to obtain a fairly comprehensive picture of the Mesoamerican "turquoise" trade.

III. EXPERIMENTAL PROCEDURES

The chemical analysis of turquoise is but one aspect of a broader field: the analytical study of archaeological artifacts. Two other minerals of archaeological importance, obsidian and jade, are also treated in this volume. Many other chemical–archaeological studies have been reported (Harbottle, in press), but almost all fall under one of three headings: analysis for the sake of information on ancient economy (progressive debasement of silver coins, for example), on technology (bronze formulae, colorants in glass, types of solder used in joining parts of metal objects), or for determination of provenience. Of this third type, the great majority of published investigations concern ancient ceramics. To our knowledge, only one analytical study directed toward establishing the origin of turquoise artifacts has been published (Sigleo 1975), although one may find in the older literature several determinations of the chemical composition of gem turquoise (Pogue 1915).

Implicit in the idea of using chemical analysis to trace artifacts to their source, or to sort out and group together artifacts of unknown sources, is what may be termed the "Provenience Postulate," namely, that there exist differences in chemical composition between different natural sources that exceed, in some recognizable way, the differences observed within a given source. These "differences" are usually simply quantitative differences in concentration of chemical elements, but they can also be differences in relationship between concentrations of two or more elements, i.e., their correlation (Beiber et al., in press). One notes that, up to now, the Provenience Postulate has not been very often tested by the exhaustive sampling and analysis of materials from single sources. Perhaps such data can be found in the geochemical literature or developed in future archaeological studies.

To try to put what has been said above in more mathematical terms, consider an equation relating the different statistical variances that might be observed in the analysis of a large number of samples or artifacts related to a particular source:

$$S_T^2 = S_N^2 + S_S^2 + S_A^2 \qquad (1)$$

where S_T^2 is the total observed variance in the group analyses, S_N^2 is the "natural" variance in the source, S_S^2 and S_A^2 are the variances due to sampling and analytical error respectively. We see instinctively that, for the Provenience Postulate to be true, the sum of terms on the right side of Equation (1) must be small enough not to cause serious overlap in the distributions of elements that may be used to discriminate one source from another.

The problem, much simplified here, is actually concerned with overlap of distributions in multivariate space, and the occurrence of single and multiple correlation of elements within a source alters somewhat the mathematical–statistical and taxonomic procedures that must be employed (Bieber et al., in press). However, for the purposes of this paper, the simpler approach will suffice.

To analyze turquoise artifacts and mining sources, we have employed neutron activation. Mining samples, usually consisting of turquoise in veins in matrix, were drilled with tungsten carbid bits in such a way as to separate, as well as possible, the turquoise from the matrix. Where necessary, an additional clean-up was done by hand-picking under a low-power lens. Source samples of more massive green stones used culturally, such as chrysocolla, were handled in the same way, except that some of the hardest stones had to be drilled with a hollow-core diamond bit because of the tendency of tungsten carbide to chip, resulting in contamination of the sample, or because of inability of the ordinary drill to pentrate. The cores were then diamond-sawed transversely into disks of suitable size. In many cases, the matrix was sampled and analyzed, as well as the "green stone" it enclosed. Powder samples of about 40 mg were sealed into very pure quartz tubes and given two separate irradiations in the Brookhaven High Flux Beam Reactor at a flux of approximately 2×10^{14} n/cm^2 sec. The first of these, for about one minute, served to activate the elements copper, arsenic, manganese, sodium, and potassium. The radioisotope Indium-116ml was also occasionally seen, but its concentration could not be computed reliably. The second, later bombardment was of two to four hours duration and activated the elements barium, lanthanum, scandium, rubidium, cesium, europium, hafnium, thorium, chromium, iron, antimony, calcium, gold, silver, and zinc. Here again other elements such as uranium and tantalum were occassionally observed but not accurately determined routinely.

For standardization, samples of the six United States Geological Survey rock standards, DTS-1, PCC-1, AGV-1, BCR-1, G-2, and GSP-1 (Flanagan 1969; 1973), were included with each bombardment. This procedure, and the table of values of element concentrations employed, have been reported in Abascal, Harbottle, and Sayre (1974). Some of the later bombardments were calibrated by means of a secondary "in-house" standard consisting of an "Ohio Red Clay" (Stewart Clay Co., New York) that had been pelletized and fired to a hard china-like ceramic "pill" at 1100°C. The Ohio Red Clay pills were in turn standardized against the six U.S.G.S rocks. Arsenic, gold, silver, and zinc were calibrated by including separate standards for these elements prepared from standardized solutions pipetted by weight. For copper, the standard was a weighed piece of pure copper foil.

Turquoise (and other blue-green stone) artifacts that have been analyzed to date include beads, small amulets, mosaic blanks, and worked pieces such as debitage from workshops. These artifacts, which weighed in the range 5–500 mg, were routinely cleaned in acetone to remove surface dirt, museum numbers, etc., and then weighed and wrapped in pure aluminum foil for bombardment. Special care was taken to eliminate interference from some batches of aluminum foil wrapping that were not sufficiently pure. Standardization was exactly as above, except that heavier standards were employed where required for heavier artifacts. It was observed in the long bombardments (see above) that some turquoise artifacts changed color from blue to a rather unpleasant gray-green. The original color partially returned with time, on standing at room temperature; the process could be accelerated by annealing in an oven at 90–100°C. In a few percent of cases, the artifact was completely destroyed, i.e., reduced to a black powder, by the long bombardment. Short irradiations, however, did not visibly affect the color or consolidation of the specimens.

After bombardment, mining samples, artifacts, and standards were transferred to counting vials and counted with a Princeton Gammatech Ge–Li counter of about 35 cm³ and 1.8 keV (cobalt-60) resolution, coupled to an ND-2400 4096-channel analyzer with magtape readout and fed by an automatic sample-changer. The gamma spectra were processed at the BNL CDC-7600 computer by the program BRUTAL, the calibration constants calculated by the program ELCALC, and elementary concentrations by the program SMPCALC. These three programs, plus NADIST and AGCLUS mentioned below, are all in use at Brookhaven. Details can be supplied on request.

It should be noted that not all the elements could be measured in every sample and artifact. Those that could be easily determined in a majority of samples included arsenic, scandium, manganese, thorium, lanthanum, iron, cobalt, europium, antimony, zinc, and, of course, copper. The alkali elements sodium, potassium, rubidium, and cesium are generally present only at very low levels in the turquoise; the last three are difficult to measure accurately. Irradiated turquoise always shows a very intense phophorus-32 beta activity owing to the activation of the phosphorus that is a part of the turquoise formula $CuAl_6(PO_4)_4(OH)_8 \cdot 4H_2O$. This same formula yields an "ideal" copper content for "chemical turquoise" of 9.8% expressed as CuO. However, our measured values from turquoise mining sources and artifacts ranged from about 3 to 10% CuO.

Having obtained the analyses of mining source samples and artifacts, one now returns to the Provenience Postulate and attempts to see whether there are groups of samples, specifically those taken from a given mine or mining area, or of artifacts that show similar chemical composition and whether samples associated with different mines can be distinguished from one another. Unfortunately, the criteria for "chemical similarity" can only be defined pragmatically, for there is no a priori reason to weight one element more heavily than another as a discriminator of sources. Compared to obsidian, or ceramic clay sources, the turquoise mines we have investigated show relative standard deviations, that is, $(S_T^2)^{1/2}$ divided by concentration of the particular element, which are very large. And yet what is important is not that the relative standard deviation be small on some absolute basis, but that it be small compared to the source-to-source variation. This is the meaning of the Provenience Postulate. We shall have more to say to justify this postulate in the next section.

Our approach to this problem of numerical taxonomy has been essentially the same as that used with archaeological ceramic analysis (Bieber et al., in press). We define an n-dimensional Euclidean hyperspace, where n is the maximum number of elements that can be measured. Each coordinate $i (0 < i \leq n)$ represents the concentration of a particular element oxide. We actually employ log concentrations in order to give equal weight to the same fractional change in any element, regardless of its concentration range. A point in n-dimensional space, then, represents the complete analytical data for a given sample, and the task of looking for samples (source and/or artifact) having similar chemical compositions becomes simply a matter of looking for clusters of points in the hyperspace. To find such clusters or groups, one employs "cluster analysis" (Sneath and Sokal 1973), a rather well studied group of numerical procedures that allows one to discover the structure inherent in multivariate data set. Such procedures almost necessarily require high-speed computers.

To begin, we define the Euclidean Distance (*ED*) between two sample points A and B in the hyperspace described above as

$$ED_{A,B} = \left(\sum_{i=1}^{n} (A_i - B_i)^2 \right)^{1/2} \qquad (2)$$

Equation (2) is nothing more than an n-dimensional Pythagorean proposition. However, since, as we mentioned above, not all n elements are measurable in every sample, we must as a practical matter limit ourselves to terms $(A_i - B_i)$ where the concentration *is* known in both A and B, and then divide by m, the number of such terms, to obtain the "Mean Euclidean Distance" (*MED*):

$$MED_{A,B} = \left(\frac{1}{m} \sum_{i=1}^{n} (A_i - B_i)^2 \right)^{1/2} \qquad (3)$$

Other similarity and dissimilarity measures such as squared *MED*, mean character difference, correlation coefficient, etc. (Sneath and Sokal 1973) exist but have not been applied by us in the numerical taxonomy of turquoise. Sigleo (1975), in processing her data on turquoise beads found at Snaketown and mining sources, employed a similarity coefficient

$$d_{A,B} = \frac{1}{n} \sum_{i=1}^{n} R_i \qquad (4)$$

where R_i is the ratio of elementary concentrations. This similarity coefficient is closely related to the "mean character difference" based on logarithmic concentrations. It should be noted that distance measures like Equation (3) average over all concentrations and weights a given fractional variation equally in all elements, provided one uses log concentration coordinates.

By means of the program NADIST, we calculate from the input analytical data a "distance matrix" or table listing all the Mean Euclidean Distances of every sample from every other. For example, if there are P samples, there are $P(P - 1)/2$ such distances. In the program NADIST these distances are not only calculated, but can be written on a disk for future use, or sorted so that, for each sample, we have a table listing all other samples from the "nearest" (chemically most similar) to the "farthest" in order. Such sorted distance tables are useful if one is clustering a small matrix, let us say $P \approx 20$; for here visual examination may reveal the structure of the data, but for large matrices it is obvious that computer-based cluster analysis must be employed.

The topic of cluster analysis has an extensive literature and need not be considered here. Suffice it to say that the particular algorithm chosen operates on the distance matrix to link up, first, the two closest points, then to add to this initial cluster either another point, or to form another cluster of two, according to the value of a "clustering criterion," which is a function of the different distances involved. We employ the clustering program AGCLUS (Oliver, n.d.), which gives the scientist a choice of seven clustering criteria. The clustering then proceeds, adding either points or clusters at ever decreasing levels of similarity, until all the points are swept up into one large cluster. This is the so-called sequential, agglomerative, hierarchical, nonoverlapping or "SAHN" group of techniques. Others are discussed in the literature (Sneath and Sokal 1973).

Of the available algorithms, we have chosen the unweighted pair–group method using arithmetic averages. Here the clustering criterion is

$$d = \frac{1}{n_1 n_2} \sum d(a, b) \tag{5}$$

This is the method referred to as "average-linkage" clustering; n_1 and n_2 are the numbers of points in the first and second clusters to be linked, respectively, and the sum is over all possible distances made up of one point in each cluster, counting each distance once. The clustering is always such that the new link chosen is that which gives the smallest new value of d.

The results of a cluster analysis are generally presented in a tree-like diagram called a "dendrogram." A description of how these are formed is found in Sneath and Sokal (1973). The dendrogram ties together points representing individual samples and clusters of points at junctions whose distance from a reference axis or margin is the value of the clustering criterion, a function of the dissimilarity. Thus the dendrogram makes visible the "clustering" of the samples; groups and subgroups can be identified through their closeness of relationship. Although the dendrogram is convenient, it is not a perfect representation of the multivariate spatial relationships of the samples. These cannot be faithfully presented in two dimensions.

IV. RESULTS

Even a cursory examination of our analytical results reveals several tendencies that are highly significant to the ultimate success of this project. These tendencies will become more concrete when we describe, below, the results of the cluster analysis of our data. First, repetitive analyses of the *same* mining sample agree closely in most elements, as they must do if all is well. One of the interesting cases of nonagreement is the element gold, which may be easily measured in one, totally missing in the other, of a pair of analyses. Such behavior is presumably due to gold's occurrence as flecks of native metal in nature, with fortuitous presence in a small sample. Second, analyses of *different* samples drawn from the same mine show a considerably greater analytical variation than we have been accustomed to see in, for example, ceramic clays or obsidian. We have not, as yet, sampled any one turquoise mine sufficiently extensively to measure a set of natural variance [see Equation (1)] of the different elements determined. It is, however, quite clear that the percentage standard deviations may be quite large although still, in general, smaller than the district to district variations. An interesting exception to this trend may be the element copper itself, where the "mine" range of variation is relatively smaller. This observation could, however, be related to the fact that we are, after all, looking for "turquoise," which can be a specific chemical compound. Thus ancient man's act of esthetic choice may be partially determining the range of copper contents one finds. Third, we have observed in several cases a surprisingly large variation from mine to mine within a given mining district. Again, the small number of samples taken precludes any firm generalizations.

In a recent publication, Sigleo (1975) has reported the neutron activation analysis of turquoise beads from the site of Snaketown (Arizona) and the matching of their chemical compositions with those of the Himalaya mine in the southern corner of Nevada. In part her success could be attributed to the very unusual trace-element composition observed in these artifacts and in this mining source, namely, extrememly low concentration of elements such as cobalt and chromium, that made this compositional group stand out. On the basis of our own experience, we do not feel that in general such a good match can be anticipated, since, as mentioned above, the variation of concentrations of a given element within one mine may be quite large.

Instead of looking for exact match-ups of the type discovered by Sigleo, we prefer to think in terms of overall chemical similarity expressed as taxonomic distance between samples, to carry through our cluster analysis, and then to see whether the results make any geochemical and/or archaeological sense. And that is what we can now report, in a preliminary and necessarily incomplete way.

We have recently prepared a dissimilarity matrix, based on mean Euclidean distance [see above, Equation (3)], for 208 samples from mining sources and artifacts for which reasonably extensive analyses had been obtained. (We have analyzed an additional 700 samples for the short-bombardment elements only.) Log concentrations of up to 13 elements per sample were the input. The dissimilarity matrix, with 21,528 entries, was clustered by the BNL CDC-7600 computer using the program AGCLUS (see above) with average-linkage clustering. (The distance, or dissimilarity matrix required 12 seconds and the cluster analysis 5 seconds; the programs can take up to 500 samples.)

The resulting dendrogram, although too large to reproduce here, is extremely interesting to study in detail. As mentioned above, samples from individual mines tend to cluster, and in several cases these clusters form subclusters to a larger cluster representing a mining district. The mines of the Cerrillos district (our Cerrillos Nos. 1, 2, and 3, the Grand Central, O'Neill, and Mount Chalchihuitl), although clustering by mine, do not cluster by district. Mines like Villa Grove, Morenci, Los Caballeros, and White Signal are also well resolved, as are most of the Mexican mines studied (Concepción de Oro, Cerro de Frijolar, Pueblo Viejo, Chalchihuites, and Ameca). We do not feel at present very confident about the depth of our analytical data. We have sampled, though only lightly, a large number of mines. Clearly many more analyses are needed; that is why we emphasize the tentative nature of our present report.

One other salient point emerges before we get to the artifacts. By and large the Mexican and New Mexican mining sources separate cleanly from one another; this includes both turquoise and nonturquoise sources. If this separation via numerical taxonomy persists when the more extensive data are in hand, it will be an extremely useful tool to the archaeologist studying trade patterns with these stones.

When we examine the positions of the artifact analyses in the dendrogram, we immediately notice that the artifacts themselves form quite good clusters. For example, the large body of artifacts (some 80 in all) from El Vesuvio and Cerro de Moctezuma, two Chalchihuites culture sites located quite near each other and also near and presumably closely athwart the turquoise trade route from the southwestern United States into Mesoamerica (see Section II), fall into two large subclusters of one grand cluster. In fact, virtually all the El Vesuvio–Cerro de Moctezuma samples are accounted for in this way. Two mining sources appear in the midst of the El Vesuvio–Cerro de Moctezuma group of artifacts: One is the Cerrillos Number 1 and the other is the Azure mine (near Tyrone, New Mexico). Most significant is the presence of one southwestern United States artifact, close to the Cerrillos No. 1 sample, in this same group: turquoise from the Arroyo Negro site, about 14 miles southwest of Santa Fe, New Mexico on the Santa Fe River. Thus our results are certainly consistent with the idea that the 80-odd artifacts from the two Alta Vista sites originated from turquoise mined in New Mexico, perhaps at Cerrillos. We can go farther than that. On the basis of the analytical and X-ray diffraction data, we can fairly certainly *exclude all of the Mexican mines* thus far sampled as possible sources of the turquoise. We can likewise exclude southwestern mines like Villa Grove, Morenci, O'Neill, White Signal, etc. Three of the El Vesuvio artifacts do bear some resemblance to one of our samples from Mount Chalchihuitl, also in the Cerrillos district.

A second large group of artifacts, which is called the Cayamungue Cache (in the Rio Grande Valley a little north of Santa Fe, New Mexico), were analyzed for the short-bombardment elements copper, arsenic, manganese, sodium, and potassium, and were found to have such closely agreeing analyses that we can scarcely doubt that they all came from a single vein or perhaps a few large nuggets of turquoise. This close agreement persisted when eight of the cache samples were given the full analysis. On our dendrogram they form a tight group, and it is no great surprise that two samples from the Cerrillos No. 2 mine fall in the midst of this Cayamungue Cache group. After all, the Cerrillos district is just south of Sante Fe. By using our computer program ADCORR, we were able to scan the totality of our short-bombardment turquoise analyses to see whether any other samples or artifacts had high probability of belonging to the Cayamungue Cache group. Several turned out to be close: These were artifacts coming from Pueblo IV sites in the Rio Grande Valley in New Mexico such as Cochiti, Nambe, Kuawa, Paako, Amoxiumqua, and Los Aguajes. Additionally, two beads from a Caddoan burial near Spiro, Oklahoma fall in this group.

Finally, most significant to the future of our project, we observed an extremely close match between a third sample from Cerrillos No. 2 and a single artifact—a turquoise fragment from Chetro Ketl in Chaco Canyon. This observation is probably the first hard evidence supporting the often-made suggestion that Chaco Canyon was processing turquoise from the Cerrillos district (see Section II). It suggests to us that careful analysis of a range of material from Chaco Canyon might well provide us with a reference baseline for describing the chemical composition of the aboriginally mined Cerrillos turquoise, as distinct from the rare samples available today from these mines.

All these suggestions and speculations have come from a single dendrogram based on data that can hardly be called complete. Every effort is now being made to improve the coverage both in width and depth, and in the next phase of the project we intend to emphasize artifacts from sites ranging well into central Mesoamerica, as well as some mining sources in new areas. At this point we can say that the technique appears to be a workable one and that, given sufficient time, it can be made to yield much hard data on the central, complex question of preColumbian "turquoise" trade routes: the economy of a luxury rare resource.

Acknowledgments

We wish to thank Madi Palmer, Tina Ortiz, Marta Levitt, Barbara Timmerman, George Sloan, Dan Levi, Don Rice, and Howard Feinberg. Without the unstinting aid of these students, this work would not have been possible. We are grateful to J. Charles Kelley, David Snow, Richard Nelson, Helene Warren, Bertha Dutton, Charles Di Peso, Gloria Fenner, Gordon Ekholm, Richard Pailes, and Marnie Mandeville for their aid in lending the project items of turquoise. At Brookhaven, we wish to thank Elaine Rowland, and the crew of the HFBR, Mike McKenna and Tom Holmquist, for constant help. Finally, we thank Emil Veakis for preparing the map.

Research has been supported in part by the United States Energy Research and Development Administration, Mesoamerican Co-operative Research Fund (Southern Illinois University Museum), and the Research Foundation of the State University of New York. Paper number BNL-21051.

References

Abascal, M. R., G. Harbottle, and E. V. Sayre
  1974   Correlation between terra cotta figurines and pottery from the Valley of Mexico and source clays by activation analysis. In *Archaeological chemistry,* edited by C. W. Beck, pp. 81–99. Washington, D.C.: American Chemical Society.
Bernal, I.
  1969   *The Olmec world.* Berkeley and Los Angeles: University of California Press.
Bieber, A. M., D. W. Brooks, G. Harbottle, and E. W. Sayre
  n.d.   Application of multivariate techniques to analytical data on Aegean ceramics. *Archaeometry,* in press.
Blake, W.
  1958   The Chalchihuitl of the ancient Mexicans: its locality and association, and its identity with turquoise. *American Journal of Science* **25**: 227–232.

Carmichael, E.
1970 *Turquoise mosaics from Mexico*. London: British Museum.
Di Peso, C.
1974 *Casa Grandes, a fallen trading center of the Gran Chichimeca*. Dragoon, Arizona: Amerind Foundation, and Flagstaff, Arizona: Northland Press.
Ekholm, G. F.
1942 Excavations at Guasave, Sinaloa, Mexico. *American Museum of Natural History, Anthropological Papers* **38**(2).
Flanagan, F. J.
1969 U.S. Geological Survey Standards—II. First compilation of data for the new U.S. G.S rocks. *Geochimica et Cosmochimica Acta* **33**:81.
1973 1972 values for international geochemical reference samples. *Geochimica et Cosmochimica Acta* **37**:1189.
Harbottle, G.
n.d. Activation analysis in archaeology. In *Chemical Society, Specialist Periodical Report* **19,** in press.
Johnston, B.
1966 Ancient turquoise mine and tunnel with tools re-discovered near Kingman, Arizona. *Lapidary Journal,* May, 309–319.
Judd, N. M.
1954 The material culture of Pueblo Bonito. *Smithsonian Miscellaneous Collections,* Vol. 124.
Kelley, J. C.
1966 Mesoamerica and the Southwestern United States. *Handbook of Middle American Indians,* Vol. 4, pp. 94–110. Austin, Texas: University of Texas Press.
1971 Archaeology of the northern frontier: Zacatecas and Durango. *Handbook of Middle American Indians,* Vol. 11, part 2, pp. 768–801. Austin, Texas: University of Texas Press.
MacNeish, R. S.
1958 Preliminary archaeological investigations in the Sierra de Tamaulipas, Mexico, *Transactions of the American Philosophical Society* **48**(6).
Millon, R.
1973 *The Teotihuacan map*. Austin, Texas: University of Texas Press.
Mountjoy, J.
1969 On the origin of west Mexican metallurgy. *Mesoamerican Studies* **4**:26–42.
Oliver, D. C.
n.d. AGCLUS, an aggregative, hierarchical clustering program. Cambridge, Massachusetts: Department of Psychology and Social Relations, Harvard University.
Pogue, J. E.
1915 Turquois. *Memoirs of the National Academy of Sciences,* Vol XII, part II.
Secretaría del Patrimonio Nacional
1970 *Minería prehispanica en la Sierra de Queretaro*. Mexico City: Secretaría del Patrimonio Nacional.
Sigleo, A. C.
1975 Turquoise mine and artifact correlation for Snaketown site, Arizona. *Science* **189**:459–460.
Sneath, P. H., and I. Sokal
1973 *A numerical taxonomy: the principles and practices of numerical classification*. San Francisco: Freeman.
Spence, M.
1967 The obsidian industry of Teotihuacan. *American Antuqity* **32**:507–514.

Vaillant, G.
  1935   Excavations at El Arbolillo. *American Museum of Natural History, Anthropological Papers* **35**:137–279.
Weigand, P. C.
  1968   The mines and mining techniques of the Chalchihuites culture. *American Antiquity* **33**:45–61.
  1974a The Ahualulco site and the Shaft-Tomb Complex of the Etzatlan area. In *The archaeology of West Mexico,* edited by B. Bell, pp. 120–131. Ajijic, Mexico: West Mexican Society for Advanced Study.
  1974b The political and economic dynamics of the northern Mesoamerican frontier. Paper presented at the 73rd Annual Meeting of the American Anthropological Association, Mexico City.
  1976   Circular Ceremonial Structure Complexes in the Highlands of Western Mexico. In *Archaeological Frontiers: Papers on New World High Cultures in Honor of J. Charles Kelley,* edited by Robert B. Pickering, pp. 183–227. Carbondale, Illinois: University Museum Studies No. 4.
  n.d.   Possible references to La Quemada in Huichol mythology. *Ethnohistory,* in press.

Chapter 3

MAYA JADE:
SOURCE LOCATION AND ANALYSIS[1]

NORMAN HAMMOND, ARNOLD ASPINALL, STUART FEATHER,
JOHN HAZELDEN, TREVOR GAZARD, AND STUART AGRELL

I. INTRODUCTION

Jade was a mineral of peculiar significance for the peoples of pre-Columbian Mesoamerica and especially for the Maya, whose civilization

[1] This research was carried out while Hammond was Leverhulme Research Fellow in New World Archaeology at the Centre of Latin American Studies, Cambridge University, and Fellow of Fitzwilliam College, Cambridge, and Gazard was a member of King's College, Cambridge and the Cambridge University Statistical Laboratory. Hazelden's participation in the project was financed by a grant from the Wenner–Gren Foundation for Anthropological Research Inc. and Gazard's by a grant from Mrs. Gail Hollenbeck. Costs of irradiation were met by the Science Research Council. The authors express their individual and collective gratitude to these supporters and also to Jennifer M. Braithwaite, Dip. A. D. (Graphics), who drew the figures, and David L. Clarke, for good advice.

flourished in the Yucatan Peninsula through most of the first millennium A.D., to whom it was "the precious stone of grace, the first infinite grace," its green color making it an allegorical metaphor of young corn, of flowing water, of life itself (Thompson 1950). At the time of Conquest, jade was also important to the Aztecs, who distinguished several types (Foshag 1955): *chalchihuitl,* which may be translated "herb-green jewel-stone," referring to ordinary grades of jade; *quetzalitztli,* from the iridescent green tail-feathers of the quetzal, a bird of the Maya highlands, probably denoting the finest translucent emerald-green jade; *tlilayotic,* which may refer to the dark green chloromelanite or to omphacite; and *iztaccichalchihuitl,* white chalchihuitl, which is most likely to be albitic jadeite.

The first European contact with the material seems to have been in the sixteenth century, when it was noted as being used for axes in Amazonia, and the word itself is of Spanish etymology, from *piedra de ijada*—"colic stone"—because of its reputed medicinal properties among some groups of Indians in South America. The term "nephrite" for one mineralogical variety of jade was coined from this by Latinization.

After the exhaustion of the current stock of precious jades in Mesoamerica following the conquest, the stone ceased to have any importance for the Spaniards; and the jade best known to later European society was the nephrite from Sinkiang worked in China from Han times onwards and, latterly, Burmese jadeite. Mesoamerican jade sources have remained unworked and mainly unknown to the present day, although the rising value of the raw material is leading to renewed exploitation.

A. Prior Research

The symbolic complexity of jade and its iconography in Classic Maya civilization has been adumbrated by Thompson (1950), but the topic has not been exhaustively investigated. The technology of jade-working has been described from archaeological material by Kidder et al. (1946), Easby and Easby (1956), and Digby (1964), and further potential data are available in the Chinese accounts of how they cut and polished this hard and refractory mineral. Considerable research on the stylistic, iconographic, and other cultural attributes of Maya carved jades has been done by Proskouriakoff (1975) in her publication of those from the Cenote of Sacrifice at Chichen Itza, and more generally by Rands (1965) and Easby (1961, 1968). The nature of the mineral itself, first defined and classified by Damour (1846, 1863), has been investigated in Guatemala by Foshag (1954, 1957) working mainly from artifact collections but including by the time of publication the *in situ* jadeite outcrop at Manzanal (Foshag and Leslie 1955); and the geological work of McBirney (1963; McBirney et al. 1967) has enlarged our knowledge of the detailed structure of central Guatemala.

B. Jade in Maya Society:
Models and Possibilities

The social function of jade in Maya civilization has not been explicitly investigated and is indeed a focus of the research on which we make interim report here, but Rathje (1970) considered its diachronic distribution in burials as one of several classes of grave goods. Rathje suggested that "burials and associated artefacts were not randomly distributed, but varied in direct relation to other aspects of Classic Maya society;" that there was a change in emphasis through time during the Classic in the breadth of social base from which elite functionaries were recruited, this base narrowing upwards so that wealth became a prerequisite for office; and that "wealth" in life correlated with "wealth" in the form of grave goods. These postulates were tested against grave inventories from the rural settlement of Barton Ramie and the major ceremonial center of Uaxactun (although Rathje had larger samples to hand for his project as a whole). They indicated that, from the Early into the Late Classic, jade became progressively more restricted to the upper echelons of Maya society. In the Early Classic jade objects were found singly in house-platform burials at Barton Ramie and in greater quantity with interments in Temple A-V at Uaxactun; but by the Late Classic the house-mounds at Uaxactun had no jade with their burials, and its distribution among the interments in the A-V palace and temple suggested that only those at the summit of the social pyramid had access to it.

Even if we may take this as being characteristic of the social distribution of jade throughout the Maya lowlands, it is still a static picture of the final disposition of jades, telling us nothing of the origin of their raw material, the means by which it was disseminated, or at what point raw jade became an artifact. In addition, the data base has been biased by half a century of excavation in which emphasis has been heavily on the major ceremonial centers, on the large public buildings within them, and on the location of burials and caches within these. The bias is thus toward jades from ritual–élite contexts in important centers, with possible further biasing factors in the greater accessibility to the archaeologist of Late Classic structures and their ritual deposits, by superposition, and in the greater number of Late Classic structures overall. Although it would be possible to compile a gazetteer of the currently known distribution of jades in space and time in the Maya Area, and indeed such a compilation will form part of the second phase of this research project, these constraints would severely limit its utility as a data base for either synchronic or diachronic models. This depressing assessment is only fully true if we wish to examine the overall significance of jade in Maya society, however. If we restrict our terms of reference strictly to its function among the Maya elite resident in, or at least buried in, major ceremonial centers, then the sample is less skewed and our hopes of obtaining useful results correspondingly sanguine.

One possible method of examining the nature of jade exchange is to compare its patterns of procurement, transportation, and distribution with those for a nonsumptuary material of similarly limited source area; the material that springs to our minds, as it does to many Mesoamericanists these days, is obsidian. Obsidian has the advantage, from our point of view, of being restricted in origin to the southern sector of the Maya area, the Guatemalan highlands, and to southern Mexico. It was exploited as a cultural resource from the Early Preclassic onwards (Pires-Ferreira 1975), can be characterized as to source, and thus used to suggest prehistoric trade networks (Hammond 1972). It functioned as raw material for both "functional" and "useful" artifacts (Tourtellot and Sabloff 1972) and is ubiquitous in all types of archaeological deposit, from household midden through construction fill (Sidrys, Chapter 5) to burials and caches. Even restricting our interest in obsidian to that utilized in the major ceremonial precincts, we may argue that it retained this dual role: useful for adding fine detail to stone, stucco, and ceramic sculpture; functional as offertory.

Obsidian shares with jade the characteristics of being a scarce good in the Maya lowlands, with a single supply zone dominant in the volcanic highlands to the south, low in bulk per finished artifact, so that a great many could be transported together in either finished or potential, roughed-out form, and thus a relatively high value : bulk ratio. It seems likely that the same mechanism of transmission, by foot-porters or canoe, would have been used for both substances, and that they would even form mixed cargo. This model, of parallel behavior from source to destination area, is one that can be explicitly tested by source attribution of jade artifacts from firm archaeological contexts to give a pattern of synchronic and diachronic source exploitation and exchange spheres that can be compared with those postulated for coeval obsidian distributions. Alternatively, a common mechanism of transmission might cover entirely different behavior.

Comparative models might be elicited from the characterization studies recently carried out by Allen et al. (1975) on steatite, Sigleo (1975) and Weigand et al. (Chapter 2) on turquoise, Brooks et al. (1974) on Palestinian ceramics, and Hammond et al. (1975) and Rands et al. (in press) on Classic Maya ceramics, all involving the movement from source to destination of largely nonutilitarian goods, while an explanatory model for such exchange in Olmec times has been advanced by Flannery (1968).

A number of trading models have been described by Renfrew (1972; 1975; Chapter 4), ranging from down-the-line through prestation to freelance and directional commercial exchange, and our artifact analyses in progress should indicate whether any or perhaps several of these apply to the Maya jade/obsidian exchange networks, or whether more complex distance : interaction models of the kind adumbrated by Hodder (1974; Hodder and Orton, in press) should be utilized. The rarity and ambient symbolism of jade in the Maya lowlands may well have removed it from the quotidian cycles of free exchange of other goods, so that the exchange network was restricted in the personnel permitted to operate it, and thus in the localities where exchange could occur and perhaps also in the commodities that could be exchanged for jade. We have at present little notion what goods were exported from the lowlands to the highlands, although the possibilities were discussed by Thompson (1964) and a strong though limited case for cacao has been made by Hammond (1975b). The assumption is, however, that exchange did occur, if only because the regions of the jade and obsidian sources were occupied at the time of their exploitation; but the possibility of "one-ended exchange," the raw material lacking value at its source and acquiring it with workmanship and distance, should not be excluded without consideration. The lack of any evidence of great prosperity, such as should mark the controller of a scarce and desirable commodity, in either the middle Motagua valley or the obsidian-bearing highlands, does suggest that some restricted variety of exchange network operated.

Whatever the means of acquisition and transmission, on arrival at their lowland destinations jade and obsidian were treated in largely, though not completely, different ways. Much obsidian arrived as, or was struck into, prismatic blades that found their way into the equipment of practically every household in sites of all degrees of magnitude, from the isolated *plazuela* group through informal and formal clusters to the several levels of minor, major, regional, and metropolitan ceremonial centers (Hammond 1975a). These were used, reused, and eventually discarded in trash. Some blades in the pristine state were used directly as grave goods, while other obsidians became caches, or tooth inlays, ear spools, and eccentrics that finished their currency as accoutrements of the dead.

Jade seems, in the lowlands at least, not to have been utilized for even the technomic artifacts to which it was suited—polished axes, for example. Most of the axes that do exist are of chloromelanite rather than jadeite. The bulk of the jade was turned into jewelry, a wide range of plaques, pendants, ear spools, and beads; some was used for tooth inlay or mosaics, even the tiniest fragment of the rock being conserved, while occasionally an entire boulder would be turned into a single artifact, such as the nine-pound head of the Sun God from Altun Ha (Pendergast 1969). A higher proportion of jade than obsidian was used for ideotechnic objects, and more of those requiring a high degree of artistic skill were of jade; but within the realm of personal adornment the two materials overlapped in artifact form and function, though with what range of nuance remains unknown.

In general jade seems to have been less socially mobile than obsidian, a greater proportion of it remaining within the possession in death of individuals who, from the location and manner of their sepulture, we assign to the upper, ruling strata of Classic Maya society. Rathje (1970) has argued that even though the bulk of Early Classic jade grave goods were already found in the major ceremonial centers, the progressive restriction of jade to such interments, in his sample almost entirely of mature adult females, was an indication of reduced social mobility. It may be that the nature of jade

artifacts underwent concomitant change, from being simply jewelery, albeit
trailing clouds of iconography, into regalia, a prescribed set of adornments
with interdependent and meshing connotations, announcing rank as well as
wealth, power reified.

We may test these hypotheses on the role of jade in Classic Maya society,
and related models for the innovation of jade as a culturally important mineral in the Preclassic, by a combination of techniques: the distribution of jade
from different sources in space and through time can be documented by
elemental analysis; the breadth of the social spectrum with access to jade can
be ascertained from the context and association of jade artifacts and their
diachronic changes; and the iconic nature of jade itself may be explored by
examining the range of objects made from it, their styles and iconographic
attributes. These are interdependent studies. The identification of a stylistic
workshop at a site such as Altun Ha may denote an important node in the
exchange network, where a major stage in the processing of jade took place
before the products were passed on or distributed out from the "style
source"; a change in mineral source and workability of the jade may dictate a
shift in style, as from a bedrock source to one yielding only rounded pebbles
from alluvial deposits.

Much information on the spatial and temporal distribution of artifact jades
and their associations is already available scattered through the literature,
while Rathje and Proskouriakoff have made significant inroads into the problems of social context and style groupings, as noted above. This paper is an
initial report on attempts to synthesize these disparate categories of information into an overall consideration of the place of jade in Maya civilization,
which we have of necessity begun by trying to find and characterize the
mineral sources of Maya jade. "Of necessity" because it is less profitable,
and even misleading, to study the final destination pattern of a resource only,
than to consider this in relation to the range, distance, and accessibility of
sources and thus to the possible means by which source and destination were
linked. The means of communication and transportation of goods are archaeologically evanescent, more so even than the goods they carry. The
characterization of sources and the attribution to those sources of artifacts
form an important part of any research design for prehistoric trade because
they provide the hooks on which the carefully woven hammock of argument
for routes and methods of carriage may be hung. In the following sections the
mineralogy is the work of Agrell, subsuming Foshag's and Hazelden's data,
the activation analysis that of Aspinall and Feather, and the statistical
analysis that of Gazard.

C. Jade Mineralogy

Modern mineralogists recognize four forms of jade, three in the pyroxene
group and one in the amphibole group; the latter, nephrite, is not known to

be present in Mesoamerica. With some degree of over-simplification, the pyroxenes that may occur in jade can be considered as being composed of varying proportions of the following components: jadeite (Jd), $NaAlSi_2O_6$; diopside (Di), $CaMgSi_2O_6$; and aegirine (Aeg), $NaFe^{+3}Si_2O_6$. Jadeite is essentially $NaAlSi_2O_6$ with less than 20% Di + Aeg. Omphacite is a jadeite–diopside solid solution in the range Jd_{20-80} Di_{80-20} with up to 20% Aeg. Chloromelanite may be regarded as an iron-rich omphacite with more than 20% Aeg. The limiting compositions chosen by different mineralogists vary; thus there can be some ambiguity in nomenclature. The particular minerals found in any deposit are controled by the physico-chemical environment during the jade forming process.

All forms of jade and its associated minerals (Figure 1) can be identified from their physical properties—density, hardness, color, etc.—and, using relatively simple techniques, their optical properties may be determined utilizing a polarizing microscope. Reference may be made to the classic work of Foshag (1957). In the past 15 years nondestructive methods of chemical analysis have advanced considerably, and all the mineral analyses quoted were obtained using an energy dispersive electron microprobe utilizing the electronic equipment developed by Kandiah (1971) and the programs developed by Statham (n.d.). The method allows for the nondestructive analysis of selected small volumes (~ 2 mm³) of minerals as seen in polished thin sections or polished mounts of the sample chosen.

Jade occurs both within serpentine intrusions and their associated mafic rocks and at the external contacts of serpentines and mafic igneous or metamorphic country rocks. The common presence near serpentines of glaucophane schists, chlorite schists, and actinolite-zoisite schists in the neighborhood of jadeite deposits enables one to use these rocks as possible indicators of nearby jadeite rocks. Commonly, but not universally, the purer jade deposits are associated with albitic jadeite rocks and albitites. The latter are either peripheral to or vein the jade-rich portions of the deposit. Most jade deposits are markedly heterogeneous (cf. Dobretsov and Ponomareva 1968). Apart from small areas in Puebla and southern Chiapas, the main occurrence of serpentine is across central Guatemala (Figure 2) in the basins of the Motagua, Polochic–Lake Izabal, and the upper Chixoy, outcropping in the Sierra de las Minas, the Sierra de Santa Cruz, the Sierra de Chuacus, and the Altos Cuchumatanes. There is also a small area on the east coast of Guanaja in the Bay Islands, a continuation of the major occurrence eastwards (Foshag 1957).

Foshag's study of Guatemalan jade was based on archaeological material in the national museum and private collections, since no geological source of jadeite was known in Mesoamerica at the time. He identified seven types, of which numbers I, II, and V were found grading into one another on the same sample, as were IIIb and VI. Clearly he intended these as descriptive types only, without any suggestion that the surface characteristics were diagnostic

Name Composition	Variety	Crystal system, β angle, habit	Specific gravity, hardness, cleavage, twinning	Color (hand specimen) pleochroism	Optic orientation optic sign, 2V dispersion	Refractive indices, birefringence
Jadeite $NaAl[Si_2O_6]$		Monoclinic 106° prismatic, equant	3.35 6–6.5 {110}g. 92°	Colorless, pale green nonpleochroic	$\beta = y$, $\gamma \wedge z = 33°–40°$ $+, 70°$ $r > v$ moderate	α 1.654–1.658 γ 1.665–1.674 $\gamma - \alpha$ 0.011–0.016
	intermediate Jadeite— Diopside					
Diopside $CaMgSi_2O_6E$		Monoclinic 105° prismatic, equant	3.25 5.5–6.5 {110}g. 92°	Colorless, white, pale green, nonpleochroic	$\beta = y$, γ $z = 38°–42°$ $+, 50°–60°$	α 1.665–1 γ 1.695–1.18 $\gamma - \alpha$ 0.020–
Pyroxenes						
Omphacite $(Ca, Na)(Mg, Al > Fe^{+2}Fe^{+3})[Si_2O_6]$		Monoclinic 106° prismatic, equant	3.3 5.0–6.0 {110}g. 92°	Green pleochroism very weak α colorless γ very pale green	$\beta = y$, $\gamma \wedge z = 39°–42°$ $+, 65°–75°$ $r > v$ moderate	α 1.669–1.691 γ 1.693–1.718 $\gamma - \alpha$ 0.024–0.027
Chloromelanite $(Ca, Na)(Mg, Al > Fe^{+2}Fe^{+3})[Si_2O_6]$		Monoclinic 106° prismatic, equant	3.4 5.0–6.0 {110}g. 92°	Dark green pleochroism weak $\alpha\beta$ green γ yellow green	$\beta = y$, $\gamma \wedge z = 45°–65°$ $+, 75°–85°$ $r > v$ moderate	α 1.690–1.703 γ 1.715–1.734 $\gamma - \alpha$ 0.025–0.031
Hornblende $(Na, K)_{0-1}Ca_2(Mg, Fe^{+2}Fe^{+3}Al)_5[Si_{6-7}Al_{2-1}O_{22}](OH, F)_2$		Monoclinic 106° prismatic, acicular	3.2–3.5 5.0–6.0 {110}g. 56°	Green to dark green black pleochroism variable green, yellow-green blue green, brown	$\beta = y$, $\gamma \wedge z = 13°–34°$ $-, 75°–85°$	α 1.608–1.688 γ 1.630–1.704 $\gamma - \alpha$ 0.022–0.016
Actinolite $Ca_2(Mg, Fe^{+2})_5[Si_8O_{22}](OH, F)_2$	var: nephrite	Monoclinic 106° prismatic, acicular, felted, fibrous	3.0–3.5 5.0–6.0 {110}g. 56°	Green α pale yellow β yellow green γ green-green blue	$\beta = y$, $\gamma \wedge z = 10°–21°$ $-, 85°–65°$	α 1.620–1.647 γ 1.640–1.667 $\gamma - \alpha$ 0.020–
Amphiboles						
Glaucophane $Na_2Mg_3Al_2[Si_8O_{22}](OH)_2$		Monoclinic 105° prismatic, acicular	3.1–3.2 5.0–6.0 {110}g. 56°	Grey, lavender blue α colorless β lavender γ blue	$\beta = y$, $\gamma \wedge z = 4°–14°$ $-, 65°–85°$ $r < v$	α 1.595–1.637 γ 1.620–1.650 $\gamma - \alpha$ 0.025–0.013
Clinozoisite $Ca_2(Al > Fe^{+3}) \cdot Al_2O \cdot OH[Si_2O_7][SiO_4]$		Monoclinic 115°	3.30 6.5 {110}g. 6{110}f	White, pale green brown nonpleochroic	$\beta = y$, $\alpha \wedge z = 0°–7°$ $-, 65°–85°$ $r < v$	α 1.697–1.714 γ 1.702–1.729 $\gamma - \alpha$ 0.005–0.015

Mineral / Formula	Crystal system	SG / H / Cleavage	Colour / Pleochroism	Optical orientation	Refractive indices
Paragonite Na₂Al₄[Si₆Al₂O₂₀](OK, F)₄	Monoclinic, ps. hex. 95° micaceous, flakey	2.9 / 2.5 / {110} v.g.	colorless nonpleochroic	$\gamma = y$, $\beta \wedge x = \pm1°$, $-$, 0°–40°	α 1.564–1.580, γ 1.600–1.609, $\gamma - \alpha$ 0.036–0.029
Micas — Muscovite K₂Al₄[Si₆Al₂O₂₀](OH, F)₄	Monoclinic, ps. hex. 95° micaceous, flakey	2.8 / 2.5 / {110} v.g.	colorless very pale green, nonpleochroic	$\gamma = y$, $\beta \wedge x = 1°–3°$, $-$, 30°–47°	α 1.552–1.574, γ 1.587–1.616, $\gamma - \alpha$ 0.035–0.042
Chlorite (Mg, Al, Fe)₁₂[(SiAl)₈O₂₀](OH)₁₆	Monoclinic, ps. hex. 97° micaceous, flakey	2.6–3.0 / 2–3 / {001} v.g.	Green pleochroism weak colorless, pale green	$\beta = y$, α or $\gamma^- = x$, $+$, 20°–0°, $-$, 0°–20°	α 1.570–1.660, γ 1.570–1.670, $\gamma - \alpha$ 0.000–0.010
Talc Mg₆[Si₈O₂₀](OH)₄ var: steatite	Monoclinic, ps. hex. 100° micaceous, flakey, slippery massive talc rock	2.6–2.8 / 1 / {001} v.g.	Colorless, white, pale green, nonpleochroic	$\gamma = y$, $\beta^- = x$, $-$, 0°–30°	α 1.539–1.550, γ 1.589–1.600, $\gamma - \alpha$ 0.050–0.050
Serpentine Mg₆[Si₄O₁₀](OH)₈ var: chrysotile var: antigorite	Monoclinic, massif, smook fibrous flakey = antigorite	2.5–2.7 / 2.5 / fibrous {001} v.g.	white, gray, green nonpleochroic	Chrysatile Antigorite x 11 fiber $\gamma = y$ $\gamma = x$ $\alpha^- = x$, $-$, 37°–61°	Chrysotile α 1.532, γ 1.545, $\gamma - \alpha$ 0.013 Antigorite α 1.558, γ 1.562, $\gamma - \alpha$ 0.005
Sphene CaTi[SiO₄](O, OH, F)	Monoclinic 119° equant, prismatic	3.5 / 5–5.5 / {110} v.g.	Brown, yellow pleochroism weak pale yellows to browns	$\beta = y$, $\alpha \wedge 2 = 40°$, $+$, 17°–40°, $r > v$ strong, $+$, 77°	α 1.843–1.950, γ 1.943–2.110, $\gamma - \alpha$ 0.100–0.160
Albite NaAlSi₃O₈	Triclinic 116° prismatic, equant	2.63 / 6–6.5 / {001}g{010}f. lamellor (010) common	Colorless, white nonpleochroic	On (010)X' $\wedge$ (001) = 20°, On (001)X' $\wedge$ (010) = 3.5°	α 1.527–1.533, γ 1.537–1.543, $\gamma - \alpha$ 0.010–0.010
Quartz SiO₂ var: chalcedony var: jasper var: chrysoprase	Trigonal prismatic equant cryptocrystalline, fibrous banded	2.65 / 7 / no cleavage	Colorless, white, pale yellow nonpleochroic gray, brown, pale yellow, red, brown green, nonpleochroic	$+$, 0°	ω 1.544, ξ 1.553, $\omega - \xi$ 0.009

Figure 1 The characteristics of jade and its associated minerals. A range of physical properties (especially specific gravity and optics) is shown by many mineral species and groups. This reflects the range of chemical composition (atomic substitution) shown by the majority of minerals.

43

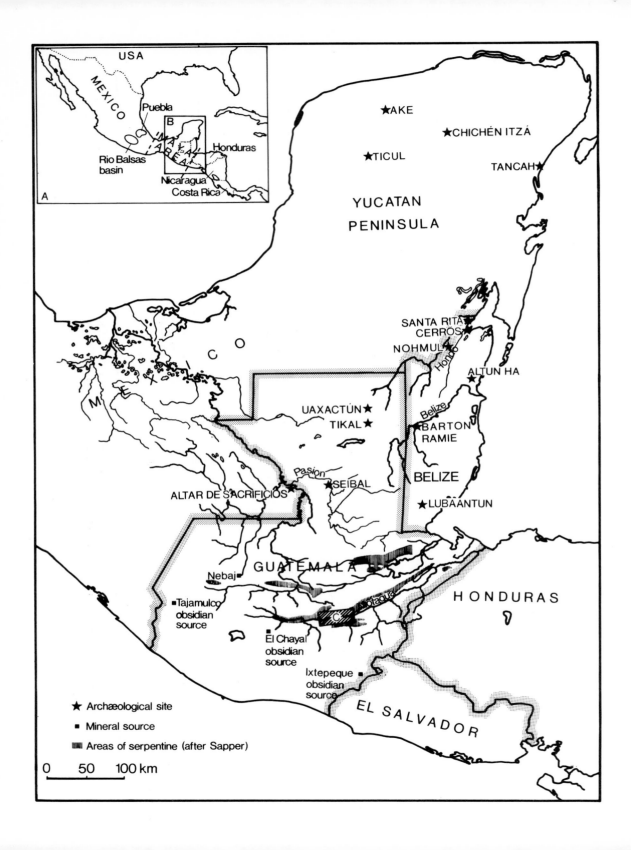

Inset A (top left):

USA

MEXICO

Puebla

Rio Balsas basin

Honduras

Nicaragua

Costa Rica

B

Main map labels:

★AKE

★CHICHÉN ITZÁ

★TICUL

TANCAH ★

YUCATAN PENINSULA

M E X I C O

SANTA RITA CERROS

NOHMUL

Hondo

ALTUN HA

UAXACTÚN ★

TIKAL ★

Belize

BARTON RAMIE

BELIZE

Pasion

●SEIBAL

ALTAR DE SACRIFICIOS

★LUBÄANTUN

GUATEMALA

Nebaj

■Tajamulco obsidian source

Motagua

HONDURAS

■El Chayal obsidian source

Ixtepeque obsidian source

EL SALVADOR

Legend:

★ Archæological site

■ Mineral source

▦ Areas of serpentine (after Sapper)

0   50   100 km

of origin. Type II was a gray-green or "blue" jadeite of the type used commonly in the Olmec period; type VII a chloromelanite, dark green to black and chemically distinct from jadeite; and type IV an albitic jadeite related to I, III, V, and VI.

This range of jade types and the often localized distribution of objects of any one type suggested that a number of geological sources were involved, though not necessarily at any great distance apart.

II. PRESENT RESEARCH

Since the first *in situ* jadeite source in the Maya area was reported in 1955 by Foshag and Leslie, it has been tacitly, and sometimes explicitly, assumed that all worked jades originated from this geological source. In 1971 a number of artifact jades from the Late Classic site of Lubaantun, Belize were compared in trace element composition with a specimen of Manzanal raw jade using X-ray fluorescence, and the immediate impression was that the compositions differed so widely that the Manzanal outcrop was an unlikely source for the Lubaantun jades. The possibility of other sources having existed and been exploited in the Classic period became palpable, and a further sample of more than 20 geological specimens from five localities in the Motagua valley was examined to determine whether intrasource homogeneity and intersource heterogeneity in trace element composition were sufficient to justify a further program of source sampling and artifact analysis[2] The results were sufficiently encouraging for us to do so, and the present project was established to locate, sample, and analyze as many mineralogical sources of jadeite in Mesoamerica as possible, to determine which of them were internally homogeneous and externally distinctive enough to be characterized, and therefore to have artifact jades assigned to source locations with some degree of probability.

A. 1973 Survey in the Motagua Valley

We began this work in 1973 with a survey by Hazelden and Hammond of a restricted area of the Sierra de las Minas on the north side of the Motagua valley, which included the Manzanal source, arguing that if jade sources

[2] The initial examination in 1971 was carried out at the University of East Anglia, Norwich, England by Dr. J. R. Cann and Mr. C. K. Winter of the School of Environmental Sciences who reported:

"It appears that there is some potential for the characterization of jade in Mesoamerica. Sources appear to be internally homogeneous and to some extent heterogeneity between sources has been demonstrated. More investigation of the distribution and character of sources in the region will be necessary before it can be certain how far this method of analysis will be successful in detail."

Figure 2 Map of the Maya area showing the location of serpentine belts and sites mentioned in the text, together with the location of the area shown in Figure 2, marked C.

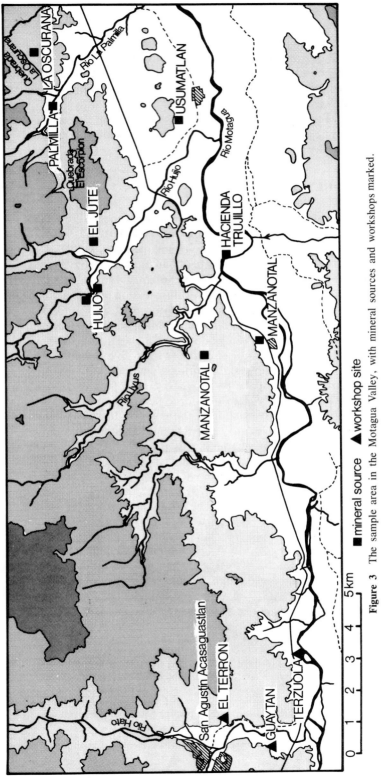

Figure 3 The sample area in the Motagua Valley, with mineral sources and workshops marked.

■ mineral source ▲ workshop site

within a small area could be successfully characterized then the same would probably apply to those over a wider area. The chosen area lay between the towns of Teculutan and San Cristobal Acasaguastlán (Figure 3). Within this area five major locations were noted where jadelike rock occurred, and a minimum of 20 samples were taken from four of them. The locations designated Manzanotal (the correct name for Foshag and Leslie's Manzanal outcrop), Usumatlan, and El Jute were *in situ* rock outcrops, while Palmilla and Huijo consisted of boulders, 0.20 m to 2.0 m in diameter, which had eroded from outcrops upstream, in the beds of the Rio Palmilla and Rio Huijo. Samples were also taken from an outcrop overlooking the Quebrada La Oscurana, which runs into the Rio Palmilla from the northeast.[3]

1. The *Manzanotal outcrop* (MA) lies some 2 km north of the *aldea* of the same name on the highway (CA9) to Puerto Barrios, at an elevation of about 450 m overlooking the Rio Uyus and the Quebrada Agua Shuca. A large number of albitite boulders, with the characteristic tough brown cortex, have eroded out from the hillside and lie on a small plateau. The "jade" inside (Figure 4b) is a pale mottled green of varying shades and differs from Foshag and Leslie's (1955) material.

McBirney et al. (1967:909) reported a jade boulder of an estimated 100 kg, with other similar material, on the line of the highway 100 m east of Manzanotal *aldea,* which on analysis proved to contain some 14% Na_2O, essentially comparable with Foshag's Manzanal material (Figure 4a). Another such boulder was sampled in the same locality by Shook (personal communication, 1975), and three chips from it submitted for analysis; this second, nonbedrock, occurrence of jadeite is coded MN in the analyses.

2. The *El Jute outcrop* (JU) is about 1 km southeast of the *pueblo* of that name on the hill above, at an elevation of about 500 m. The beds seem to be outcropping almost horizontally, at four distinct levels, each of which was sampled separately ($n = 5$) as well as a general collection of 20 samples from the source as a whole. The rock is of a distinctive apple-green color with brown mottling and a fibrous rather than crystalline appearance, but it takes a high polish.

3. The *Usumatlan outcrop* (US) lies 8 km almost due east of the Manzanotal outcrop, on a south-facing hillside overlooking the *pueblo* of Usumatlan at just over 300 m elevation. At the source is a hollow 3 m deep and a 5 m in diameter with a mound of weathered backdirt beside it; the

[3] The Quebrada La Oscurana samples were collected by Mr. Charles Farrinton of Antigua, Guatemala and sent for analysis by Mr. Edwin M. Shook, who also collected the El Terron workshop material and the MN source samples. We acknowledge with gratitutde the encouragement and assistance that Shook has given us.

It is perhaps worth reiterating here that the possible jade source in the Maya Mountains suggested by Thompson (1964) on the basis of the 1886 survey notes of C. Wilson has been demonstrated by both Hazelden (in Hammond 1970:222) and Bateson and Hill (personal communication, 1970) not to exist, on the basis of the nonultramafic geology of the region.

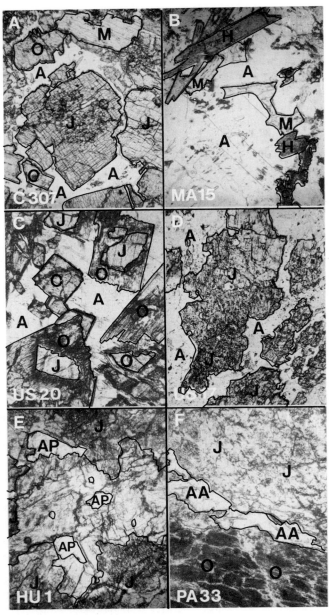

Figure 4 Jadeite-bearing rocks from the sample area: (a) Jadeite (J), albite (A), rock with subordinate omphacite (O), and white mica (M) from Manzanotal (McBirney C307). (b) Albitite with albite (A), horblende (H), clinozoisite (C), and muscovite (M) from Manzanotal (Hammond and Hazelden MA15). (c) Jadeite (J), with overgrowths of iron-poor omphacite (O) set in albite (A); O = Foshag's ''jadeite-diopside.'' From Usumatlan (Hammond and Hazelden

hollow is well silted up and clearly not of recent date, and its proximity to the mineral outcrop suggests that it was an opencast mine for extracting jade boulders. The lack of postconquest exploitation of Mesoamerican jade would intimate that it is of pre-Columbian date and the first aboriginal jade mine to be discovered; it would clearly repay excavation. The jade from the Usumatlan outcrop (Figure 4c and d) is a pale mottled green similar in appearance to that from Manzanotal.

4. The boulders in the bed of the *Rio La Palmilla* (PA) above Pueblo Nuevo now lie at just below 300 m elevation, while the hills around rise to over 1000 m; the Quebrada El Escorpion cutting back into the Cerro Joya Grande to the west might be the source of the boulders.[4] The Palmilla boulders consist of very crystalline material, extremely hard and pale green in color (Figure 4f).

5. Two boulders were found at Las Majadas in the bed of the Rio Huijo (HU), 1.5 km west of El Jute *pueblo* at an elevation of 300–325 m. They must have been brought down by the stream from up toward Los Vados. Cerro Joya Grande lies on the east side of this valley, and the Huijo jade is similar in crystalline appearance to that from Palmilla, although darker green in color (Figure 4e). Only the two boulders located were sampled from this putative source.

6. The *Quebrada La Oscurana outcrop* (OS) lies on the south side of the valley between 400 and 500 m elevation, some 2 km upstream from its confluence with the Rio La Palmilla. The rock is of apple-green color similar to that from El Jute; only a few samples were submitted for analysis.

The *in situ* sources of the stream-bed material must lie somewhere within the restricted catchment areas of the streams. The size of the larger boulders suggests that they are not far distant, but we did not locate them on the 1973 survey. Samples were taken from all available jadelike boulders, however. The whole of the area surveyed drains south into the Motagua valley, which contains terrace deposits with boulders of various rocks up to 0.30 m diameter, including serpentine and other basic rocks. Although we noted no jade in an admittedly cursory survey of erosion profiles, a substantial boulder of jadeite was found on the Hacienda Trujillo, just downstream from the confluence of the Uyús and the Motagua, in 1952 (Foshag and Leslie 1955:81); the battered surface suggested that it had been roughed out preparatory to removal to a workshop. It is thus possible that the ancient Maya obtained

---

[4] H. Chollot, personal communication, 1970.

US20). (d) Jadeite-albite rock with sieved porphyroblasts of jadeite (J) set in albite (A) from Usamatlan (Hammond and Hazelden US17). (e) Jadeite (J) dusty with inclusions replaced by omphacite (O) and clear apatite (JP) between some of the pyroxenes. From Huijo (Hammond and Hazelden HU1). (f) Jadeite (J) rock with lens of dark green omphacite (O) separated by a late vein of albite and analcite (AA) with needles of hornblende. From Palmilla (Hammond and Hazelden PA33).

some of their jade from these terrace deposits, and the attribution of an artifact to a source may not necessarily mean that the jade was collected from the outcrop itself. On the other hand, the putative pre-Columbian jade mine at the Usmatlan outcrop suggests that outcrop sources were exploited in the past, as does the amount of debris at the Manzanotal outcrop reported by Foshag and Leslie (1955:82).

Other sources of jadelike rock certainly exist outside our sampled area. Chollot (personal communication, 1970) found what he considered to be jadeite near Nebaj, El Quiche (incidentally a noted area for artifact jades). McBirney (1963; McBirney et al. 1967) reported detrital jadeite in terrace deposits of the Motagua valley some 70 km west of Manzanotal, in Baja Verapaz, while Shook (personal communication, 1975) noted at least one jadeite boulder on the southern side of the valley between McBirney's area and Manzanotal. Mr. J. Ridinger of Antigua, Guatemala is exploiting several locations commercially, which he is not prepared to reveal beyond a general "Department of Zacapa" designation; since our Huijo, El Jute, La Palmilla, Quebrada La Oscurana, and Usumatlan source locations lie in Zacapa, with the two Manzanotal sources MA and MN just to the west in El Progreso, it seemed probable that Ridinger's sources included at least some of ours, but the seven samples submitted were analyzed under a general Zacapa (ZA) designation.

Two further samples were provided by an assistant of H. Chollot after the latter's death. The samples were claimed to come from a source at Los Tecomates in the southern part of El Progreso, not far from Guatemala City. Although the samples looked much like Chollot's Manzanotal and Usumatlan material, we included them in the analysis under designation TE.

In general, it seems likely that jadeite occurs in many places in the serpentine belts of central Guatemala and that, even if only a small proportion of these outcrop, we are still unaware of more than a few of the exposures that could have been exploited by the ancient Maya. A careful survey of the serpentine belts is an essential prerequisite for any further useful work on jade sources in the Maya area.

B. Workshops

At a number of localities in the vicinity of the jade sources sampled in 1973, fragments of jade rock in various stages of processing into artifacts have been reported, from sites including San Augustin Acasaguastlán and Quirigua; and, similarly, the boulder from Trujillo reported by Foshag and Leslie (1955:81) showed the marks of initial shaping. That some jade was exported in boulder form is shown by the large example with saw cuts found at Kaminaljuyu (Kidder et al. 1946:Figure 154) and the unworked material from Altar de Sacraficios (Willey 1972:154), and can with some likelihood be argued from the common composition of associated artifacts in sites distant from the source region (*infra*).

We attempted to assess which, if any, of the sources we had sampled had been locally utilized in ancient times by submitting a number of jade-like rock fragments collected from three workshop sites to the same activation analysis as the source samples. The sites were (a) the Terzuola Site (TZ), located at km 93 on CA9 from Guatemala City to Puerto Barrios. The site lies on low bluffs south of the highway and overlooking the river flood plain and consists of scatters of jade and other rock fragments, including obsidian and Late Classic ceramics. It has been described by Feldman et al. (1975), and some samples were provided by Feldman. (b) The El Terron site (ET), reported and collected by Shook (personal communication, 1974) lies in the mouth of a small *barranca* of that name draining west into the Rio Hato 1 km downstream and southwest of the *pueblo* of San Austin Acasaguastlán. (c) Guaytan (GT), investigated by the Carnegie Institution (Smith and Kidder 1943), lies 1.8 km south of San Agustin on the west bank of the Rio Hato at the same 300 m elevation as El Terron upstream on the other bank. The sample analyzed here consists of rock fragments collected by Hammond and Hazelden in 1973.

C. Artifacts

Artifact analysis was not part of this initial phase of the project during which we merely wished to establish whether jade sources were characterizable, but nine artifact samples were included in the activation analysis. These consisted of (a) six "blue jade" beads from Costa Rica,[5] for which we wished to obtain a range of element concentrations that could later be compared with both Rio Balsas blue jade and Olmec artifact jades of this color in the hope that some indication of the general source area of Olmec blue jade might be obtained. These were coded CR. (b) One green jade bead from Honduras,[5] coded HN, included out of interest in whether artifacts from southeast of the Motagua might prove to be of jade from our sample area. (c) Two Late Preclassic jades, coded NM, a bead and a bib-head pendant, from a foundation cache excavated in 1974 at the lowland Maya site of Nohmul, northern Belize (Hammond 1974:Figure 7). Such heads have a north Yucatecan distribution similar to that of Ixtepeque obsidian in the Classic period (Hammond 1972:Figure 1), suggesting that an east coast canoe trade route from the Motagua might have determined the distribution if the pendants were both as raw material and as artifacts from that region rather than further west in the Guatemalan highlands. We therefore included the only two artifacts from the cache small enough to undergo irradiation in order to compare their

[5] Supplied by Dr. Doris Z. Stone.

	1 US20 SA50	2 US20 SA51	3 PA50 SA78	4 MA3 SA120	5 GT2 SA71	6 MA3 SA124	7 PA5 SA23	8 MA8 SA80	9 US17 SA120	10 PA5 SA24	11 MA8 SA84	12 US20 SA107	13 US20 SA108
SiO_2	59.03	57.16	54.83	56.29	54.42	49.02	41.60	68.74	68.25	51.90	49.71	46.93	39.75
TiO_2	0.00	0.13	0.00	0.00	0.00	0.25	0.13	0.00	0.00	0.00	0.59	0.00	0.00
Al_2O_3	24.75	13.06	11.15	11.40	0.87	9.46	18.83	19.17	19.74	24.59	28.12	40.14	32.18
Cr_2O_3	0.00	0.00	0.00	0.00	0.00	0.00	0.00	0.00	0.00	0.00	0.00	0.00	0.00
FeO	0.00	1.77	5.69	4.11	1.93	9.91	12.72	0.00	0.00	0.00	1.59	0.12	1.11
MnO	0.00	0.00	0.24	0.10	0.00	0.26	0.60	0.00	0.00	0.00	0.00	0.00	0.00
MgO	0.00	7.09	6.32	7.54	16.53	14.70	8.28	0.00	0.00	0.00	2.90	0.00	0.00
CaO	0.31	11.12	12.55	12.70	24.86	10.42	7.54	0.11	0.00	0.00	0.00	0.17	24.98
Na_2O	14.92	8.83	7.63	7.54	0.94	3.05	6.38	11.91	11.52	12.75	0.34	7.95	0.00
K_2O	0.09	0.00	0.00	0.00	0.00	0.37	0.15	0.00	0.00	0.24	10.10	0.28	0.00
Total	99.10	99.16	98.41	99.68	99.55	97.44	96.43	99.93	99.51	89.48	93.35	95.59	98.02
Unit formulas	$O = 6$	$O = 6$	$O = 6$	$O = 6$	$O = 6$	$O = 23$	$O = 23$	$O = 8$	$O = 8$	$O = 6$	$O = 20$	$O = 20$	$O = 13$
Si	2.00	2.01	2.00	2.01	1.99	7.02	6.19	3.00	2.99	1.95	6.12	5.43	3.15
Ti	—	0.01	—	—	—	0.03	0.01	—	—	—	0.06	0.00	—
Al^{IV}	—	—	—	—	0.01	0.98	1.81	—	—	—	1.88	2.57	—
Al^{VI}	0.99	0.54	0.48	0.48	0.03	0.61	1.49	0.99	1.02	1.09	2.20	2.90	3.00
Cr	—	—	—	—	—	—	—	—	—	—	—	—	—
Fe^{+3}	—	—	0.06	—	—	0.19	0.02	—	—	—	—	—	—
Fe^{+2}	—	0.05	0.12	0.12	0.06	1.00	1.56	—	—	—	0.16	0.01	0.07
Mn	—	—	0.01	0.01	—	0.03	0.03	—	—	—	—	—	—
Mg	—	3.38	0.34	0.40	0.90	3.14	1.84	—	—	—	0.53	—	—
Ca	0.01	0.42	0.49	0.49	0.97	1.60	1.20	0.01	—	—	0.05	0.02	2.12
Na	0.98	0.60	0.54	0.52	0.07	0.85	1.84	1.01	0.98	0.93	0.08	1.78	—
K	0.00	—	—	—	—	0.07	0.03	—	—	0.01	1.59	0.04	—

Figure 5 Electron-probe analyses of rock samples from the Motagua Valley. (1) Jadeite, cave of crystal overgrown by jadeite-diopside of analysis 2. (2) Jadeite-diopside, overgrowth of jadeite of analysis 1. (3) Omphacite, dark green from lens in jadeite rock. (4) Omphacite, resorbed crystal in albitite with hornblende of analysis 6. (5) Diopside, in felted mass associated with dilorite. (6) Hornblende, acicular green crystal in albitite with residual omphacite from analysis 4. (7) Hornblende, green crystal late thin albite analcite vein in jadeite rock. (8) Albite, colorless untwinned crystal in albitite. (9) Albite, colorless untwinned crystal in jadeite albite rock. (10) Analcite, colorless material in core of albite analcite hornblende vein; hornblende analysis. (11) Muscovite, sporadic crystals in albitite; albite analysis 8. (12) Paragonite, associated with albite, jadeite-diopside analysis 2 and clinozoisite analysis 13. (13) Clinozoisite, crystal associated with albite and paragonite of analysis 2.

element concentrations with those for our jade sources. In addition, all seven of the jades in the cache (four pendants, two earspools, one bead) were examined by X-ray fluorescence (see Figure 9) to estimate whether they were likely to be from the same source. The first widespread use of jade in Yucatan occurs in the Late Preclassic, and the diversity or unity of sources for this iconographically rather homogeneous class of bib-head pendants might be a factor of some importance in establishing the intial character of the Preclassic exchange network. Analysis of all extant bib-head pendants will be a priority of the second phase of this project, artifact analysis and source attribution.

III. CHARACTERIZATION PROCEDURES

Mineralogical identification of the source samples, workshop debris, and artifacts was made by macroscopic inspection and comparison with reference collections in the Department of Mineralogy and Petrology at Cambridge University; selected source samples were thin-sectioned for petrographic analysis and examined with the electron microprobe. Source and workshop samples and most of the artifacts were submitted to neutron activation analysis, and all the artifacts were examined by X-ray fluorescence spectrometry. Data from the activation analysis were clustered on an iterative program developed specifically for this project.

A. Petrographic Analysis

This is presented here only as a summary and an assessment of recognizable groupings; the detailed descriptions will be published elsewhere, although the electron-probe analyses are displayed in Figure 5. Sample numbers cited, e.g., PA57, are field numbers and do not coincide with numbers US01-09, MA01-09, PA01-13, etc. used to tag the activation analysis samples 1–75. At present overlap between the individual samples examined by the two methods is small, the populations having been randomly but separately sampled from the field collections; but PA5 = activation sample 19 and HU8 = 33, and workshop samples GT1-2 = 56-57. The activated samples are now being examined petrographically.

The rock types studied here consist of two groups. The first, comprised of source locations HU, US, MA, PA, ranges from jadeite rocks with a variable amount of jadeite diopside or omphacite and subordinate albite, paragonite, and apatitie, to albitites with subordinate omphacite, hornblende, clinozoisite, muscovite, paragonite, quartz, and sphene. Some of the pyroxene-rich rocks are extensively sheared, residual paler pyroxene rock lenses being surrounded by a dark greenish-black fine-grained albitite enclosing many small hornblende needles. The latest alteration to which the pyroxene-rich rocks are subject are narrow (1–2 mm) brittle fracture veins filled in with albite, analcite, and minor acicular green hornblende.

The second group, comprised of source locations JU and OS, consists of cherty green silexite often shattered and veined by recrystallized quartz. Some of these correspond to chrysoprase, the green color being due to chromium held in a small amount of microcrystalline disseminated Cr-muscovite. No transitions to members of the first (HU, US, MA, PA) series have been observed.

The mineral assemblages of the first series are very similar to those described by Dobretsov and Ponomareva (1968) for the jadeite-bearing rocks associated with serpentines in the Polar Urals and Prebalkhash regions of the U.S.S.R. Certain Russian localities contain "sugar quartz rocks," but these do not resemble the fine-grained silexite of the JU–OS series. The latter were probably deposited from very low temperature siliceous hydrothermal fluids that have traversed serpentines.

Recognizable groupings on a petrographic basis are as follows:

Silexites—cherty "chrysoprase": JU, all samples; OS, all samples; GT1 (activation sample 56). Very distinctive, with no basis for distinguishing GT1 from JU and OS.

Albitites, with acessory omphacite, hornblende, sphene, clinozoisite, muscovite: MA, all samples (Figure 4b). Very distinctive; differ in texture but not in mineralogy from the albite-rich replacement areas in some PA and US samples.

Diopside-chlorite rock: GT2. Very distinctive; only one sample.

Massive granoblastic jadeite rocks with or without lenses of *dark green omphacite:* Without: PA 5, 18; with: PA 33 (Figure 4f), 50. Distinctive.

Massive granoblastic jadeite-pale green jadeite-diopside (Fe-poor omphacite) *rocks with platey matrix albite* (± 0.5 cm) and accessory hornblende, clinozoiste, paragonite: US 20 (Figure 4c), PA1, PA57 (the PA samples with veins and rosettes of horblende); HU 8 has albite plates but is distinctive with pyroxene (omphacite) richer in Fe. Distinctive.

Massive jadeite-Fe-rich omphacite rocks with accessory apatite: HU 1 (Figure 4e), 8. Distinctive.

Highly sheared jadeite–omphacite rocks with dark greenish black fine-grained albite and hornblende in shear zones: PA 20, 43. Distinctive.

Jadeite–albite rocks with sieved porphyroblastic jadeite in granulitic albite (sub parallel orientation): US 5, 19, 17 (Figure 4d). Distinctive.

Therefore distinctive subgroups exist and, on the basis of the present source collection, some may be diagnostic of specific localities. But the range, internal variability, and transitional nature of the PA series, even though collected as river cobbles, suggests that any individual source outcrop will be variable, although what was utilized may have been a relatively specific rock type.

B. Neutron-Activation Analysis

A total of 75 samples ranging in number from 13 for the La Palmilla (PA) source down to 2 for Huijo (HU) and the claimed Los Tecomates (TE) source was selected for irradiation, with 3 samples from the E1 Terron (ET) workshop, 2 from Guaytan (GT) and 2 from Terzuola (TZ), together with the 6 blue jade beads from Costa Rica (CR), the two Preclassic Nohmul jades (NM), and the single Honduras (HN) bead. The general desirability of separating the jadeite itself from jadeite rock has been emphasized by Foshag (1954, 1957) and McBirney et al. (1967), and its advantages from the statistical point of view are reiterated in this paper by Gazard. However, if source material is to be compared with jade artifacts that cannot be sampled sufficiently for such separation to be carried out because of their artistic and intrinsic value, it is necessary to analyze the whole rock sample and to rely on the statistical significance of large numbers of samples and multielement analysis to provide a basis for comparison with nondestructive analysis of the artifacts. Even so, the latter must be small enough to undergo irradiation if activation analysis is to be used, and residual radioactivity may remain in some cases for a considerable period. A preferable course of action, and one that we shall attempt to pursue as far as is practicable in the second phase of this project, is to obtain small expendable artifacts such as beads from which the jadeite component may be separated for comparison with that of source samples. We hope that the potential usefulness of the project as discernable from this paper may persuade excavators and curators that the odd bead is worth sacrificing in the interests of prehistory.

The analyses were therefore made on complete source samples ranging in mass from 80–1800 mg. After cleaning they were irradiated in batches of 10 together with a multielement standard (Perlman "standard pottery") for 48 hours in the A.W.R.E. Aldermaston "Herald" reactor at a flux density of 2×10^{12} neutrons/cm²/sec. The long period that elapsed between removal from the reactor and examination at Bradford, a function of logistics *inter alia*, limited our analysis to those isotopes with half-lives in excess of 24 hours, with the exception of Na, which provided the major "short-lived" activity. Analysis was carried out in the School of Archaeological Sciences at Bradford University using large-volume Ge–Li detectors linked to 1024 channel analyzers and the data processed with the aid of computer program SPECT, evolved at Bradford. A total of 23 elements was recognized. Fourteen were selected as giving reliable data, but, even so, the statistical accuracy of measurement is very variable and depends on the actual concentration measured. Results are thus generally given with last-figure reliability.

The measured concentrations and masses are displayed in Figure 6. Where an element has not been observed, an estimated minimum detectable concentration has been quoted in parentheses, e.g., (0.01). It can be seen that specimens from any one source are not homogeneous in terms of element concentration, although internal homogeneity is greater than heterogeneity between sources. Even major elements such as Na and Fe range over a factor of 2, and minor elements frequently over a factor of 10. This variability was verified for several single samples by splitting and reanalyzing them.

C. Cluster Analysis

The raw data from the neutron-activation analysis are too complex for immediate assertions on the characterizability of sources to be made, and the data were therefore analyzed by means of the iterative clustering program LIKEPART, evolved by Gazard at the Cambridge University Statistical Laboratory, the operation of which is described in detail in Hammond et al. (1976). In this program the data were presented for each sample as a vector of proportions by weight of the various metallic elements found during analysis. Thus each sample would sum to unity to represent the relative proportions of the metallic elements in a sample from a multinomial distribution, so that the effect of intrusions of other materials into the jade is eliminated. Then, given a group of samples that have been assigned to the same source, we can find the maximum likelihood estimate for the normalized source proportions. This is the weighted average of the proportions vectors for each piece in the group, with the weight for a piece proportional to the total mass of metallic elements present. From this we can derive an expression for the loglikelihood for any given assignment of the pieces into groups, with a common source being postulated for each group. The objectiveness of the criterion lies in its direct relation to the standard statistical concept of loglikelihood, and as such it is an improvement on previous methods of cluster analysis.

The algorithms devised to perform the maximization are also new. The first is based on the standard nearest neighbor iterative method. At each stage it examines the partition produced; and, if a piece has been assigned to a cluster although its vector of proportions is nearer to the estimate of source distribution for another cluster, it is reallocated to the second group. "Nearer" is being used in the sense that the reallocation will effect an increase in loglikelihood using the estimates for the source distributions as they stand. After the reallocation the source distributions will have to be recalculated,but that will only produce a further increase in loglikelihood. These transfers are repeated one piece at a time, and the process stops because there are only a finite number of partitions. Since at each stage a strict increase in loglikelihood is effected, there is no possibility of cycling through the same partition twice. When the transfers have to finish, the partition is said to be admissible; otherwise it is inadmissible. We can always improve an inadmissible arrangement to an admissible one, so clearly we are only interested in admissible partitions.

The second method carried two partitions at any stage and generates two more from each by finding the amalgamations that cause the smallest and second smallest decrease in loglikelihood, before checking for admissibility. The four partitions are then made admissible, and the best two differing arrangements are selected to be carried forward to the next stage. This algorithm has produced better arrangements than the first, particularly in the later stages of the clustering where the number of clusters is relatively few.

The clustering algorithms continue until all of the pieces are amalgamated into one cluster. It is therefore important to be able to set a level at which sufficient large clusters have been formed to show the structure that is present, but not as far as the point at which archaeologically unrelated material is being forced into the same groups. In this paper we have analyzed the clusters formed at level 66 of the partition.

The method works best with data in which the concentrations for each element are at least approximately of the same order of magnitude; but several of the elements in the jade rock are not detectable in some samples and yet may occur at concentrations of up to 1% in others. In view of this the data set was split in four ways: The first clustering used only Na and Fe concentrations; the second used the remainder; the third used Na, Fe, and Cr; and the fourth used the remaining trace elements. This gave four sets of clusters, which were not identical. To combine them, first the subgroups appearing in all four sets were isolated. Then any sample linked to each member of such groups in any three sets was added. Finally the remaining samples were allocated to groups to which they link in at least two sets. The final result is displayed in Figure 7.

Several strong groups emerge, in general consistent with the petrographic analysis. The JU and OS material separates out well into groups (vii) and (viii), and there is even some separation between these groups in terms of the separate strata sampled at the JU source. The second and third strata go together, the fourth links with the OS material, while the topmost layer is ambivalent and the two samples from the surface collection have a high Fe content that links with the GT workshop material in group (xi). Group (xii) consists of the CR beads, identified petrographically as chalcedony. The two HU jadeite samples fall into group (ix), linked on three runs with one of the TZ workshop samples and on two runs with the Preclassic artifacts NM01–02 and source sample ZA04.

Groups (i)–(vi) contain a mixture of MA, US, PA, MN, and TE source samples, with the ET workshop material and one of the two TZ workshop samples. The ZA samples, except ZA04, spread themselves across these groups. No source is distinctive in spite of the mineralogical separation of MA (which is, however, by texture and not mineralogy). In an attempt to solve this, two-element scatter diagrams were made. The most successful was Na:Fe (Figure 8), in which the PA material just separates from US, MA, and TE. These latter three are inseparable by activation analysis.

Although the individual four runs produce variable groupings, the combined clusters differentiate clearly, as might be expected, between the jadeite and nonjadeite rocks, and to some extent between individual jadeite sources.

	Sample	Na%	Sc	Fe%	Co	Hf	Eu	Cs	La	Cr	Th	Rb	Ba	Ta	Sb	Mass (mg)
1	US01	6.20	0.530	0.258	0.49	3.40	0.038	(0.01)	(0.1)	0.75	(0.01)	(2)	22	(0.005)	(0.05)	1843
2	US02	8.82	0.082	0.228	0.52	0.45	0.121	(0.01)	0.33	(0.1)	(0.01)	(2)	(5)	(0.005)	(0.05)	603
3	US03	8.47	0.067	0.169	0.20	1.10	(0.001)	(0.01)	(0.1)	(0.1)	(0.01)	(2)	(5)	(0.005)	(0.05)	1774
4	US04	7.47	0.093	0.223	0.76	1.44	0.0046	0.61	(0.1)	1.39	(0.01)	10	123	(0.005)	(0.05)	664
5	US05	7.64	0.116	0.220	0.76	0.98	0.0042	0.069	(0.1)	(0.1)	(0.01)	(2)	364	(0.005)	(0.05)	699
6	US06	7.75	0.089	0.208	0.34	1.43	0.011	(0.01)	(0.1)	(0.1)	(0.01)	(2)	(5)	0.029	(0.05)	759
7	US07	8.83	0.189	0.326	1.14	0.84	0.017	(0.01)	(0.1)	14.3	(0.01)	(2)	(5)	(0.005)	(0.05)	602
8	US08	9.58	0.186	0.330	1.01	2.86	0.0093	1.44	(0.1)	0.29	(0.01)	(2)	(5)	(0.005)	(0.05)	1569
9	US09	6.86	0.085	0.153	0.30	1.49	0.013	(0.01)	(0.1)	0.23	(0.01)	(2)	20	0.016	(0.05)	1254
10	MA01	6.00	0.069	0.208	0.681	1.18	0.044	0.08	0.31	1.99	0.01	(2)	29	(0.005)	(0.05)	945
11	MA02	8.95	0.170	0.253	0.68	2.63	0.0065	(0.01)	(0.1)	(0.1)	0.09	(2)	21	(0.005)	(0.05)	728
12	MA03	8.30	0.061	0.186	0.68	0.11	(0.001)	(0.01)	(0.1)	0.75	(0.01)	(2)	(5)	(0.005)	(0.05)	845
13	MA04	6.79	0.097	0.174	0.19	1.83	0.015	0.023	(0.1)	(0.1)	(0.01)	(2)	11	(0.005)	(0.05)	1360
14	MA05	8.84	0.132	0.366	0.82	1.09	0.01	(0.01)	(0.1)	1.53	(0.01)	(2)	(5)	(0.005)	(0.05)	1430
15	MA06	7.45	0.029	0.155	0.31	0.77	0.0066	(0.01)	(0.1)	(0.1)	(0.01)	(2)	(5)	0.017	(0.05)	1172
16	MA07	5.86	0.079	0.253	0.57	0.14	0.015	(0.01)	(0.1)	(0.1)	(0.01)	3	(5)	(0.005)	(0.05)	1658
17	MA08	9.73	0.091	0.149	0.88	0.65	0.016	(0.01)	(0.1)	5.4	(0.01)	(2)	43	(0.005)	(0.05)	335
18	MA09	4.94	0.445	0.182	0.62	0.60	0.090	0.06	1.34	3.74	0.09	(2)	85	0.019	0.08	1151
19	PA01	8.84	0.750	0.544	1.37	1.11	0.007	(0.01)	0.1	0.14	0.06	(2)	131	0.020	(0.05)	628
20	PA02	10.70	0.79	0.451	0.93	0.27	(0.001)	(0.01)	(0.1)	(0.1)	(0.01)	(2)	(5)	(0.01)	0.14	88
21	PA03	9.79	0.30	0.336	0.55	0.27	0.014	(0.01)	(0.1)	(0.1)	(0.01)	(2)	(5)	(0.01)	(0.05)	226
22	PA04	10.20	0.45	0.546	1.21	0.84	0.016	(0.01)	(0.1)	(0.1)	(0.01)	(2)	(5)	(0.01)	(0.05)	338
23	PA05	10.55	0.63	0.417	0.54	0.85	0.030	(0.01)	0.36	(0.1)	(0.01)	(2)	(5)	(0.014)	(0.05)	1364
24	PA06	10.10	0.33	0.361	0.41	1.05	0.064	(0.01)	(0.1)	(0.1)	(0.01)	(2)	(5)	0.063	(0.05)	1008
25	PA07	7.60	0.53	0.769	1.83	0.45	0.030	14.1	19.6	(0.1)	0.34	(2)	106	0.015	(0.05)	1609
26	PA08	10.50	0.24	0.230	0.62	1.74	0.006	(0.01)	(0.1)	(0.1)	(0.01)	5	(5)	0.020	0.12	222
27	PA09	10.56	0.29	0.212	0.43	2.91	0.016	(0.01)	(0.1)	(0.1)	(0.01)	(2)	(5)	(0.01)	(0.05)	345
28	PA10	9.62	0.97	0.527	0.90	0.66	0.010	0.34	(0.1)	(0.1)	(0.01)	(2)	(5)	(0.01)	(0.05)	1238
29	PA11	10.85	0.32	0.301	0.55	1.70	0.004	(0.01)	(0.1)	(0.1)	(0.01)	(2)	(5)	(0.01)	(0.05)	314
30	PA12	8.91	0.42	0.518	1.44	0.73	0.076	2.46	(0.1)	(0.1)	(0.01)	(2)	206	(0.01)	(0.05)	591
31	PA13	8.24	0.389	0.439	0.55	2.29	0.018	(0.01)	(0.1)	(0.1)	0.05	2	37	0.036	0.05	784
32	HU01	9.00	2.45	1.78	7.25	2.55	0.104	11.1	2.16	8.6	1.04	(2)	(200)	(0.005)	(0.05)	423
33	HU02	9.85	1.64	1.70	6.86	2.97	0.193	1.4	4.88	(0.1)	2.14	(2)	(200)	(0.005)	(0.05)	181
34	TE01	6.83	0.065	0.207	0.48	0.06	0.007	(0.01)	(0.1)	(0.1)	(0.01)	(2)	(5)	(0.005)	(0.05)	428
35	TE02	7.44	0.154	0.225	0.62	1.84	(0.001)	(0.01)	(0.1)	(0.1)	(0.01)	(2)	43	(0.005)	(0.05)	550
36	JU01	0.005	4.55	2.97	50.2	(0.2)	(0.001)	0.90	(0.1)	1990	(0.2)	(2)	(200)	(0.005)	27	663
37	JU02	0.012	5.24	5.72	43.8	(0.2)	(0.001)	0.78	0.20	1950	(0.2)	(2)	(200)	(0.005)	90	567

No.	ID															
38	JU03	0.006	1.00	0.042	5.15	(0.2)	(0.001)	3.30	(0.1)	2580	(0.2)	19	358	(0.005)	61	876
39	JU04	0.022	4.58	0.163	59.8	(0.2)	(0.09)	2.50	(0.1)	2820	(0.2)	(2)	(200)	(0.005)	56	11944
40	JU05	0.023	7.16	0.133	28.7	(0.2)	0.079	6.35	0.64	3470	(0.2)	(2)	(200)	(0.005)	287	345
41	JU06	0.026	2.61	0.043	17.4	(0.2)	(0.001)	1.55	(0.1)	2120	(0.2)	(2)	(200)	(0.005)	129	629
42	JU07	0.017	7.10	0.464	112.8	(0.2)	(0.001)	7.38	(0.1)	8280	(0.2)	(2)	(200)	(0.005)	380	385
43	JU08	0.025	2.822	0.435	27.0	(0.2)	(0.001)	1.50	(0.1)	2410	(0.2)	(2)	(200)	(0.005)	234	700
44	JU09	0.020	3.77	0.210	23.9	(0.2)	(0.001)	1.60	(0.1)	4490	(0.2)	(2)	(200)	(0.005)	371	427
45	JU10	0.006	5.69	0.114	6.18	(0.2)	(0.001)	5.10	(0.1)	2820	(0.2)	25	(200)	(0.005)	58	1119
46	JU11	0.015	5.00	0.131	8.95	(0.2)	(0.001)	4.70	0.32	3200	(0.2)	16	(200)	(0.005)	66	221
47	OS01	0.018	5.71	0.230	8.9	(0.2)	(0.001)	2.40	0.90	6520	(0.2)	104	620	(0.005)	72800	67
48	OS02	0.022	14.5	0.158	34.3	(0.2)	(0.001)	1.60	(0.1)	7760	(0.2)	92	(80)	(0.005)	10100	107
49	OS03	0.019	4.11	0.276	15.8	(0.2)	(0.001)	2.00	0.17	5640	(0.2)	64	190	(0.005)	49600	183
50	MN01	27.86	0.84	2.188	5.76	4.93	(0.001)	1.57	(0.1)	5	(0.01)	26	840	(0.005)	(0.05)	75
51	MN02	25.97	0.88	1.782	4.90	11.5	0.02	1.72	(0.1)	5	(0.01)	30	970	(0.005)	(0.05)	175
52	MN03	25.07	0.36	0.332	1.50	2.43	0.02	4.95	0.33	2	(0.01)	11	1520	(0.005)	(0.05)	538
53	ET01	27.63	0.82	1.007	5.76	0.72	(0.001)	37.5	(0.1)	79	(0.01)	28	3860	(0.005)	(0.05)	188
54	ET02	26.86	0.51	0.713	4.48	5.00	(0.001)	25.5	(0.1)	50	(0.01)	10	370	(0.005)	(0.05)	280
55	ET03	26.95	0.62	0.672	4.58	13.3	(0.001)	32.1	(0.1)	79	(0.01)	11	370	(0.005)	(0.05)	447
56	GT01	0.0174	12.1	2.18	62.3	(0.2)	0.01	2.06	0.14	1073	(0.01)	16	(200)	(0.005)	6030	1049
57	GT02	0.0175	3.25	2.32	39.1	(0.2)	0.03	0.72	0.20	900	0.14	11	(200)	(0.005)	4300	938
58	TZ01	0.0162	1.54	0.066	11.0	(0.2)	(0.001)	4.57	0.17	1570	(0.01)	21	200	(0.005)	7720	717
59	TZ02	6.45	0.90	0.967	11.7	17.1	0.02	17.9	(0.1)	131	(0.01)	8	260	(0.005)	(0.05)	126
60	ZA01	6.95	0.480	0.648	3.24	3.52	0.019	1.43	(0.1)	6.6	(0.01)	(2)	749	(0.005)	(0.05)	3024
61	ZA02	10.47	1.01	0.531	0.66	4.60	0.025	(0.01)	0.2	(0.01)	(0.01)	(2)	(5)	(0.005)	(0.05)	1747
62	ZA03	10.06	2.04	0.066	1.69	0.86	0.101	0.75	(0.1)	0.7	(0.01)	(2)	(5)	0.150	(0.05)	1934
63	ZA04	7.10	0.148	1.23	5.53	1.64	0.096	0.29	0.14	0.3	(0.01)	(2)	304	(0.005)	(0.05)	2352
64	ZA05	9.60	0.256	0.452	0.97	2.63	0.008	(0.01)	(0.1)	(0.01)	(0.01)	(2)	412	(0.005)	(0.05)	2034
65	ZA06	7.06	2.59	0.865	3.63	0.92	0.064	0.32	(0.1)	7.3	(0.01)	(2)	349	(0.005)	(0.05)	2642
66	ZA07	9.78	0.139	0.336	1.03	2.32	(0.001)	1.31	0.1	0.4	(0.01)	(2)	179	(0.005)	(0.05)	1839
67	NM01	6.88	0.697	1.15	8.75	3.54	0.022	0.38	(0.1)	148	(0.01)	(2)	415	0.013	(0.05)	4892
68	NM02	7.46	2.33	1.34	6.56	0.92	0.010	0.07	(0.1)	291	(0.01)	(2)	91	0.027	(0.05)	14606
69	CR01	0.025	0.097	0.126	0.129	0.03	0.067	0.02	1.05	0.3	(0.01)	3	15	(0.005)	(0.05)	1608
70	CR02	0.048	0.401	1.18	0.568	0.02	0.180	0.13	3.85	0.6	(0.01)	19	38	(0.005)	(0.05)	1447
71	CR03	0.029	0.250	0.609	0.795	0.02	0.093	0.20	1.31	0.6	(0.01)	12	(5)	(0.005)	(0.05)	249
72	CR04	0.091	0.553	0.811	0.955	(0.01)	0.333	0.20	5.47	(0.1)	0.04	19	57	(0.005)	(0.05)	189
73	CR05	0.062	3.17	0.824	0.734	0.31	0.256	0.30	3.33	6.6	0.35	9	(5)	(0.005)	(0.05)	176
74	CR06	0.180	9.11	1.97	2.64	4.06	0.408	1.73	3.58	7.6	2.47	55	6300	0.440	(0.05)	26
75	HN01	7.29	2.60	0.939	6.49	(0.01)	0.149	0.45	0.34	2890	(0.2)	(2)	(5)	(0.005)	(0.05)	198

Figure 6 Neutron-activation analyses of source, workshop, and artifact samples. Note: The exceptionally high Na levels quoted for 50–55 have caused us some concern. Second samples of these will be analyzed to check the reliability of the assignments. The quoted ends are used in Figure 8, but the clustering in Figure 7 has been carried out using a lower level (50% of that observed) more in accordance with the mineralogical composition.

59

FINAL SET OF CLUSTERS

i	2	3	6	12	15	26	27	29	34		62
ii	4	34			18	53	66				5	52	74
iii	11	13			54	55			9		5	17
iv	8	14	16	20	21	23	24		7		1	10
v	19	30	51	64					31		52	74
vi	22	28	61
vii	40	41	44		42	43					38	39	58
viii	45	49			46	48			47		38	39	58
ix	32	33							59		63	67	68
x	50	60	65								25
xi	56	57									36	37
xii	69	72			70	71	73				74

Piece not allocated:

| xiii | | | | | | | | | 75 |

Figure 7 Final set of clusters produced by amalgamation of the four sets formed at level 66 of the LIKEPART program. Numbers on the left of the line and on the same horizontal level represent groups of objects in which each piece links to all the others in its group in at least three of the four clusterings. Adjacent numbers represent groups that link up in all four of the clusterings. A space between two such groups indicates that the composite group does not appear in all four runs. Numbers to the right of the line represent objects that join with all the members of the cluster on their left in at least two of the runs, except as detailed in the notes. Only pieces that cannot be put anywhere else are included: Piece 5 joins with the second set on the trace-element clusterings but with the third group on the runs involving iron and sodium. Pieces 38, 39, and 58 join with 40, 41, and 44 and 46 and 48, but not with the others in the groups with which they are linked. Piece 17 joins with 54 and 55, but not 11 and 13. Piece 74 joins on 69 and 72, but not with 70, 71, and 73. This is on the sodium and iron clusterings. On the trace-element runs piece 74 links with two possible groups, both containing similar material. Piece 52 also joins 74 on the trace-element analyses. Na levels for ET and MN have been halved for this chemistry. See Figure 8 for key to symbols.

IV. CONCLUSIONS

A. Source Analysis

The combination of mineralogical examination by electron probe and thin section and elemental analysis by neutron activation has differentiated between sources of jadelike rocks with some success. Jadeites and albitites have separated from nonpyroxenes on both methods; and within the jadeitite-albitite range it has been possible to isolate HU material by both methods and PA material on a two-element plot, in spite of the variety of individually distinctive rock types within the PA sample. MA and US are mineralogically but not chemically distinct. The postulated TE source would seem not to exist, the samples given us in good faith coming in fact from the MA/US sources; and the range of ZA samples would seem to have been taken from the same sources as our MA/US/PA/HU material. The MN boulder is closer in composition to PA than to the nearer MA source. At present characterization of individual jade sources such as HU is possible, but a number of sources may prove indistinguishable. A larger number of samples from more sources is essential if this somewhat indeterminate conclusion is to be improved upon.

B. Workshops

The ET material clusters with MA source samples in groups (ii)–(iii), with links with US; it seems likely that the MA source, 12 km in airline and about 17 km along the valleys, was exploited. Of the two TZ samples one proved to be a chrysoprase similar to the JU and OS material, the other a jadeite similar to HU. We suggest that the bed of the Rio Huijo or the bedrock sources upstream, some 12 km in airline and 18 km or so along the valleys, together with the nearby E1 Jute outcrop, were exploited for both jade and chrysoprase, the latter being worked also and used as "social jade." The two GT workshop samples form a separate group, with loose links to the high-Fe samples from the JU source on the activation analysis; but mineralogically they are different, one being a chrysoprase indistinguishable from JU/OS, the other a diopside-chlorite. Here again we have green rocks being worked as "social jade." The three workshops are all near the major archaeological site of San Agustin Acasaguastlán, which was known to be a center for pre-Columbian jade-working (Smith and Kidder 1943); and the analyses show that the inhabitants were traveling up to 20 km for their raw material, but that the slightly more distant PA jades were not being exploited from this workshop zone.

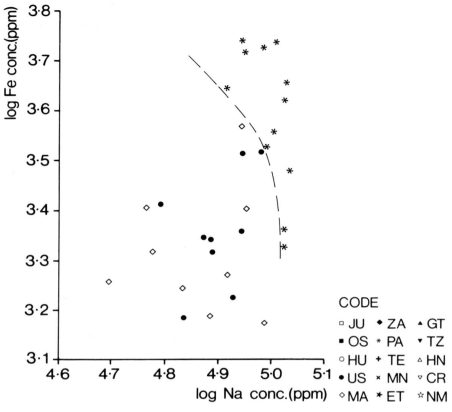

IRON/SODIUM PLOT FOR ALL JADE SOURCES

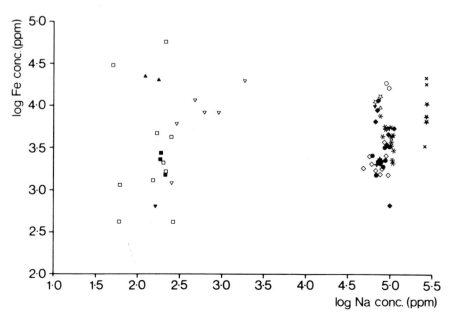

C. Artifacts

The six Costa Rica beads (CR) proved to be of blue chalcedony and not jadeite; in future the application of the term "jade" to blue-stone Olmec artifacts will need to be more carefully considered and backed up by mineralogical determinations. The placing of the beads in one cluster does not necessarily indicate a single source, since their chalcedonic composition renders them more similar to each other than to the jades or chrysoprases.

The bead HN remained outside all groups in the clustering, so that, in spite of being mineralogically jadeite, it is unlikely to have come from any of the sources sampled so far; such negative conclusions may prove to be of some interest.

The two NM artifacts proved to be of similar chemical composition, as the X-ray fluorescence analysis also suggested, and to have loose links with the HU material and one of the TZ workshop pieces. It is possible that the NM jade came from the HU source, if from any of those sampled here, and unlikely that it came from US, MA, or PA. The two samples NM01–02 were also examined by X-ray fluorescence together with the other three head pendants and the two earspools from the same cache. The resulting spectra (Figure 9) are sufficiently similar to suggest that all seven objects were made from jade from a common source, perhaps the same boulder. This raises the question of whether the jades were carved at source or in northern Belize. Any answer can only be a balance of improbabilities, but it seems the more likely that separation of the original block into artifact roughouts occurred nearer the place of deposition in view of the improbability of a cache consisting entirely of similar jade or of similar jades manufactured at source remaining together otherwise. On conventional archaeological grounds, of their similar iconography and stratigraphic association, we would also have argued that manufacture from a single block was the more likely, and the analyses do not run counter to this.

D. Summary and Prospects

Our research to date has shown that multiple mineral sources of jadeite rock exist in the Motagua valley serpentine belt in both bedrock outcrops and boulders in stream beds eroded from them, together with albitites and other nonpyroxene greenstones similar in appearance to jade. All of these were collected by the ancient Maya inhabitants of the area and worked into artifacts. Some of the sources sampled within a very small test area prove to

Figure 8 Two-dimensional scatter diagram of Na and Fe concentrations, with an enlargement to show the separation of PA from US and MA (TE and Za omitted from enlargement). For the high Na levels of ET and MN see caption to Figure 6.

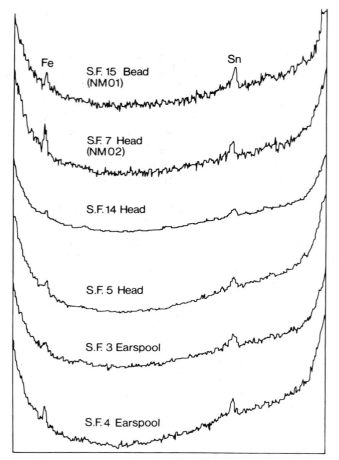

Figure 9   X-ray fluorescence spectra for the Nohmul Preclassic jade cache, including samples NM01–02 (67–68) from the neutron-activation analysis. The presence of Fe and Sn peaks and the absence of others in all spectra indicate that all objects could be of jade from the same source.

be characterizable using a combination of mineralogical and chemical analysis, while others are indistinguishable. This combination of electron-probe and neutron-activation techniques promises to characterize at least some jade sources firmly, but a larger number of located and sampled sources and more samples from each source are necessary for the further development of the study.

The results of this pilot project seem to us sufficiently encouraging for the work to proceed into a second phase in which the source inventory will be enlarged by fieldwork and refined by larger samples, and in which a large number of Maya jade artifacts from firmly established stratigraphic contexts selected from properly excavated sites over as much of the Maya area as possible will be analyzed and as far as possible attributed to located, or unlocated, source groups. We shall then be able to assess the role of jade and its exchange in the processes that led to the rise, florescence, and decline of Classic Maya civilization in a manner that the ''precious stone of grace'' merits.

References

Allen, R. O., A. H. Luckenbach, and C. G. Holland
  1975 The application of instrumental neutron activation analysis to study of prehistoric steatite artifacts and source materials. *Archaeometry* **17**:69–83.
Brooks, D., A. M. Bieber Jr., G. Harbottle, and E. V. Sayre
  1974 Biblical studies through activation analysis of ancient pottery. In *Archaeological Chemistry,* edited by K. W. Beck. *Advances in Chemistry Series* 138:48–80.
Damour, A.
  1846 Analyses du jade oriental. *Annales de Chimie et Physiques* 3(16):469–474.
  1863 Notice et analyse sur la jade verte. Réunion de cette matière mineral a la famille de wernerites. *Comptes Rendues Paris* **56**:861–865.
Digby, A.
  1964 *Maya jades.* London: British Museum.
Dobretsov, N., and L. G. Ponomareva
  1968 Comparative characteristics of jadeite and associated rocks from Polar Ural and Prebalkhash regions. *International Geology Review* **10**:221–242, 247–279.
Easby, E. K.
  1961 The Squier jades from Tonina, Chiapas. In *Essays in pre-Columbian art and archaeology,* edited by S. K. Lothrop et al., pp. 60–80. Cambridge, Massachusetts: Harvard University Press.
  1968 *Pre-Columbian jade from Costa Rica.* New York: Emmerich.
Easby, E. K., and D. T. Easby
  1956 Apuntes sobre la tècnica de tallar jade en Mesoamerica. Buenos Aires: *Annales del Instituto de Arte Americano,* No. 6.
Feldman, L. H., R. Terzuola, P. Sheets, and C. Cameron
  1975 Jade workers in the Motagua valley. *Museum Briefs,* No. 17. Columbia, Missouri: Museum of Anthropology, University of Missouri–Columbia.
Flannery, K. V.
  1968 The Olmec and the Valley of Oaxaca: a model of inter-regional interaction in formative times. In *Dumbarton Oaks Conference on the Olmec,* edited by E. P. Benson, pp. 119–130. Washington, D.C.: Dumbarton Oaks.
Foshag, W. F.
  1954 Estudios mineralògicos sobre el jade de Guatemala. *Anthropologia e Historia de Guatemala* **6**:3–47.
  1955 Chalchihuitl: a study in jade. *American Mineralogist* **40**:1062–1070.
  1957 Mineralogical studies on Guatemalan jade. *Smithsonian Miscellaneous Collections* **135**(5).
Foshag, W. F., and R. Leslie
  1955 Jadeite from Manzanal, Guatemala. *American Antiquity* **21**:81–82.
Hammond, N.
  1970 Excavations at Lubaantun, 1970. *Antiquity* **44**:216–223.
  1972 Obsidian trade routes in the Mayan area. *Science* **178**:1092–094.
  1974 Preclassic to Postclassic in northern Belize. *Antiquity* **48**:177–189.

1975a   Maya site hierarchy in northern Belize. *Contributions of the University of California Archaeological Research Facility* **27**:40–55.

1975   Lubaantun: a Classic Maya realm. *Monographs of the Peabody Museum, Harvard University,* No. 2. Cambridge, Massachusetts.

Hammond, N., G. Harbottle, and T. Gazard
1976   Neutron activation and statistical analysis of Maya ceramics and clays from Lubaantun, Belize. *Archaeometry,* **18:**147–168.

Hodder, I.
1974   Regression analysis of some trade and marketing patterns. *World Archaeology* **6:**172–189.

Hodder, I , and C. R. Orton
n.d.   *Spatial archaeology.* Cambridge: Cambridge University Press (in press).

Kandiah, K.
1971   High resolution spectrometry with nuclear radiation detectors. *Nuclear Instrumentation and Methods* **95:**289–300.

Kidder, A. V., J. Jennings, and E. M. Shook
1946   Excavations at Kamilaljuyu, Guatemala. *Carnegie Institution of Washington Publication* **561.** Washington, D.C.

McBirney, A. R.
1963   Geology of a part of the Central Guatemalan Cordillera. *University of California Geological Science Publications* **38:**177–242.

McBirney, A. R., K-I. Aoki, and M. N. Bass
1967   Eclogites and jadeite from the Motagua fault zone, Guatemala. *American Mineralogist* **52:**908–918.

Pendergast, D. M.
1969   Altun Ha, British Honduras (Belize): the sun god's tomb. *Royal Ontario Museum of Art and Archaeology Occasional Paper* **19.**

Pires-Ferreira, J. W.
1975   Formative Mesoamerican exchange networks with special reference to the Valley of Oaxaca. *Memoirs of the Museum of Anthropology, University of Michigan,* No. 7. Ann Arbor, Michigan.

Proskouriakoff, T.
1975   Jades from the Cenote of Sacrifice at Chichen Itza, Yucatan, Mexico. *Memoirs of the Peabody Museum, Harvard University.* **10**(1). Cambridge, Massachusetts.

Rands, R.
1965   Jades of the Maya lowlands. *Handbook of Middle American Indians,* **3:**561–580. Austin, Texas: University of Texas Press.

Rands, R. P. H. Benson, R. L. Bishop, P-y Chen, G. Harbottle and G. V. Sayre
n.d.   Western Maya fine paste pottery: chemical and petrographic correlations. *XLI Congreso Internacional de Americanistas, Actas* (in press). Mexico City.

Rathje, W. L.
1970   Socio-political implications of lowland Maya burials: methodology and tentative hypothesis. *World Archaeology* **1:**359–374.

Renfrew, C.
1972   *The emergence of civilization: the Cyclades and the Aegean in the third millennium B.C.* London: Methuen.

1975   Trade as action at a distance: questions of integration and communication. In *Ancient civilization and trade,* edited by J. A. Sabloff and C. C. Lamberg-Karlovsky, pp. 3–59. Albuquerque, New Mexico: University of New Mexico Press.

Sigleo, A. C.
1975   Turquoise mines and artifact correlation for Snaketown, Arizona. *Science* **189:**459–460.

Smith, A. L., and A. V. Kidder
  1943   Explorations in the Motagua Valley, Guatemala. *Carnegie Institution of Washington Publication* **546**:101–182. Washington, D.C.
Statham, P. J.
  n.d.   A comparative study of techniques for quantitative analysis of X-ray spectra obtained with a Si(Li) detector. *X-ray Spectrometry* (in press).
Thompson, J. E. S.
  1950   Maya hieroglyphic writing: introduction. *Carnegie Institution of Washington Publication* **589**. Washington, D.C.
  1964   Trade relations between Maya highlands and lowlands. *Estudios de Cultura Maya* **4**: 13–49.
Tourtellot, G., and J. A. Sabloff
  1972   Exchange systems among the ancient Maya. *American Antiquity* **37**:126–134.
Willey, G. R.
  1972   The artifacts of Altar de Sacrificios. *Papers of the Peabody Museum, Harvard University,* Vol. 64, No. 1. Cambridge, Massachusetts.

Part III

Descriptive Models of Exchange

Chapter 4

ALTERNATIVE MODELS FOR EXCHANGE AND SPATIAL DISTRIBUTION

COLIN RENFREW

I. INTRODUCTION

Characterization methods and the development of efficient field recovery procedures have now made possible the quantitative investigation of trade or distribution patterns in a detailed manner. The most obviously suitable subjects for such studies are classes of artifact, such as pottery or chipped stone, which are of relatively frequent occurrence at the sites where they do occur so that quantitative measures, in terms of frequency (whether absolute or relative) or quantity recovered per unit volume, can be established. The focus of investigation has thus moved beyond simply the identification of the source of origin for individual finds and hence the demonstration of contact. Instead the underlying regularities in the patterns observed are being sought, with the aim of understanding the mechanisms of exchange involved and hence of gaining an insight into the economic and social processes at work in the society in question.

It is the aim of this paper to draw attention to some of the regularities that are now becoming apparent and to ask to what extent we are justified in associating these with specific kinds of trade or exchange. (Exchange is here interpreted in the widest sense; indeed in the case of some distributions it is not established that the goods changed hands at all. Trade in this case implies procurement of materials from a distance, by whatever mechanism.)

In particular two different models for the traffic in goods are shown to produce distributions of the same form. Their coincidence raises questions of a more general nature.

II. THE LAW OF MONOTONIC DECREMENT

When a commodity is available only at a highly localized source or sources for the material, its distribution in space frequently conforms to a very general pattern. Finds are abundant near the source, and there is a fall-off in frequency or abundance with distance from the source. This pattern is observed in many archaeological instances, and fall-off patterns of this kind are familiar to geographers. Frequency of occurrence declines with distance. That this should not be so is not unduly surprising, since, in general, the transport of goods from a source requires the input of energy and, other things being equal, the greater the distance the greater the energy input required. The generality, that there is a fall-off in frequency or abundance with distance from source, shows signs of implying further and more interesting regularities. Moreover, departures from it are likely to be of interest and significance. It can be stated as follows:

In circumstances of uniform loss or deposition, and in the absence of highly organized directional (i.e., preferential, nonhomogeneous) exchange, the curve of frequency or abundance of occurrence of an exchanged commodity against effective distance from a localised source will be a monotonic decreasing one.

This implies little more than that frequency decreases with increasing distance. The first proviso is an important one (see Ammerman et al. 1977). And we are dealing here with *effective* distance, which is not necessarily the same as the distance between points, since the ease of traversing terrain has to be considered. Deserts and mountains, acting as barriers or impediments, will increase effective distance. In certain circumstances rivers and sea will decrease it, depending always on the transport available. Effective distance may indeed be regarded as a measure of the energy required to move goods between two points, and it is crucially dependent upon the mode of transport available. The development of new travel technologies—the inception of long distance maritime travel or the use of the camel in desert lands—fundamentally alters effective distance.

The absence of directional exchange is a crucial point, and on the adequate definition of it rests the status of the law. For if directional trade were recognized solely by departure from the regularity, the "law" would become a tautology. Directional exchange and concentration effects are discussed in Section X below.

The geographical literature about distance decay effects is already extensive (cf. Haynes 1974; Claeson 1968; Olsson 1965). It embraces many aspects of the spatial distribution of human interaction and offers stimulating insights for the archaeologist. But while we stand to learn much from the rigor with which some geographers have approached their data, the models offered should not be accepted without some consideration of the underlying theory.

Various approaches have now been made toward a regression analysis of the fall-off with distance of traded commodities (cf. Renfrew, et al. 1968; Hodder 1974). In each case some measure of abundance or frequency is plotted against distance from the source in question. The choice of the measure of abundance used is an important one. Naturally it is preferable to select a measure that is not massively biased by recovery techniques in the field, where so often a high frequency is a measure of intensity of archaeological activity rather than of real variations in the archaeological record itself. In operational terms the choice of an appropriate measure is crucial.

It is the possibility of reaching general conclusions of wider application that makes this field of research such an interesting one at present. Demonstrable regularities conforming to mathematically simple forms are still disappointingly few in archaeology, and their analysis raises new and interesting questions. For there is hope that many archaeological distributions from different times and places, and entirely independent in the circumstances of their formation, can be expressed in this way. If it is the case that these distributions share basic, simple properties, the same may be true also for the processes generating them. And the understanding of these cultural processes is the ultimate goal of our investigation.

III. SHAPE OF FALL-OFF

Three principal classes of curves have, up to the present time, been considered relevant as possible approximations for the distance regressions observed. In each the variation of some measure of frequency or abundance I (whether expressed in occurrence per unit area or ratio of occurrence to that

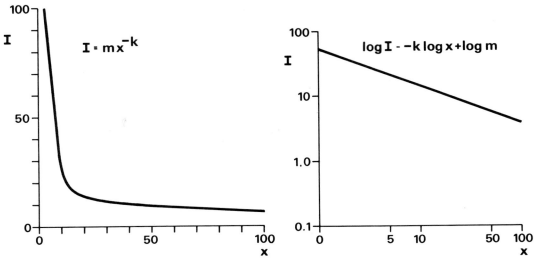

Figure 1 The Pareto model. On the left, interaction and distance are both on a linear scale; on the right, both are on a logarithmic scale.

of some other material) at a point is related to the distance X of the point from the source locality.

$$I = f(x) \tag{1}$$

A. The Pareto Model

The first of these is a power function known as the Pareto model (see Figure 1).

$$I = mx^{-k} \tag{2}$$

where k and m are constants. To those reared on Newtonian mechanics and the inverse square law, such a formulation seems a natural one to describe action at a distance. But there is no clear theoretical basis for the application of such an expression to human interactions, and geographers have in general found that it does not fit their data well.

To investigate such a relationship, logarithmic plotting may be used. For

$$\log I = -k \log x + \log m \tag{3}$$

so that when a power relationship holds, the logarithm of interaction plotted against the logarithm of distance on log–log paper will give a straight line with slope $-k$ and intercept $\log m$ on the ordinate. Wright (1970) has used such a plot for obsidian in the Near East.

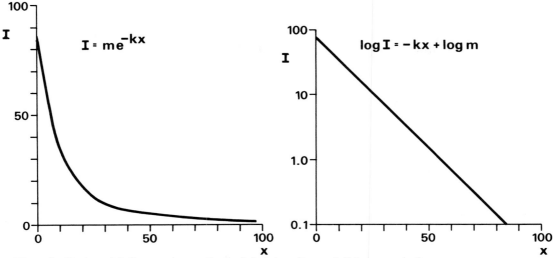

Figure 2 Exponential distance decay. On the left, interaction and distance are both on a linear scale; on the right, interaction is on a logarithmic scale, distance on a linear one.

B. Exponential Distance Decay

$$I = m \cdot e^{-kx} \tag{4}$$

$$\log I = \log m - kx \tag{5}$$

In this case e is the base of the natural logarithms, and fall-off is dependent on e raised to the power of the distance. When an exponential relationship holds, log (interaction) plotted against distance—*not* against the logarithm of distance—will give a straight line of slope $-k$ and with intercept $\log m$ on the ordinate (see Figure 2).

C. Gaussian Fall-Off

Since the work of Pearson and Blakeman (1906), Gaussian (normal) fall-off has been associated with the idea of random flights (see Figure 3).

$$I = m \cdot e^{-Kx^2} \tag{6}$$

It follows that

$$\log I = \log m - kx^2 \tag{7}$$

So that if $\log I$ is plotted on the ordinate against x^2 on the abscissa, a straight line will result, of slope $-k$ and intercept $\log m$ on the ordinate. The idea of random flights was first applied to archaeological distributions by Hogg

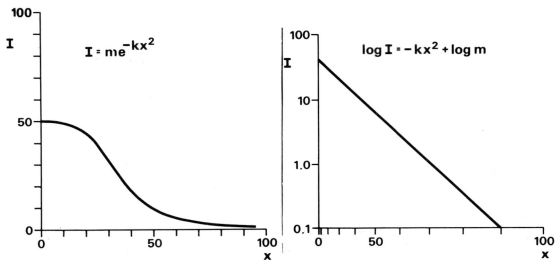

Figure 3   Gaussian fall-off. On the left, interaction and distance are both on a linear scale; on the right, interaction (on a logarithmic scale) is plotted against the square of distance.

(1971) when considering the distributions of Iron Age coin types in Britain and the distance of the findspot from the issuing mint.

It should be noted that Equation (4) and (6) are specific cases of the more general relationship

$$I = m \cdot e^{-Kx^\alpha} \tag{8}$$

where α, the exponent, is a constant. Its value is 1 in the exponential case and 2 in the Gaussian.

Other fall-off patterns may yet be sought in the data; log normal, Pareto exponential, and square root exponential have been considered by geographers (Morrill 1963; Morrill and Pitts 1967).

IV. STEEPNESS OF FALL-OFF

The shape of the fall-off curve is discussed further below. Clearly, in the expressions given, it depends first on whether a power or exponential relationship is chosen and secondly on the value of the constant k, which in Equations (5) and (7) determines the slope of the line produced when the transformed variables are plotted.

It is in fact intuitively fairly obvious that some commodities will travel farther than others, and this has been confirmed in quantitative studies by geographers, demonstrating the greater traveling power of high-value goods.

This relates in some cases to the distinction between what I have called down-the-line exchange and prestige-chain exchange (Renfrew, 1972) (see Figure 4).

The underlying idea is that the commodity or artifact has reached its destination as a result of a number of exchange transactions. The two models in question envisage a chain of exchange transactions by which the artifact finds its way from the source to the place where it finally enters the archaeological record. Four features of the latter were put forward (Renfrew 1972:465–468).

That formulation fails to do justice to the complexity of the situation and the number of factors operating, nor does it follow that high-value goods are necessarily prestige goods, which amount to what George Dalton (cf. Chapter 11 of this volume) calls "primitive valuables" (by implication belonging to a different sphere of exchange), although this is often the case. Among the relevant factors governing the distance a given object travels are mean distance transported between exchange transactions (in prestige exchange, it is expected that the distances are greater); transportability (expressed as a ratio of value to weight and breakage rate in transit) and effective life, considering frequency of use, breakage rate in use, reuse–discard after breakage, loss–recovery rate, and deliberate burial.

A consideration of these factors—and no doubt there are others—makes it clear that "high-value" commodities will have a smaller slope than others. The exchange of prestige goods involves at least two further considerations: namely, a restriction in the number of those for whom it is appropriate to have them, and the existence of "spheres of conveyance" restricting the free exchange of one class of good for another. The exchange of *Spondylus* shells in neolithic southeast Europe may be one such instance. Hammond et al. (Chapter 3) discuss the Maya jade trade in comparable terms, and Pires-Ferriera (1973:257) has considered iron ore mirrors in Oaxaca in this way.

V. THE DOWN-THE-LINE MODEL: LINEAR ATTENUATION AND EXPONENTIAL FALL-OFF

In 1968, when working with obsidian data from the Near East (Renfrew et al. 1968:Figure 2), I noticed that an approximately linear pattern was obtained by plotting the percentage of obsidian in the total chipped stone industry on a logarithmic scale (distance being plotted on a linear scale). As indicated above, this implies an exponential fall-off. A possible generating model was proposed as follows (cf. Renfrew 1972:446).

Imagine a line of villages linked in a trading network in a linear manner and equally spaced a distance *l* apart. Each receives a supply of a particular

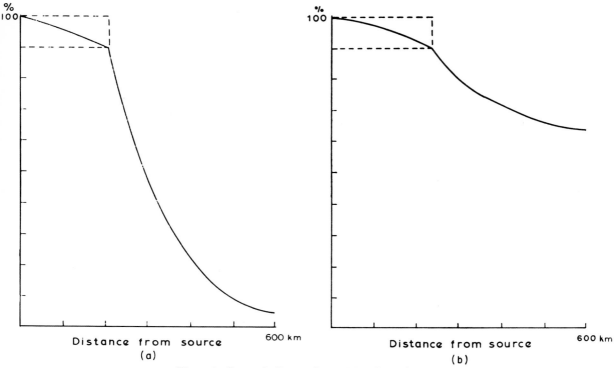

Figure 4 Down-the-line exchange (a) and prestige-chain exchange (b). Interaction and distance are shown on a linear scale. Dotted lines indicate the supply zones.

commodity from its neighbor nearer the source, returns some for its own use (which ultimately finds its way into the archaeological record as debris, etc.), and passes the remainder on. If each village passes on a proportion k of what it receives (k being less than 1), then

Village 1 at distance l passes on Nk
Village 2 at distance $2l$ passes on Nk^2
Village 3 at distance $3l$ passes on Nk^3
Village n at distance nl passes on Nk^n

At distance x the amount passed on is $N \cdot k^{x/l}$. An exponential fall-off is generated by this series of exchange transactions.

The assumption of a chain of villages at uniform spacing is, however, a needlessly special case of a more general condition for exponential decay, namely a uniform distribution of population. Assume first that reduction in number of artifacts or quantity of material is proportional to the number or quantity left at the point in question, namely I. Assume further that this population is uniformly distributed and takes a constant fraction before passing the remainder on.

$$-dI \propto I\,dx$$
$$\int \frac{dI}{I} = -\int k \cdot dx \qquad \text{where } k \text{ is constant}$$
$$\log I = -kx \qquad \text{where } I_0 \text{ is constant}$$
$$I = I_0 e^{-kx} \tag{9}$$

This model makes no statement about a number of transactions but states simply that there is a continual attrition or attenuation proportional to the flow of goods at the point. Exponential distance decay has been well discussed by Haynes (1974). He is using a slightly different model, that of the journeys or trips from the source along a line away from the source.

The key condition here is that the reduction is proportional to the number or quantity at the point in question. If this assumption were modified so that the reduction were independent of the number left but dependent only on change in distance, we would have (in one dimension) simply a linear fall-off:

$$-dI \propto dx$$
$$\int -dI = \int k \cdot dx \qquad \text{where } k \text{ is constant}$$
$$I - I_0 = -k \cdot x \qquad \text{where } I \text{ is constant}$$
$$I = I_0 - kx \tag{10}$$

VI. RANDOM WALK OR FLIGHT. GAUSSIAN FALL-OFF

Pearson (1906) was faced with the problem of the infiltration of a species into a new habitat. He therefore conducted a mathematical analysis of the distribution of mosquitoes departing from a point source. For the archaeologist the analogy is that of transactions involving the transport of commodities, each period of ownership being the counterpart of a single flight, an exchange transaction terminating one flight and starting another. When a large number of transactions (flights) are included, the situation is clear. Pearson's expression is

$$\phi(r^2) = N/2^{ps2} \exp(-\tfrac{1}{2}r^2\sigma^2) \tag{11}$$

where ϕ is the frequency of individuals in a small area distant r from the center of dispersion, N is the number of individuals starting from that center, and $\sigma^2 = 2nl^2$, where l is the length of each flight and n the number of random flights.

Although containing more constants, this is of the same form as our Equation (6):

$$I = m \cdot e^{-kx^2}$$

since r is the equivalent of x.

When n is fairly small, the concentration is near the center of dispersion. But when n is much larger, the distribution is more widely dispersed.

This generative model indicates clearly how a Gaussian distribution may occur in many cases analogous to the random flights of mosquitoes. It should be noted, however, that in this case the term "random" refers only to the direction of flight. The model is highly nonrandom in other respects, for each mosquito is constrained to undertake precisely n flights, each of length exactly l. In most real cases, however, the length of flight is not fixed but could be given by a frequency distribution. More seriously for the archaeological cases likely to be encountered, the objects in question certainly do not undertake the same number of flights or walks. The archaeological record is in fact the sum of the random walk functions for $n = 1$, $n = 2$, and so on up to a high value for n. Once again a frequency distribution could be constructed for the number of flights. A further necessary modification may be to allow the source to produce further individuals as the successive flights of existing individuals take place.

The essential point here remains that a large number of uncoordinated events will, in certain circumstances, produce a coherent, quantifiable fall-off curve in this way. The world offers many examples of such behavior— Brownian motion is one—and there are analogies here for the diffusion of innovation as well as for the exchange of goods.

VII. ATTENUATION IN TWO DIMENSIONS

In Section V, fall-off along a line was discussed for the situation in which the reduction of goods at each point is proportional to the quantity/frequency of goods at the point in question. The result was an exponential fall-off. It is interesting to extend this assumption to exchange in two dimensions, making the same assumptions as in the one-dimensional case. This, then, is the general situation of diffusion or attenuation in two dimensions. As Dr. R. H. Dean has kindly indicated to me, the result is once again a Gaussian distribution.

Assume

1. That the reduction at a point is proportional to the number or quantity left, I.

2. That the population is uniformly distributed and takes a constant fraction.

i.e.,
$$-dI \propto I \cdot 2\pi x \, dx$$
$$\int -dI/I = \int 2kx \, dx \qquad \text{where } k \text{ is constant} \tag{12}$$

or
$$\log I/I_0 = -kx^2$$
$$I = I_0 e^{-kx^2} \tag{13}$$

This is an important result, since it takes the same form as Equation (6), although the generating model is a very different one.

In order to complete the examination of random walk, uniform attenuation, and constant fall-off in one and two dimensions, two other cases should be considered at this point. Again I owe their formulation to Dr. Dean.

(1) *Reduction independent of number left; two dimensions.* Here we are making the same assumption that led, for one dimension, to Equation (9). The reduction in number or quantity is independent of the number or quantity left.

i.e.,
$$-dI \propto 2\pi x \, dx$$
$$\int -dI = 2kx \cdot dx \qquad \text{where } k \text{ is constant}$$
$$I - I_0 = kx^2 \tag{14}$$

This is parabolic.

(2) *Random walk in one dimension.* A particle or object has an equal probability of going to the right or to the left at each decision. After N steps let it be dispaced n steps to the right. What is the probability of this? The total number of choices is 2^N. The "successful" number (i.e., the number of ways of producing a shift of n) is

$$^N C_{(N+n)/2} = \frac{N!}{\left(\dfrac{N+n}{2}\right)! \left(\dfrac{N-n}{2}\right)!}$$

Therefore the probability is

$$\frac{N!}{\left(\dfrac{N+n}{2}\right)! \left(\dfrac{N-n}{2}\right)! \, 2^N}$$

If there are many steps, this becomes

$$\text{Probability} = 1 \, \sqrt{\pi N} \, \exp(-n^2/N) \tag{15}$$

This is again a Gaussian expression.

We are thus in a position to summarize the shape of fall-off curves obtained

TABLE 1

The Shape of the Curves Resulting from Distance
Fall-Off Effects from a Point Source, Along a Line,
and On a Plane, With a Uniform Distribution
of Population

Model	One dimension	Two dimensions
Reduction in number independent of number left	Linear (10)[a]	Parabolic (14)
Reduction in number proportional to number left	Exponential (9)	Gaussian (13)
Random walk	Gaussian (15)	Gaussian (11)

[a] Figures in parentheses refer to equations in the text for functions derived.

for each of three models in one and two dimensions, always assuming that the distribution of population is a uniform one (see Table 1).

VIII. EQUIFINALITY AND THE CHOICE OF MODELS

In Sections VI and VII two different models for prehistoric exchange are discussed that might explain fall-off effects. The first represents exchange transactions in two dimensions in terms of random flights, where the direction of travel is random although other features (length of flight, number of flights) are fixed. The second postulates exchange transactions in two dimensions originating from a point source, the quantity of commodity retained at any location being a given constant proportion of that which reaches it. The remarkable circumstance is that the shape of the two distributions is identical: it is Gaussian.

Dr. Dean has kindly pointed out another case. We have assumed throughout that the distribution of population is uniform. To modify this assumption varies the results. For example in Equation 12, we have

$$-dI \propto I \cdot 2\pi x \, dx$$

But if the population density falls off as $1/x$ from the center of distribution or dispersal, this becomes

$$-dI \propto I \cdot 2\pi \, dx$$

which again gives rise to Equation (9), the exponential case.

The circumstance in which different initial conditions and different processes lead to the same end-product in the archaeological record suggests at first the notion of equifinality in general systems theory. There is no difficulty, of course, in defining the formation processes and preservation process of the archaeological record as a *system*. As Kast and Rosenzweig (1972:23) express it:

> In physical systems there is a direct cause and effect relationship between the initial conditions and the final state. Biological and social systems operate differently. The concept of *equifinality* says that final results may be achieved with different initial conditions and in different ways. This view suggests that the social organisation can accomplish its objectives with varying inputs and varying internal activities. Thus the social system is not restrained by the simple cause and effect relationship of closed systems.

Equifinality is a fascinating concept because of the great scope of the cases to which it is applicable (cf. Von Bertalanffy 1950:157f.). But I am not sure that it is applicable here, or rather that it relates to the behavior of the culture system, which is the focus of our interest. For there is no suggestion that the culture system in the cases under discussion did in fact reach a final, steady state to which the term equifinality could be applied. In a sense, I suppose, the formation processes did reach a steady state, namely the state in which we find the archaeological record. But this realization does not help us in the choice between two models, both producing the same patterning in the data. A more effective resolution must be to seek for independent tests for the different assumptions on which those models rest.

IX. COMPARISONS OF FALL-OFF DATA

The most systematic investigation to date of distance decay data from archaeological contexts has been undertaken by Ian Hodder (1974). In his thoughtful and wide-ranging survey he has for the first time collected sufficient instances to make the distinctions discussed above of more than academic interest. At the same time, the treatment given above of the models generating the different patterns puts some of these real cases in a new light.

Hodder used the very general expression, Equation (8) above, in the form

$$\log I = a - bD^{\alpha} + C \tag{16}$$

His method was to use a computer program to calculate the best fit regression line, performing the calculation for several values of α in succession (varying in steps of 0.1 from $\alpha = 0.1$ to $\alpha = 2.5$). As we have seen, in the exponential case, $\alpha = 1$; in the Gaussian case, $\alpha = 2$.

Hodder reported that his data fell into two groups, and such a division is reflected in the work of geographers studying distance decay effects. In the first group α was around 1 or greater. He cites Anatolian obsidian ($\alpha = 0.9$), Dobunnic coins ($\alpha = 1.3$), Roman fine ware from Oxford and Hampshire ($\alpha = 1.0$ and 1.3), neolithic pottery from Cornwall ($\alpha = 1.6$), and neolithic axes ($\alpha = 2.5$) (cf. Hodder 1974: Figure 17).

In the second group are materials whose fall-off shows a very low alpha value, between 0.1 and 0.6. Examples are Roman roofing tiles, Roman coarse pottery, and Middle Bronze Age palstaves.

In the discussion it must be remembered that the value of α determines the shape of the curve and hence the nature of the model. It is not merely some expression for the value of a constant in an equation.

The first group, with value of α around 1, suggests some conformity with the exponential decay situation. Higher values of α, around 2, indicate Gaussian fall-off. It is not correct to suggest that a figure near unity ($\alpha = 0.9$) for Anatolian obsidian may be seen as the result of a random walk process. The very thrust of Hodder's elegant regression analysis must be to show that, for a random walk, $\alpha = 2$.

The analysis tends to suggest exponential rather than Gaussian fall-off for some commodities, and our models indicate that this implies some linear patterning. Attenuation down a line produces exponential decay, while attenuation in two dimensions or random walk along a line produce Gaussian fall-off ($\alpha = 2$). Down-the-line trade of this kind has to be seen in terms of trading chains and trading *networks*.

Hodder's second group suggests to me something very different. When α is near zero, neither exponential decay nor random walk can apply at all. He has documented that many of the goods in question are common, bulky, and supplied in a limited area: for instance, Roman roofing tiles near Cirencester. In some cases the slope of the regression line is also very steep. This leads me to suggest that the models discussed above, which are framed in terms of repeated transaction, do not apply in such cases. In some of them the pattern may not be very far from the linear one described above [Equation (10)] or even the parabolic [Equation (14)].

I suggest that this is *supply zone* behavior (Renfrew et al. 1968:327), where we are dealing with a pattern arising largely from single journeys. In many cases the user is traveling direct to the source or manufacturing center, or the producer is traveling with his goods direct to the purchaser. The result is an extreme localization in the distribution of the product that is not in general handed on in subsequent transactions. There is a radius beyond which the specific product is very rarely found, and this radius is usually the length of a single journey that the producer or user will normally undertake to sell it or to fetch it. In some cases there may be an intermediate transaction at a local market. But in general, within the supply zone, the goods are distributed by means of a single exchange transaction. This is mode 2 of a recent formulation of trading types (Renfrew 1975:42).

This is to be contrasted with *contact zone* behavior, where commodities are worth exchanging beyond the limits of the supply zone (although the distance traveled may be limited by the effect of competing sources—cf. Section XI). Often they are distributed by down-the-line exchange. As Hodder well brings out, these are usually either more desirable, or easier to transport, or both.

X. CONCENTRATION EFFECTS AND DIRECTIONAL TRADE

We have discussed so far distributions in which the exchange is taking place from hand to hand in a homogeneous population. That is to say, no one individual or place is particularly distinguished from any other. In these circumstances any location will receive less of a commodity than its neighbor nearer to the source.

Not infrequently, however, this principle, the law of monotonic decrement, is violated, and a more distant source obtains not only more of the commodity but a greater per capita frequency of it. This can only mean that it is being supplied preferentially (with respect to its neighbors), and it is here that the term directional trade is appropriate.

In the first place, it is relevant to see in this the development both of larger centers of population and of central places. A large center of population, whatever its nature, will attract a large absolute quantity of any commodity (see Section V). But this will not of itself guarantee any larger quantity *per head* of population.

The concept of "central place" implies, however, more than simply larger size. The central place is a locus for exchange activity, and more of any material passes through it (per head of population) than through a smaller settlement (see Figure 5).

The hierarchy of settlement is here accompanied by a hierarchy of exchange activity. Suppliers from a distance bring their goods first to the central place, and they are disseminated from the central place to smaller localities. In other words, the central place is used for break of bulk. The effect here is that, in terms of supply, the central place is nearer to the source than are lower-order localities supplied by it, even if these may in reality be geographically closer to the source.

If the archaeological record is formed in proportion to the quantity of material handled, the central place will show a greater frequency than its population alone would warrant, since it is acting as a supply center for its hinterland.

In practice, however, the effect is sometimes more marked than this. For accompanying the hierarchy of places is a hierarchy of persons. And those persons in the upper parts of the hierarchy have preferential access to the material and will accumulate greater quantities, per head, of commodities they desire.

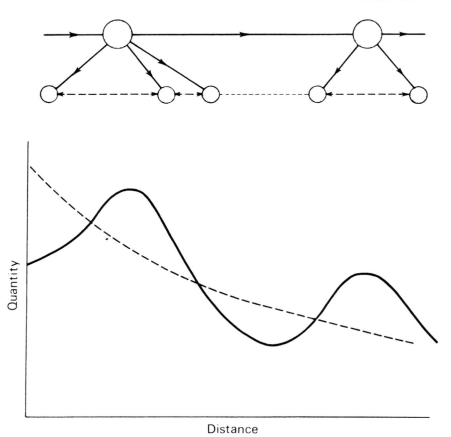

Figure 5 Directional trade: the effect of central places (above) on the fall-off. The dashed curve shows down-the-line exchange: exponential fall-off generated by exchange in a linear chain (quantity and distance on linear scales).

Here, then, are two concentration effects. The first arises from the central place or market function of a center, with the break of bulk of the commodity. The second arises from preferential access of prominent or wealthy individuals who are generally located at central places. Both these concentration effects result in a greater frequency (per head of population or per cubic meter of excavated soil) than would otherwise be the case. Were it not for them, the total of a commodity at a large population center would be greater than in surrounding settlements, but the frequency would not.

Directional trade is to be recognized by indications of break-of-bulk operations (storehouses, organizational systems, waste materials) and by signs of preferential supply in large quantity. In favorable cases, both of these will result in a higher frequency of finds and hence in a departure from the monotomic decrease effect encountered with nondirectional trade.

This argument has been used (Renfrew and Dixon 1977) to explain the decline in the concentration of obsidian at rural sites in the Near East in the middle and late neolithic period, it being suggested that the emergence of central places was actually impairing the supply of obsidian at lower-order localities. Sidrys (Chapter 5) has elegantly documented the concentration effect operating for obsidian at Classic Maya ceremonial centers.

XI. COMPETING SOURCES

Care is needed in the use of gravity models for the prediction of traded materials as reflecting interaction with centers of population. For, as implied in the last section, the larger population attracting a larger quantity of material need not result in any greater frequency, expressed in frequency per head or per cubic meter of soil.

The impact of a second source of the same commodity, however, is important. Bradley (1971) suggests that the asymmetrical spread of various pottery products, as well as of obsidian, in the Near East may be interpreted in these terms. An equally interesting case has arisen in the obsidian distribution of the Sardinia, Lipari, and Parmarola sources of southern Italy (Hallam et al. 1976).

If we use a modification of the Law of Retail Gravitation (Reilly 1931), this impact can be explained. Let the material traded have a desirability factor or attractiveness A_1. Then source S_1 will supply a quantity Q_1 directly proportional to its attractiveness A_1 and inversely proportional to some function of the distance D_1 from the source. (In this formulation the square of the distance is used.) That is

$$Q_1 \propto A_1/D_1{}^2$$

When dealing with two sources

$$Q_1/Q_2 = A_1/A_2 \times D_2{}^2/D_1{}^2 \tag{17}$$

And if we take the locus of equal interaction, $Q_1 = Q_2$, and

$$A_1/A_2 = D_1{}^2/D_2{}^2 = k^2 \tag{18}$$

where k is the ratio of the "attractiveness" of the sources. If d is the effective distance of separation of the sources, then it is easy to show that the locus of equal interaction is a circle of radius $kd/1 - k^2$ with a center lying on the line joining the landfalls and displaced a distance $k^2d/1 - k^2$ from the least attractive source (see Figure 6).

It is quite possible for two sources a distance X apart to give rise quite independently to fall-off patterns, which taken together might suggest the behavior of competing sources discussed here. The two patterns superimposed, as if they were contemporary, will give a first approximation to that

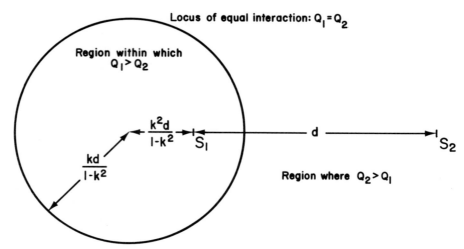

Figure 6   The locus of equal interaction for two competing sources S_1 and S_2. (After Hallam et al. 1976.)

predicted by the Law of Retail Gravitation. It is therefore necessary to distinguish the effect of straightforward, independent distance fall-off from that of sources simultaneously in competition. A "test" of the model, apparently supporting its application, would be of little worth. Moreover, it is probably inappropriate to use an inverse square relationship for distance, as explained in Section III and within much of the preceding discussion. Until these problems have been carefully thought out, applications and modifications of the Reilly formula should perhaps be viewed with suspicion.

XII. MODES OF EXCHANGE

A recent attempt (Renfrew 1975: Figure 10) to identify the spatial correlates of various specific modes of trade, in the vocabulary of Polanyi, must be viewed with some sobriety in the light of the foregoing discussion.

Central place redistribution and central place market exchange are spatially identical (although concentration effects are facilitated by redistributive control or by tax).

These two modes should, however, be distinguishable from symmetrical, homogeneous, reciprocal exchange networks. I suggest that a useful field for further study will be the range of organizational devices through which the law of monotonic decrement is circumvented by human exchange systems, particularly those that are hierarchically structured.

Acknowledgments

I am very grateful to Dr. R. H. Dean of the Department of Physics, University of Southampton, for kindly setting down for me the derivations of a number of the distance decay functions, especially those given in Section VII; to Dr. Ian Hodder for discussion; and to the editors for their encouragement.

References

Ammerman, A. J., C. Matessi, and L. L. Cavalli-Sforza
  1977   Some new approaches to the study of obsidian trade in the Mediterranean and adjacent areas. In *The spatial organisation of culture,* edited by I. A. Hodder, London: Duckworth (forthcoming).
Bradley, R.
  1971   Trade competition and artefact distribution. *World Archaeology* 2:347–352.
Claeson, C. F.
  1968   Distance and human interaction. *Geografisker Annaler B* 50:142–161.
Hallam, B., S. Warren, and C. Renfrew
  1976   Obsidian in the West Mediterranean. *Proceedings of the Prehistoric Society* 42 (forthcoming).
Haynes, R.
  1974   Application of exponential distance decay to human and animal activities. *Geografisker Annaler B* 56.
Hodder, I.
  1974   Regression analysis of some trade and marketing patterns. *World Archaeology* 6:172–189.
Hogg, A. H. A.
  1971   Some applications of surface fieldwork. In *The Iron Age and its hillforts,* edited by M. Jesson and D. Hill. Southampton, England: University of Southampton Press.
Kast, F. W., and J. E. Rosenzweig
  1972   The modern view: a systems approach. In *Systems behaviour,* edited by J. Beishon and G. Peters. London: Open University.
Morrill, R. L.
  1963   The distribution of migration distances. *Papers and Proceedings of the Regional Science Association* 11:75–84.
Morrill, R. L., and F. R. Pitts
  1967   Marriage, migration and the mean information field: a study in uniqueness and generality. *Annals of the Association of American Geographers* 57:401–422.
Olsson, G.
  1965   Distance and human interaction: a review and bibliography, *Regional Science Research Institute Bibliography Series* 2.
Pearson, K.
  1906   A mathematical theory of random migration. *Drapers Company Research Memoirs, Biometric Series* 3:3–54 (with J. Blakeman).
Pires-Ferreira, J. W.
  1973   *Formative Mesoamerican exchange networks.* Ph.D. dissertation, Ann Arbor, Michigan: University of Michigan.
Reilly, W. J.
  1931   *The law of retail gravitation.* New York.

Renfrew, C.
   1972   *The emergence of civilization: the Cyclades and the Aegean in the third millennium BC.* London: Methuen.
   1975   Trade as action at a distance: questions ot integration and communication. In *Ancient civilization and trade,* edited by J. A. Sabloff and C. C. Lamberg-Karlovsky, pp. 3–59. Albuquerque, New Mexico: University of New Mexico Press.
Renfrew, C., and J. Dixon
   1977   Obsidian in western Asia: a review. In *Studies in economic and social archeology,* edited by I. Longworth and G. Sieveking, pp. 137–150. London: Duckworth.
Renfrew, C., J. E. Dixon, and J. R. Cann
   1968   Further analysis of Near Eastern obsidians. *Proceedings of the Prehistoric Society* **34:**319–331.
Von Bertalanffy, L.
   1950   An outline of general system theory. *British Journal of the Philosophy of Science* **1:**134–165.
Wright, G. A.
   1970   On trade and culture process in prehistory. *Current Anthropology* **11:**171–173.

Chapter 5

MASS–DISTANCE MEASURES FOR THE MAYA OBSIDIAN TRADE

RAYMOND SIDRYS

I. INTRODUCTION

This study examines the quantitative and geographic distribution of imported obsidian in the Maya sphere during both the Classic (250–900 A.D.) and Postclassic (1000–1450 A.D.) periods. The Classic Maya of eastern Mesoamerica (present day Guatemala, Belize, the Mexican states of Yucatan, Quintana Roo, Campeche, Chiapas, and Tabasco, and sections of Honduras and El Salvador) have long been noted as a culture in which knowledge of astronomy, calendrics, mathematics, and hieroglyphic writing figured prominantly in the lives of the ruling class. For over a half millenium this cultural system apparently enjoyed a remarkably successful man–land relationship. The large populations estimated for Maya settlements (Haviland 1970) and the impressive energy expenditure represented in their monumental architecture has spawned much debate as to whether Maya social institutions show a closer evolutionary fit to an "advanced chiefdom" or a "primitive state" (Sanders and Price 1968; Willey 1972b).

Long-distance trade has been cited as an important factor in both the rise of Maya civilization (Rathje 1972) and in its dramatic demise (Culbert 1973; Webb 1964). The large lowland civic–ceremonial centers may have functioned as the commercial loci for this long-distance trade. This is suggested by the presence of long-distance imports and spacious public plazas within the centers, as well as their locational distribution in a hexagonal lattice-like network (Hammond 1974; Marcus 1973).

The present research project examines two problems: (1) whether the lowland centers did, indeed, serve as commercial nuclei of Maya culture, and (2) whether evolutionary trends are evident in the development of Maya exchange systems from the Classic through the Postclassic periods. Accordingly, the project was divided into two research phases.

II. RESEARCH PHASE I: CENTRAL PLACE OF CEREMONIAL CENTERS

In the first research phase, transport distance and commodity mass (as critical measures of the intensity of trade activity at a site) were determined from the obsidian artifacts excavated from the fill of 18 Classic Maya sites. Within the regional pattern, the commodity mass of obsidian consumed in central places should appear as anomalies of transport distance. In other words, it was expected that the per capita consumption of obsidian would be higher within central places than in neighboring sites that had equal transport distances to obsidian sources.

Trade indices that use the ratio between artifact classes or the ratio between materials in a single artifact class do not measure the quantity of material consumed by a given population. For example, such ratios include obsidian to flint, which has been used in the Maya area (Moholy-Nagy 1974; Rathje 1972; Urban n.d.), in California (Ericson, Chapter 6), and in the Near East (Renfrew et al. 1968; Wright 1969). For this reason a new index was derived, which is sensitive to per capita consumption. The obsidian density index, abbreviated OD, was calculated as the mass of obsidian per unit volume.

$$\text{Obsidian density} = \frac{\text{Obsidian mass}}{\text{Excavated volume}} \tag{1}$$

In this paper, the obsidian density (OD) index is calculated by the number of grams per cubic meter of excavation fill. The OD index serves as a measure of obsidian per capita at each site. For example, if Site A had a population twice the size of Site B, but both sites had the same OD, then individuals at both sites would have consumed comparable amounts of obsidian. This assumption is permissible as long as the density of residence units is fairly constant between Maya population centers.[1] Thus an increase in OD represents a true increase in obsidian deposition between comparable residence unit populations (relative obsidian per capita) rather than simply registering the additional deposition of a higher population density. In addition, there are two other important research concerns which make the OD preferable. It provides an estimate of the quantity of the consumed material that can be directly compared to the quantity produced (c.f. Singer and Ericson, Chapter 10). Secondly, as discussed by Wright (1969:48), mass is a critical factor in a primitive transport system based on human manuport. The index provides a means to estimate the number of personnel involved in transport.

The representativeness of the OD estimates must, however, always be considered carefully. For Maya residential structures, artifacts are usually recovered from "secondary" contexts (c.f. Schiffer 1972:159), as it was a common practice to use refuse as fill for the house platform (Haviland 1963:76; Willey et al. 1965:454). Since the small size of obsidian artifacts ensures that they were not deposited as special fill, the samples may be considered representative of normal household midden (for a more extensive discussion of specific sampling problems for the Maya, see Sidrys 1973:20–27). Within a site, contributions from all special purpose deposits like caches or burials were excluded to avoid their bias.

The obsidian data were obtained primarily from published site reports, including personal clarifications, when necessary, from several of the excavators. Archaeological recovery techniques varied between excavations, but two-thirds of the excavation reports stated that special efforts had been made to recover all of the obsidian. After the excavation volumes were determined from plans and profiles, the mass of obsidian was estimated in the following manner. The average dimensions of a "fragmentary prismatic flake-blade," using data from Barton Ramie, San Jose, Zacualpa, Uaxactun, and Yaxha, were found to be thickness, .3 cm; width, 1.1 cm; length, 3.1 cm. The mass of this "average" fragment was estimated as a 2 gm standard for converting counts of prismatic blade fragments to an obsidian mass. Similarly cores were estimated to be 25 gm, knife blades at 9 gm, and "waste" flakes at 2 gm. Complete statistical data and methodology for this study is reported elsewhere (Sidrys 1973: 113–141).

The dating of artifacts is greatly complicated by their redeposited context. Refuse piles probably had a high reuse rate in view of incessant Maya constructional activity, and it may be that redeposited refuse generally was not much older than the construction date of the building, especially for small

[1] Only Mayapan and perhaps Tulum approach an urban settlement pattern (Willey 1972b:13). Furthermore, since the fill at Zaculeu, Tajumulco, El Baul, Bilbao, and Altar (as picked for the study) comes from large plazas or pyramids, they represent collective deposits, which may bias the site samples.

structures (Willey 1972a:2). At present, however, there is insufficient data to derive an OD for each ceramic phase at any given site. Most of the data in the OD study overlaps throughout the Classic period.[2] By excluding time as a factor, the general data patterns are somewhat dependent on the assumption that relative site hierarchy was fairly stable through the Classic. The stable size of the Great Plaza–North Terrace of Tikal from 100 B.C. to 700 A.D. offers support for such an assumption (Coe 1962:504).

A. Source Distance

The present study uses the linear distance from each site to the nearest obsidian source area as the source distance for the final statistical tests. The sources used for the study were those eleven potential sources that were most likely exploited regularly by the Classic Maya (Figure 1). The numerous but more distant sources (about 1000 km) in the Central Mexican Highlands are excluded, since this obsidian is only occasionally found in the Maya area. For example, 1.6% of the obsidian recovered at Tikal (to 1967) is of a green variety probably from Pachuca, Hidalgo (Moholy-Nagy 1974). This report does not incorporate any source assignations based on trace-elemental research. The present state of the art in Mesoamerican "sourcing" research is still uncertain (Stross et al. 1976; Sidrys et al. 1976), and the few Maya sites that have been sourced, such as Tikal (Moholy-Nagy 1974), Yaxha (Sidrys and Kimberlin n.d.), and Seibal (Graham et al. 1972), tentatively indicate multiple-source exploitation at each site.

B. Fall-Off Model

As a function of transportation cost, the abundance of any object falls off with increasing distance from source (c.f. Renfrew, Chapter 4). Generally this decrease is exponential, as shown by modern freight movements (Haggett 1969:34) or in the distribution of Near Eastern obsidian during the neolithic (Renfrew et al. 1968:328). For the 18 Maya sites, the fall-off model will predict the trend of the data, but only in a very limited and general way. That is, a net decrease in the average OD exists between the seven highland sites, closest to the obsidian sources, and the eleven lowland sites presented in Table 1. However, the exponential nature of the fall-off model would predict a linear decrease of OD as a function of distance on a log–log plot. Regression analysis of the OD (log–log) and distance data for the 18 sites showed a low Pearson's r correlation coefficient, $r = -.56$. Clearly this fall-off model does not provide the best "fit" for the data.

---

[2] The Postclassic sites of Tulum, Mayapan, and Zaculeu were included to obtain a better geographic sample.

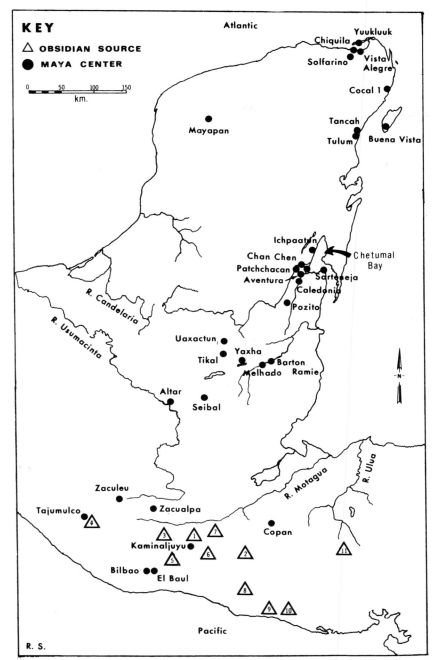

Figure 1 Obsidian sources and Maya centers used in the OD and O:S analyses. Note that Santa Rita Corozal, shown at the southwestern corner of Chetumal Bay, is not labeled. Numbered obsidian sources: (1) El Chayal, Guatemala; (2) Ixtepeque, Guatemala; (3) San Martin Jilotepeque, Guatemala; (4) Tajumulco, Guatemala; (5) Amatitlan, Guatemala; (6) Media Cuesta, Guatemala; (7) Jalapa, Guatemala; (8) Santa Ana, El Salvador; (9) Zaragoza, El Salvador; (10) Rio Comalapa, El Salvador; (11) La Esperanza, Honduras.

Indeed, upon reexamination, this result was not surprising in view of the different economic functions of the 18 sites that range from undifferentiated agricultural hamlets to nucleated centers. This differentiation suggested a stratification within the data set. Thus, when the major centers were distinguished from the other sites, two discrete but parallel patterns emerge (Table 1). Within each group there is a significant negative correlation between source distance and OD (respective Pearson's r is $-.81$ and $-.93$). The group of major centers (Line 1 in Figure 2) includes large sites described as political "capitals" (Tikal, Copan, Bilbao, Kaminaljuyu, Mayapan) or trade ports (Tulum and Cozumel). The other group (Line 2 in Figure 2) is com-

TABLE 1

OBSIDIAN DENSITIES AND EXCAVATION DATA

Site[a]	Excavation volume used in study (m³)	Obsidian mass (g) found in excavation volume	Obsidian density (g/m³)	Source distance (km)	Nearest potential source[b]
Altar	6790	3500	.5	195	San Martin Jilotepeque
Barton Ramie	2213	700	.3	315	El Chayal
Zacualpa	681	6116	9.0	30	San Martin Jilotepeque
Zaculeu	600	565	.9	55	Tajumulco Volcano
Tikal	544	8297	15.3	285	El Chayal
Tajumulco	466	2143	4.9	15	Tajumulco Volcano
Cozumel (Buena Vista)	275	140	.5	710	El Chayal
Uaxactun	213	481	2.3	305	El Chayal
Seibal	197	220	1.1	196	San Martin Jilotepeque
Kaminaljuyu	178	6776	38.1	18	El Chayal
Tancah	165	10	0.6	682	Ixtepeque
Mayapan	159	583	3.7	690	El Chayal
Tulum	150	212	1.4	680	Ixtepeque
El Baul	79	263	3.3	50	Amatitlan
Bilbao	67	1160	17.3	53	Amatitlan
Copan	38	1046	27.5	87	Ixtepeque
Yaxha	19	246	12.8	280	El Chayal
Melhado	16	3	.2	305	El Chayal

[a] Site obsidian densities are listed in order of reliability, i.e., according to the size of the excavation volume examined.

[b] The La Esperanza source may be slightly closer than Ixtepeque for Cozumel, Tulum, and Tancah.

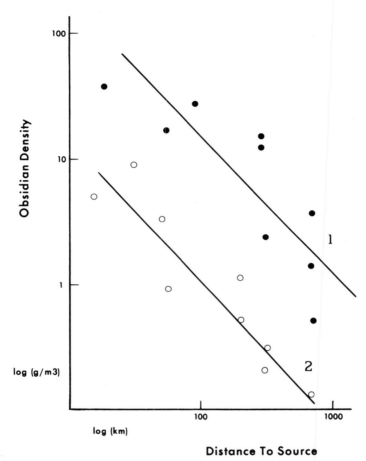

Figure 2 Fall-off of obsidian density (grams of obsidian/m³ of excavated fill) with increasing distance from source. Line 1 is the estimated regression line for the major centers, while line 2 is the estimated regression line for the minor centers. The average OD for the major centers is about six times higher than that of the minor centers.

posed primarily of villages and less important centers (Seibal and, perhaps, Altar are exceptions). The major centers have nucleated civic–ceremonial areas (wall-boundaries, acropoli, group-complexes) that average 6.7 times larger than their minor center counterparts and average 4.3 times as many public monuments (Table 2). The data indicate that major centers were able to import about six times more obsidian per capital than the smaller centers (which had a much smaller average source distance, 205 km versus 345 km). This result suggests that the lowland ceremonial centers did in fact serve as the commercial nuclei of Maya culture during the Classic period.

TABLE 2

TRADE INDEX RANKS AND CEREMONIAL ATTRIBUTES

Site	Trade index (obsidian density × source distance)	Civic– ceremonial area (k m²)	Nontransportable monuments
Major Centers			
(1) Tikal	4361	4.0	206
(2) Yaxha	3584	.6	62
(3) Mayapan	2553	4.0	38
(4) Copan	2393	.18	82
(5) Tulum	952	.12	9
(6) Bilbao	917	.10	77
(7) Uaxactun	702	1.4	69
(8) Kaminaljuyu	685	.15	30
(9) Cozumel (Buena Vista)	355	.18	1
Means	1834	1.2	64
Minor Centers			
(1) Zacualpa	270	.24	2
(2) Seibal	216	1.1	30
(3) El Baul	165	.04	30
(4) Altar	98	.08	47
(5) Barton Ramie	95	.005	0
(6) Tajumulco	74	.006	27
(7) Melhado	62	.0004	0
(8) Zaculeu	50	.04	1
(9) Tancah	41	.13	0
Means	119	.18	15

C. The Trade Index Model: A Technique for Comparing Hierarchical Stratified Sites

The problem encountered with the fall-off model was that a few regional centers could "mask" the fall-off pattern in regression analysis, particularly in small data sets. Likewise, the process of stratifying sites as to their hierarchical ranking without a priori knowledge is problematic. The trade index, abbreviated TI, allows the comparison of a relatively small sample of economically dissimilar sites at varying distances from a source. This index simply weights a given OD value by the source distance as shown in Equation (2).

$$TI = OD \times SD \tag{2}$$

where TI is the trade index, OD is the obsidian density (obsidian grams/m³ of excavated fill), and SD is the source distance from site to source (km). Weber (see Haggett 1969:142) devised a similar economic index in 1909 to explain the problem of "eccentric" locations of specialized industrial centers. In his analysis the distance a commodity was transported was multiplied by the commodity mass to produce *ton-mile* units.

The TI has important applications. As an index, it couples two significant variables of exchange, namely the amount of material consumed (mass) and transport distance (source distance). Since the index measures energy expenditure, it is amenable to studying least work effort. The relationship of force and distance from classical physics is described in Equation (3).

$$W = F \cdot D \tag{3}$$

where W is work, F is force, and D is distance. The TI is equivalent to the form of the work equation (3), since a gravitational constant makes force directly proportional to [obsidian] mass, which is represented in the TI as OD. As a generalized index, TI allows the analyst to study other independent variables of exchange.

For these purposes the TI was calculated for the 18 Classic sites. It can be seen in Table 2 that the nine major centers have, as expected, the highest TI values. The size of the TI establishes a hierarchical sequence among the major centers in terms of the intensity of trade activity. Furthermore, the regression of the log–log of TI with site civic–ceremonial area has a correlation of Pearson's $r = 70$. Although the explained variability (r^2) is not great, at least this analysis is suggestive. Nonparametric statistical analysis showed similar results (Spearman's $r = .72$; Kendall's $\tau = .55$). These results tend to support the relationships discussed in the fall-off model. Following the hierarchical ranking propositions of locational geographics, an increase in attributes of "ceremonialism" at a site (which may be equated to some degree as the administrative accoutrements of a managerial group) is apparently related to the increase in trade activity for obsidian per capita.

III. RESEARCH PHASE II: DIACHRONIC STABILITY OF EXCHANGE SYSTEMS

The second phase of research examined the diachronic stability of the exchange systems. In Maya culture, it appears that obsidian import may begin (to some degree) in the earliest occupations of most of the larger sites (Moholy-Nagy 1974; Willey 1972a:217; Graham et al. 1972:111).

Several studies have emphasized the apparent widespread abundance of obsidian during the Classic period as the major evidence for its everyday technoeconomic use (Rathje 1972; Moholy-Nagy 1974). While it is true that obsidian may be randomly distributed at a site in the qualitative or nominal sense (i.e., presence/absence), there are other data (see Sidrys n.d.) that indicate it is not randomly distributed in the quantitative sense. Evidence for the high status of imported obsidian includes its differential concentration near the residences of wealthy individuals as well as its lavish use in caches and burials at many sites. The issue deserves further research and clarification.

The enormous obsidian caches in the Early and Middle Classic (Coe 1962:498; Willey 1972a:214) further suggest the presence of political "pot-latching patterns": the intentional removal from potential use of a useful imported commodity during a public ritual. Likewise, the manufacture of Late Classic ritualized "eccentric" obsidian items is somewhat analogous to the production of the geometrically-shaped "coppers" that were used in Northwest Coast potlatch ceremonies (c.f. Drucker 1967:492). To sum-marize, obsidian use during the Classic period undoubtedly did have some specialized utilitarian functions (surgery, shaving, fish-cleaning, etc.). But, for the most part, it maintained a specific system of social stratification through its extensive use in ritualistic behavior and as a useful item in the elite or upper-class households. However, the transition from the Classic to the Postclassic period apparently brought a radical reorganization of obsidian import, which will be discussed in the next section.

A. The Obsidian:Sherd Count Index (O:S)

As discussed earlier, the ratio of obsidian artifacts to an abundant different artifact type serves as an alternative trade measure. For Mesoamerica, Thompson (1948) and Parsons (1969:80) have used the ratio of obsidian blades to sherds, and Cobean et al. (1971:666) have used the ratio of obsidian artifacts to grinding stones. The primary disadvantages of artifact count ratios are that there is often a poor correlation between numbers of artifacts and their weight, different breakage rates distort the ratio, and there is a differential recovery and classification of artifact classes by different re-searchers, particularly the "unutilized" flake (c.f. Brose 1975).

As sherds are the best artifactual measures of the site population size and activity (Cook 1972), they were selected for the second research phase. This study utilizes an obsidian:sherd count index (O:S), which is the ratio of obsidian artifacts to sherds for a sample of 31 Classic and Postclassic sites. The obsidian artifact count from a given excavation was "weighted" by the associated sherd number to standardize population differentials. this statis-tic was more readily available in the archaeological literature than the OD, and the sample size permitted a temporal separation (Classic and Postclas-sic). However, the sample size from the Classic is almost 13 times larger than its Postclassic counterpart, which, unfortunately, lessens their comparability. Another limitation of the available data required the lumping of obsidian artifacts from both utilitarian and ceremonial contexts into a single group.

B. The Fall-Off Model

The fall-off of the Classic O:S data with increasing distance, shown in Table 3, is comparable to that demonstrated in the first research phase. For example, the average obsidian artifact/sherd ratio (O:S) for the four highland sites is 1:22, whereas the lowland sites average is 1:232. The fall-off is more clearly demonstrated in a plot of the O:S versus source distance (Figure 3). Again, hierarchical ranking of sites appears to be operating in that most of the minor centers and villages are on the lower side of the least square line, which suggests their participation in a less efficient or less active system of obsidian trade.

A comparable fall-off pattern of the Postclassic O:S data with increasing distance can not be drawn in Figure 3, since all but two sites are clustered at a 450–825 km distance from source. It is significant, however, that the range of variation of the O:S for these distant sites is comparable to that for the Classic sites, which were closer to the sources (18–450 km). It suggests that Postclassic North Yucatecan settlements had a greater accessibility to obsidian sources (because of more efficient transport methods?) than did their Classic period counterparts. This diachronic anomaly is more evident in the following section.

C. The Trade Index

The utility of the distance-weighted trade index is demonstrated in discerning the diachronic trend in the exchange systems. The O:S data were multiplied by the source distance, following the format of Equation (3). By inspection, the mean distance-weighted Postclassic trade index is substantially higher than that of the Classic period (2.1 to 1.5), even with the exclusion of the three unusually high Postclassic cases that may be due to sampling (shown in Table 3). The results indicate a significant increase in the volume of obsidian exchange from the Classic through Postclassic.

The distance-weighted trade index in Table 3 (like its counterpart in Table 2) also shows that most of the Classic major centers have higher indices than the minor centers. The small center of Caledonia appears as an anomaly, which might be a function of sampling. For this site, the high proportion of obsidian was found in an Early Classic elite midden within a huge structure with a basal area of 14,300 m^2 (Sidrys n.d.; Hammond 1973:69).

D. Discussion of Results

The significance of the observed diachronic change in the exchange system warrants further discussion. Between the Classic and Postclassic, it seems

TABLE 3

OBSIDIAN: SHERD COUNT RATIOS FOR THE CLASSIC AND POSTCLASSIC PERIODS

Site	Total obsidian in association with sherd total (number)	Sherd total used in study (number)	Obsidian: sherd ratio	Source distance (Km)	Distance-weighted trade index $\left(\dfrac{\text{obsidian}}{\text{sherd}}\right) \times$ distance = TI
Classic Occupations					
Uaxactun, Guat.	150	7669	1:51	305	6.0
Caledonia, Bel.	29	4500	1:155	436	2.8
Yaxha, Guat.	213	23000	1:108	280	2.6
Bilbao, Guat.	461	9973	1:22	53	2.4
Tikal, Guat.	3952	525150	1:133	285	2.1
Kaminaljuyu, Guat.	25000	215000	1:9	18	2.0
Copan, Hon.	320	16353	1:51	87	1.7
Sarteneja, Bel.	1	450	1:450	470	1.0
Sta. Rita Corozal, Bel.	10	4450	1:445	457	1.0
Patchchacan, Bel.	7	5550	1:793	454	.6
El Baul, Guat.	—	—	1:90	50	.6
Aventura, Bel.	22	18600	1:845	447	.5
Barton Ramie, Bel	334	200000	1:600	315	.5
Tancah, Mex.	5	6972	1:1394	682	.5
Chan Chen, Bel.	6	5700	1:950	460	.5
Altar, Guat.	1948	800000	1:411	195	.5
Melhado, Bel.	1	1889	1:1889	305	.2
				$n = 17$	mean = 1.5
Postclassic Occupations					
Sarteneja, Bel.	39	400	1:10	470	47.0
Cocal 1 Mex.	2	56	1:28	767	27.4
Yuukluuk, Mex.	1	60	1:60	825	13.8
Ichpaatun, Mex.	110	9414	1:86	484	5.6
Tulum, Mex.	96	12491	1:130	680	5.2
Mayapan, Mex.	1955	500000	1:256	690	2.7
Solfarino, Mex.	1	436	1:436	812	1.9
Sta. Rita Corozal, Bel	8	2000	1:250	457	1.8
Patchchacan, Bel.	12	3000	1:250	454	1.8
Vista Alegre, Mex.	1	587	1:587	812	1.4
Chan Chen, Bel.	8	4250	1:531	460	.9
Zacualpa, Guat.	310	14100	1:45	30	.7
Chiquila, Mex.	1	1206	1:1206	805	.7
Zaculeu, Guat.	—	—	1:268	55	.2
				$n = 14$	mean = 7.9

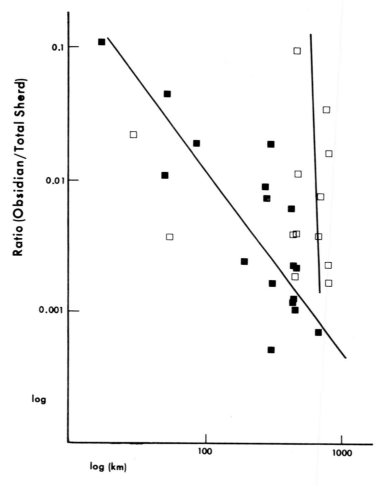

Distance To Source

Figure 3   Fall-off of obsidian artifact/sherd ratio with increasing distance from source for 17 Classic sites and 13 Postclassic sites. Solid squares represent Classic sites. Note that while most of the Postclassic sites are far from the source, the range of variation of their O:S ratios is similar to that of the Classic sites.

likely that transport efficiency of obsidian import increased. It is suggested here that the evolution of sea canoe transport made obsidian more readily available, irrespective of increasing source distance. In this case, we would expect that the transport routes would shift from overland to predominantly riverine and sea coast routes. On his fourth voyage, Columbus encountered a trading canoe said to be as long as a Spanish galley, eight feet wide and holding more than 25 men (Las Casas bk. 2, ch. 20), near the Bay Islands.

Ceremonial canoes in Hispaniola sometimes reached a length of 96 feet (Rouse 1966:236). Although trading canoes relied primarily on paddlers, the chronicler Bernal Diaz del Castillo claims to have seen the use of a lateen sail.

There is at least preliminary archaeological evidence that the Postclassic exchange patterns did shift to the coast. A recent survey in the Northern Belize coastal region confirms that obsidian import increased from the Classic to the Postclassic in terms of both the OD and O:S measures (Sidrys n.d.). Other Late Postclassic coastal or riverine sites such as Ichpaatun and Tulum (Sanders 1960), Marlowe Cay (Craig 1966:28), Wild Cane Cay (N. Hammond, personal communication), Corozal Beach, Indian Church (D. Pendergast, personal communication), and Buena Vista, Cozumel (Rathje, personal communication) also show large deposits of obsidian in the archaeological record, which appears to support the ethnohistoric documentation of an active Late Postclassic coastal trade network (Roys 1943).

This change may be directly linked to the growth of an economic institution termed "ports of trade" as a device that facilitated Postclassic long-distance trade (Chapman 1957). The hypothesis is that certain coastal regions were set aside by Central Mexican alliances to serve as neutral meeting areas for merchants traveling along the Yucatan Coast. The possible political administration of this trade is, however, still unresolved. Alternatively, it is quite possible that local fishermen may have acted as middlemen for much of the northern lowland obsidian market centers. At Sarteneja, as much of the obsidian was apparently found in a utilitarian context, associated with fishing equipment, it is possible that it was procured directly by local fishermen (Sidrys n.d.).

In conclusion, it is suggested that the Late Classic, and certainly the Late Postclassic, increases in transport efficiency "devalued" the exotic status of obsidian in the Maya lowlands and permitted a more regular and widespread utilitarian use. Whether the whole exchange pattern shifts from overland to sea coast remains an interesting, although unresolved, problem at present.

IV. CONCLUSIONS

The large lowland Maya civic–ceremonial centers served as commercial nuclei or central places in long-distance [obsidian] exchange during the Classic period. Empirical data indicate that these major centers were able to import about six times more obsidian per capita than could smaller centers, in spite of a larger average travel distance to obsidian sources. This difference in the volume of obsidian exchange between the two groups appears to be consistent throughout the Yucatan Peninsula.

The Classic–Postclassic transition brought a reorganization in lowland obsidian import. Mass-distance obsidian trade indices show that Postclassic settlements enjoyed greater access to obsidian (source distances being equal) than did their Classic period counterparts. As the archaeological distribution of obsidian in Postclassic Northern Yucatan clusters around coastal or riverine sites, it seems likely that efficient sea canoe transport together with institutionalized "ports of trade" were significant factors in shifting Post-classic exchange patterns to the coast. The huge canoes, occasionally equipped with sails, that were seen by the Spaniards upon their arrival apparently had no Classic period counterparts.

In summary, Postclassic advances in long-distance trade network logistics "devalued" the earlier exotic status of obsidian in the Maya lowlands and allowed a wider access to this useful natural glass.

Acknowledgments

This paper is a revision of an earlier one presented at the 38th Annual Meeting of the Society for American Archeology, 1973, San Francisco. I am grateful to Timothy Earle and Jon Ericson for valuable advice during several revisions of the paper.

References

Adams, R. E. W.
  1971   The ceramics of Altar de Sacrificios. *Peabody Museum Papers* **63**(1).
Brose, D.
  1975   Functional analysis of stone tools: a cautionary note on the role of animal fats. *American Antiquity* **40**:86–93.
Chapman, A. M.
  1957   Port of trade enclaves in Aztec and Maya civilizations. In *Trade and market in the early empires,* edited by K. Polanyi, C. Arensberg, and H. Pearson, pp. 114–153. Glencoe, Illinois: The Free Press.
Cobean, R., M. Coe, E. Perry, Jr., K. Turekian, and D. Kharkar
  1971   Obsidian trade at San Lorenzo Tenochtitlan, Mexico. *Science* **174**:666–671.
Coe, W. R.
  1962   A summary of excavation and research at Tikal, Guatemala: 1956–61. *American Antiquity* **27**:479–507.
Cook, S.
  1972   Can pottery residues be used as an index to population? *University of California Archaeological Research Facility Contributions* **14**:17–40.
Craig, A.
  1966   Geography of fishing in British Honduras and adjacent coastal waters. Baton Rouge, Louisiana: *Louisiana State University Press, Coastal Studies Series* **14**.
Culbert, T. P. (editor)
  1973   *The classic Maya collapse.* Albuquerque, New Mexico: University of New Mexico Press.
Diaz del Castillo, B.
  1908
  –16   *The true history of the conquest of New Spain,* translated by A. P. Maudslay. London: The Hakluyt Society.

Drucker, P.
  1967 The potlatch. In *Tribal and peasant economies,* edited by G. Dalton, pp. 481–493.
        New York: Natural History Press.
Graham, J., T. Hester, and R. Jack
  1972 Sources for the obsidian at the ruins of Seibal, Peten, Guatemala. *University of
        California Archaeological Research Facility Contributions* **16**:111–116.
Haggett, P.
  1969 *Locational analysis in human geography.* London: Edward Arnold.
Hammond, N.
  1973 British Museum–Cambridge University Corozal Project. *Centre of Latin American
        Studies.*
  1974 The distribution of late classic Maya major ceremonial centres in the central area. In
        Mesoamerican archaeology: new approaches, edited by N. Hammond, pp. 313–334.
        Austin, Texas: University of Texas Press.
Haviland, W. R.
  1963 Excavations of small structures in the northeast quadrant of Tikal, Guatemala. Unpub-
        lished Ph.D. Thesis, Department of Anthropology, University of Pennsylvania.
  1970 Tikal, Guatemala, and Mesoamerican urbanism. *World Archaeology* **2**:186–197.
Las Casas, B. de
  1877 *Historia de las indias,* 2 vols. Mexico.
Marcus, J.
  1973 Territorial organization of the lowland classic Maya. *Science* **180**:911–916.
Moholy-Nagy, H.
  1974 Obsidian at Tikal, Guatemala. Paper read at 41st International Congress of
        Americanists, Mexico City.
Parsons, L.
  1969 Bilbao, Guatemala, an archaeological study of the Pacific Coast Cotzumalhuapa re-
        gion, Vol. II. *Milwaukee Public Museum, Publications in Anthropology* **12**.
Rathje, W.
  1972 Praise the gods and pass the metates: a hypothesis of the lowland rainforest civiliza-
        tions in Mesoamerica. In *Contemporary archaeology,* edited by M. Leone, pp. 365–
        392. Carbondale and Edwardsville, Illinois: Southern Illinois University Press.
Renfrew, C., J. Dixon, and J. Cann
  1968 Further analysis of near eastern obsidians. *Proceedings of the Prehistoric Society*
        34:319–331.
Rouse, I.
  1966 Mesoamerica and the eastern Caribbean area. In *Handbook of Middle American In-
        dians,* Vol. 4, General Editor, R. Wauchope. Austin, Texas: University of Texas
        Press.
Roys, R.
  1943 The indian background of colonial Yucatan. *Carnegie Institute of Washington, Publi-
        cation* **548**.
Sanders, W.
  1960 Prehistoric ceramics and settlement patterns in Quintana Roo, Mexico. In *Carnegie
        Institute of Washington, Contributions* **12**(60).
Sanders, W., and B. Price
  1968 *Mesoamerica: The evolution of a civilization.* New York: Random House.
Schiffer, M.
  1972 Archeological context and systemic context. *American Antiquity* **37**:156–165.
Sidrys, R.
  1973 Utilitarian trade indices for the ancient Maya. M.A. paper, on file at University of
        California, Los Angeles, Department of Anthropology.

n.d. The 1974 UCLA excavations in Corozal, Belize. In *Archaeological investigations in northern Belize, Central America*, edited by N. Hammond. London: British Museum (in press).

Sidrys, R., and J. Kimberlin
n.d. Obsidian sources used at Yaxha, Guatemala. Paper on file at University of California, Los Angeles, Department of Anthropology.

Sidrys, R., J. Andresen, and D. Marcucci
1976 Obsidian sources in the Maya area. *Journal of New World Archaeology* **1**(5).

Stross, F., T. Hester, R. Heizer, and R. Jack
1976 Chemical and archaeological studies of Mesoamerican obsidians. In *Advances in obsidian glass studies: archaeological and geochemical perspectives*, edited by R. Taylor. Park Ridge, New Jersey: Noyes (in press).

Thompson, J. E. S.
1948 An archeological reconnaissance in the Cotzumalhuapa region, Escuintla, Guatemala. *Carnegie Institute of Washington, Publications* **574**(44).

Tourtellot, G., and J. Sabloff
1972 Exchange systems among the ancient Maya. *American Antiquity* **37**:126–134.

Urban, P. J., Jr.
n.d. A proposed method to measure the efficiency of long-distance trade of the Maya. M.S. at Tempe, Arizona, Arizona State Museum.

Webb, M.
1964 The post-classic decline of the Peten Maya: an interpretation in the light of a general theory of state society. Doctoral dissertation, University of Michigan.

Willey, G. R.
1972a The artifacts of Altar De Sacrificios. *Peabody Museum, Harvard University, Papers* **64**(1).
1972b Urban trends of the lowland Maya and the Mexican highland model. In *Verhandlungen des 38 Internationalen Amerikanistenkongresses, Stuttgart, Munchen, 12.bis 18. August, 1968*, Bd. 4.

Willey, G. R., W. R. Bullard, Jr., J. Glass, and J. Gifford
1965 Prehistoric Maya settlements in the Belize Valley. *Peabody Museum, Harvard University, Papers* **54**.

Wright, G.
1969 Obsidian analyses and prehistoric near eastern trade: 7500 to 3500 B.C. *Museum of Anthropology, University of Michigan, Anthropological Papers*, **37**.

Chapter 6

EGALITARIAN EXCHANGE SYSTEMS IN CALIFORNIA: A PRELIMINARY VIEW

JONATHON E. ERICSON

I. INTRODUCTION

The value of a methodology that can describe the detailed spatial patterning of exchanged items within a given region is immense, because it would permit the analysis of systemic variables responsible for the observed trends and anomalies. More importantly, however, this analysis would permit the isolation and ranking of these systemic variables as to their effect on exchange. Such a methodological framework would also be amenable to the study of a regional exchange system and its development in an evolutionary framework incorporating analyses of spacetime, systemic, and cultural variability. Toward these desired ends, the egalitarian exchange systems in California, defined by the prehistoric utilization of a given obsidian source, are described and analyzed, using the methodological framework developed in this preliminary study.

The quantitative analysis of prehistoric exchange systems is a recent and developing field in archaeology. Beginning with the work of Renfrew et al. (1968), researchers have evaluated exchange systems by the observed changes in the quantity of an exchanged item as a function of distance from its source. In this method, an exchange index, representing the quantity of a particular item in its archaeological context, is plotted or statistically regressed as a function of distance between the point of observation and its specific source. These analyses of distance-dependent trends in regional exchange systems have been useful for comparative analysis. For example, Hodder (1974) has investigated differences in transport systems reflecting the bulk weight of the exchanged items, and Sidrys (Chapter 5) has identified the hierarchical ranking of central places within a regional trend. Although this methodology, termed two-dimensional analysis, is frequently employed in quantitative studies, it has several limitations.

Since, in two-dimensional analysis, *only* the magnitude of an observation and its distance from a source is considered, the spatial position of the observation is not considered in its local context; and this simplification often masks significant variability in the data. For example, although a regression line can be fit to the data, the statistical "outliers" and other data may represent other significant trends that can be easily overlooked by the analyst. The analyst should expect that within a spatial data array, each observation represents orders of variability: (1) "large-scale" systematic changes, such as the decrease of an item as a function of distance or the Law of Monotonic Decrement (Renfrew, Chapter 4); (2) "small-scale" fluctuations, including (a) nonsystematic variation, such as changes in the quantity of an item due to effects of a central place hierarchy (Sidrys, Chapter 5) and (b) systematic local variations, such as changes in the quantity resulting from the bifurcation of a network system; and (3) chance variation, such as would result from sampling error (Krumbein and Graybill 1965). The collapsing of orders of variability with the resultant masking of other important trends in the data imposes a definite limitation on two-dimensional analysis.

The validity of two-dimensional analysis is dependent on the overall symmetry of the regional system (i.e., that there is more or less an equivalent decrease in the quantity of the item as a function of increasing distance, regardless of the direction from the source). For symmetrical systems, linear regression analysis can be used to define the regional trend. However, in asymmetrical or directed systems one would expect that linear regression of distance would be inappropriate. For example, in the analysis of an asymmetrical system, many regional trends could be defined, depending on the selected sample. This raises the question: which trend would be most characteristic of the system or "type of system" under investigation? It is maintained that all the directed trends are significant in terms of understanding the operation of multiple systemic variables. In this perspective, the operation of these yet unidentified parameters may be the direct variables of a system; whereas, in such cases, "distance" would be an indirect variable. For example, population and its fluctuation, not distance, is shown as an important variable in utilitarian exchange (cf. Wright and Zeder, Chapter 13).

In summary, the masking of significant sources of variability in the data, the dependency of the results on the symmetry of the system, and the significance of the distance-dependent trends impose major limitations on the applicability of two-dimensional analysis. The need for the development of a different methodological approach is apparent, particularly one that overcomes these limitations.

Unlike two-dimensional analysis, the new method is characterized as a three-dimensional approach. This process describes the spatial patternings of the exchange items, the degree of symmetry of the exchange system, the regional trends, local trends, spatial anomalies, and, to some degree, the nature of the observational error. With this comprehensive description of the system, both qualitative and quantitative analysis of the variables operating on the system can be conducted.

The operation of a set of independent variables can be qualitatively defined by inspection or by superimposition of data over the spatial patterning, particularly focusing on the observed trends and anomalies. The final phase, the testing of these variables, can be accomplished by multiple regression analysis.

The methodology proposed in this chapter is applied to archaeological and ethnohistoric data in California. The details and results of its application are discussed in the following sections.

II. THE CONTEXT OF STUDYING EXCHANGE IN CALIFORNIA

California offers an ideal setting in which to study the development and operation of egalitarian exchange systems that have been documented for this region (Davis 1961). Ample ethnographical, ethnohistorical, and archaeological data are available on the aboriginal, hunter-gatherer populations. Although the complex forms of regionally centralized organizations are not manifested here, there appears to be evidence for a complex integration of people and resources through the early development of exchange systems (cf. Singer and Ericson, Chapter 10). It is expected that the high diversity of the environment, which creates a mosaic of localized raw materials (e.g., obsidians and salt) and biological communities, sets the necessary preconditions for the development of exchange. Nevertheless, without centralized organization, these egalitarian systems were integrated by exchange between trade partners and independent sociopolitical units.

The important question, which can be addressed in California, is the following: What are the conditions and factors favoring the development, maintenance, and stability of exchange systems among hunter-gatherer economies? This problem is currently under investigation, utilizing the three-dimensional approach. As employed in studying the regional exchange systems in California, it involves three research phases: (1) the description of the exchange systems through synagraphic mapping, (2) a qualitative analysis of certain systemic variables, and (3) a quantitative analysis of space specific variables through multiple regression analysis. Each phase is detailed in the following discussion.

III. A DESCRIPTION OF EXCHANGE SYSTEMS

In three-dimensional analysis, the need for a technique that describes the spatial distributions of exchanged items within their local context has been established. The technique, utilized in this paper, is borrowed from locational geography. Specifically, synagraphic mapping by the use of the computer program SYMAP, developed by Fisher (1963) and modified by Lankford (1974), has been designed to display, relate, and weigh spatial data. Through interpolation, SYMAP describes the distributions of an exchanged item in space. SYMAP performs the interpolations of the data through multiple regression analysis. In general, the interpolation of the value of a given point is determined by the values of seven nearby data points. The interpolated values are assigned to a contour interval and plotted as a two-dimensional contour map. Thus, synagraphic mapping of exchange data is the vital first phase of three-dimensional analysis.

Four basic steps in sampling and compilation of the exchange data are used to produce the exchange distribution map (Figure 1). The initial step is to select an exchange item for analysis. Obsidian was chosen because many of its characteristics are ideal for a regional study: (1) The high chemical and physical durability of obsidian (cf. Ericson et al. 1975) contributes to its preservation in archaeological sites; (2) its use as a raw material in the manufacture of chipped stone tools appears to be utilitarian and, as such can be compared to the use of alternative lithic materials for internal consistency; (3) obsidian and other lithics were collected with relatively little bias by the archaeologist; (4) there are many obsidian sources, well distributed throughout California (cf. Ericson et al. 1976), providing an opportunity to study competition among sources; (5) the particular source of obsidian can be identified by both X-ray fluorescence (Jack and Carmichael 1969; Jackson 1974; Jack 1976) and instrumental neutron activation (Ericson and Kimberlin n.d.) analyses; (6) there exists a potential for direct dating by obsidian hydration (cf. Ericson 1975).

The second step is to establish an exchange index. Several different types of indexes can be used as measures of exchange, each having certain advantages and disadvantages. The exchange index was derived as the percentage of obsidian in the total chipped stone tool category at each site, defined by

Renfrew et al. (1968:327). This index was selected as having the least bias introduced by the techniques of recovery. It is important to note that the index represents the relative degree of the occurrence of obsidian rather than its absolute quantity.

The next step is to select and tabulate data for synagraphic mapping. Fifty-two late Horizon sites were chosen to give an area coverage using the compiled site information file (Ericson and Hagan n.d.). The following information on each site was recorded: the percentage of obsidian tools in the total chipped stone tool category was calculated as the exchange index from the raw material specifications; and the sites were assigned coordinate numbers within an $X–Y$ rectangular grid system using the plane coordinate intersections (United States Department of Commerce 1954) to minimize curvilinear distortion.

At this point, the exchange index data and grid coordinates of the sites were entered as the data in the SYMAP program. In order to divide the range of the exchange index into equivalent values, from 0–100, a 10% contour interval was chosen to describe the spatial pattern of the distribution of obsidian. The resulting synagraphic map of the exchange index distributions is shown in Figure 1. Two options of SYMAP were used to refine the map. (1) The outline of California was established by 84 points along its boundary. (2) The coordinates of each obsidian source were entered as data to identify its location.

The synagraphic contour map (Figure 1) describes the obsidian exchange systems of the Late Horizon in California. Some of the salient features of these systems are quite interesting.

The areas of highest percentage value of the exchange index enclosed the location of the obsidian sources. In other words, the obsidian sources appear to be the "sources" used in prehistoric obsidian exchange. If a major source of obsidian had been missed in prior obsidian source surveys, it would have "appeared" on the map.

The quantity of obsidian falls off as predicted by the Law of Monotonic Decrement (Renfrew, Chapter 4). However, the patterns are *not* symmetrical around the obsidian sources. In fact, the systems appear to be directed, in terms of their observed gradients, defined as the direction of maximum rate of change. This "directedness" might be due to the locations of the sources of other exchange items, such as shell and salt, which have not been considered in this paper. Notably, the "directedness' is generally perpendicular to major ecozones.

There is no indication of the existence of hierarchial centers (or central places), which would be observed as abrupt, localized anomalies within the regional pattern (cf. Sidrys, Chapter 5). This result is expected, since hierarchial-ranked central places are not considered to be characteristic of egalitarian exchange systems.

The size or extent of each system appears to be different. One would

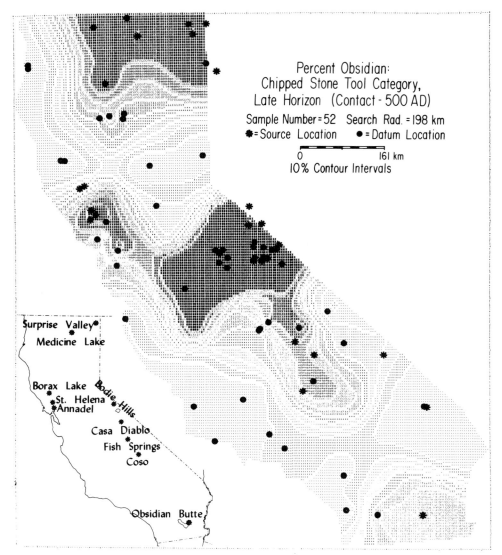

Percent Obsidian:
Chipped Stone Tool Category,
Late Horizon (Contact - 500 AD)
Sample Number = 52   Search Rad. = 198 km
✳ = Source Location   ● = Datum Location
0   161 km
10% Contour Intervals

Figure 1 A synagraphic map of the prehistoric egalitarian exchange systems in the Late Horizon of California. The ten sources enumerated in the bottom lefthand corner are evaluated through systems analysis.

expect that the sizes would be similar or at least operate to fill the space between sources, assuming that the modes of production and transportation (through exchange) are approximately equivalent between systems.

The patterns suggest the overlap of many systems, particularly illustrated by the trans-Sierran systems originating from Bodie Hills and Casa Diablo obsidian sources. In these cases, the isolation of independent systems would require chemical characterization of artifacts. In sum, the differences in extent, shape, symmetry, and "directness" characterize each system. The variability of these properties suggests the operation of specific systemic variables within each system. In the following sections, a number of variables are evaluated as to their effect on 10 systems, enumerated in Figure 1.

IV. A QUALITATIVE ANALYSIS OF CERTAIN SYSTEMIC VARIABLES

As a preliminary procedure of analysis, certain variables that might have influenced the distribution of obsidian were evaluated qualitatively. The influences of trials, regional geology, and ethnolinguistic boundaries were examined by superimposing data on their distribution over the exchange system map.

Superimposition of the trails (Figure 2), as described by Davis (1961), indicates that the gradients of several exchange systems coincided with the location of the trails. The notable examples are (1) the north–south trail west of the Medicine Lake obsidian source and (2) the two east–west trails over the Sierra Nevadas originating from Casa Diablo obsidian source. These examples strongly suggest that the trails operated as lines for exchange. It appears that on a local scale the quantity of obsidian received is a function of distance from the trail and, possibly, the rank of the trail (primary, secondary, tertiary), as hypothesized from network analysis (cf. Irwin-Williams, Chapter 8). This evidence suggests that the best measure of distance would be a measure of the trail lengths.

For California, it was assumed that obsidian as a lithic material was used primarily in a utilitarian context. Thus it was expected that the location of alternative lithic resources, such as other obsidian sources, and alternative raw materials would influence both the symmetry and extent of individual exchange systems. For these reasons, a selected portion of the regional geology of California was superimposed over the original exchange system map (Figure 3). The Monterey and Franciscan Formations, containing local supplies of chert, and the nongranitic portions of the Sierra Nevada batholith were selected, because they provided potential sources of alternative lithic materials for aboriginal California. It was impossible to determine potential sources of all lithic material for this report, but the three examples illustrate the effect that the presence or absence of alternative lithic sources had on the exchange of obsidian. (1) The most notable examples are the trans-Sierran systems originating from Casa Diablo and Bodie Hills, which includes the granite mastiff of the Sierra Nevadas. One might expect that the work expended crossing rugged terrain and additional limitations imposed by short

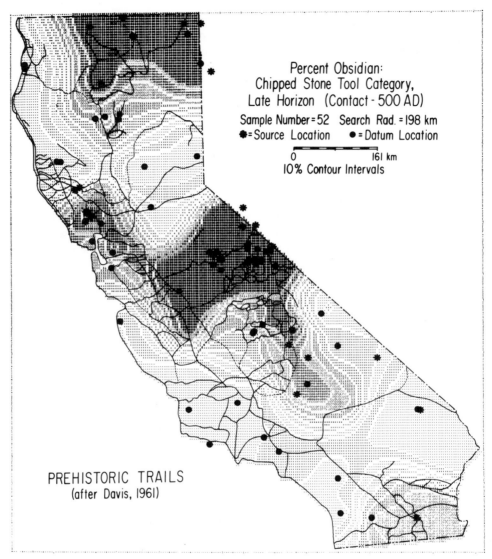

Percent Obsidian:
Chipped Stone Tool Category,
Late Horizon (Contact - 500 AD)

Sample Number = 52   Search Rad. = 198 km
● = Source Location   ● = Datum Location

0   161 km
10% Contour Intervals

PREHISTORIC TRAILS
(after Davis, 1961)

Figure 2 A demonstration of the correspondence of the major trails and gradients of the distributions of obsidian within the exchange systems. The major trails are superimposed over the original synagraphic map. (After Davis 1961).

snowless seasons would have discouraged the development of exchange over the mountains. However, the absence of alternative lithic materials appears to have been a dominant and overriding factor in the development of the systems. (2) It is also interesting to note the abrupt termination of these systems along the boundary of the Franciscan Formation, where extensive

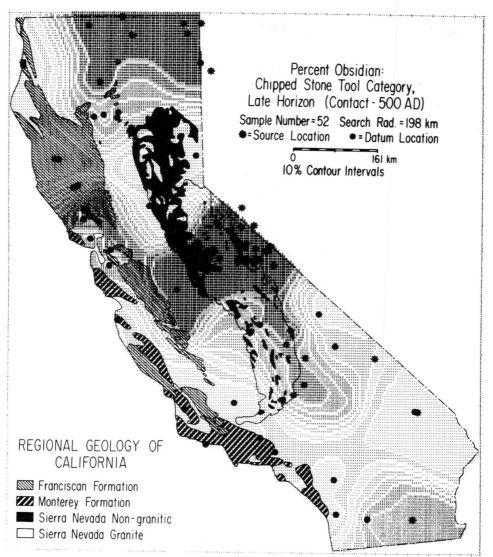

Percent Obsidian:
Chipped Stone Tool Category,
Late Horizon (Contact - 500 AD)

Sample Number = 52   Search Rad. = 198 km
● = Source Location   ● = Datum Location

0   161 km
10% Contour Intervals

REGIONAL GEOLOGY OF
CALIFORNIA

Franciscan Formation
Monterey Formation
Sierra Nevada Non-granitic
Sierra Nevada Granite

Figure 3 A demonstration of the effects of alternative regional resources on the distributions of obsidian within the exchange systems. The geological formations, containing abundant alternative materials for the manufacture of chipped stone tools, are superimposed over the original synagraphic map.

chert resources would have offered alternative materials. (3) The attenuation of the systems originating from the St. Helena, Annadel, and Borax Lake sources most likely can be explained by the presence of chert sources. When one considers the limited extent of these three systems, nearly at sea level

(500–1000 ft), and the extent of the trans-Sierran systems that begin at 8000–10,000 ft, one is struck by the influence of alternative resources on the respective systems!

The important implication of these findings suggests that the resource base (i.e., the distribution of resources) is an extremely important factor in the development of utilitarian exchange systems, which determines their extent and symmetry.

Sahlins (1972) proposes in his model of reciprocity that the form of reciprocity is a function of social distance. If it is assumed that the social distance of communities within an ethnolinguistic group is less than between ethnolinguistic groups, then it would be expected that discontinuities in quantity of exchange items would be observed at ethnolinguistic boundaries. For these reasons, the ethnolinguistic boundaries, described by Kroeber (1925: Map 1), were superimposed over the original exchange system map, shown in Figure 4. The expected discontinuities do not appear. Although these results are discordant with Sahlin's model, in all fairness two additional factors should be considered. Kroeber (1925) describes that in many cases ethnolinguistic boundaries were mitigated by intermarriage between members of contiguous groups. Secondly, the original data set, selected to provide area coverage, does not necessarily provide sufficient control to resolve localized discontinuities. Nevertheless, the boundary effect does not appear to be important.

In conclusion, the distribution of resources is seen as an important factor in the development of exchange systems. The control of this variable will be important to gain a further understanding of the extent and symmetry of the systems and the process of exchange of utilitarian items. Secondly, the major trails appear to have served as lines of exchange. If this is correct, then the distance along the trails will be a better measure than straightline distance currently employed in two-dimensional analysis. In addition, there is some evidence, supporting a prediction of network analysis, that the rank of a trail within a hierarchical trail system determines the net quantity of certain items. Thirdly, the existence of ethnolinguistic boundaries does not appear to affect the exchange of goods in the system. If this is correct, then the model of reciprocity, presented by Sahlins, requires modification. Finally, the qualitative analysis of the three selected variables demonstrates its simplicity in evaluating and ranking variables prior to undertaking quantitative analysis.

V. SYSTEMS ANALYSIS: QUANTITATIVE ANALYSIS OF SPECIFIC VARIABLES

A. A Discussion of Distance as a Variable

Distance remains as an established measure and variable of diminishing supply within an exchange system. For the analyst, it is a simple measure of

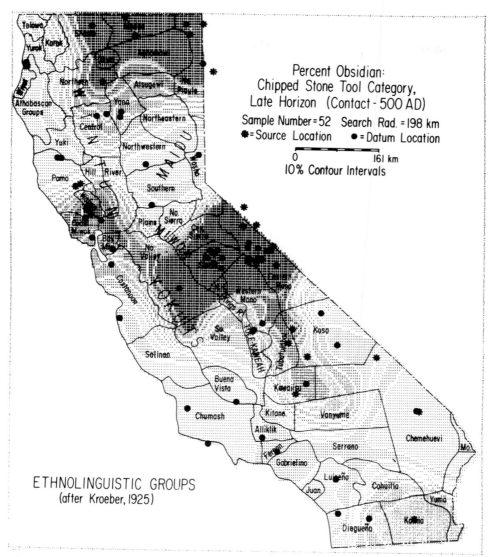

Figure 4 A demonstration of the lack of correspondence between the boundaries of ethnolinguistic groups and changes in the distributions of obsidian within the exchange systems. The territories are superimposed over the original synagraphic map. (After Kroeber 1925.)

the basic trend within the exchange system. However, it is not clear to me as to what distance is really measuring within the system or its cultural significance. The resolution of this problem is vital to our further understanding of exchange systems.

To start, a basic differentiation is made between modes of acquisition. If an item is obtained by direct access, then it is assumed that distance can be equated with work expenditure in acquiring an item. Alternatively, if an item is obtained through exchange, the conversion of distance as a measure of work expenditure may be inappropriate. For example, in the simulated binary system of salt and axe exchange, the middlemen receive both items without much effort (Wright and Zeder, Chapter 13). The real work performed by the middlemen is minimal—only that expended in traveling between trade partners. In effect, the energy expenditure with many people traversing short-range links within the system is much less than that expended by the same population using direct access, thereby making the exchange system much more efficient. In this system, a great deal of the work is expended in procuring or producing the item at its source for exchange. Thus, the apparent functional dependence of an item with distance which cannot be directly related to work expenditure, must be related to the operation of other variables.

The dependency of a given group on an exchange item or its degree of being utilitarian, is an important consideration. If an item is absolutely necessary for a given group or area (i.e., "absolutely utilitarian"), then it is expected that the quantity of the item remains constant and can be directly related to the number of consumers. In this case, the quantity of the item is independent of distance. For example, this relationship seems to be demonstrated by the existence of the "supply zones," described by Renfrew et al. (1968) and illustrated by the trans-Sierran systems (Figure 1). The boundary of the "supply and contact zones" (Renfrew et al. 1968) most likely is determined by the location and availability of alternative materials of the same class. Nevertheless, within a "contact zone" an item is "relatively utilitarian" and, thus, related in some way to the number of consumers. As an item passes through the system, quite possibly the amount of the item decreases as a function of the increasing number of potential consumers. For example, zones of high population density would tend to deplete the number of utilitarian items. Without an adjustment within the system, the item would be greatly attenuated with distance. Hypothetically, the system can respond by an increased production of obsidian at its source or restricting its use to certain tool categories. The relationship between the number of consumers and diminishing supply warrants further examination.

In summary, it is suggested that the significance of distance as a variable depends on the mode of acquisition and its local importance. In direct access, distance can be related to work expenditure. However, in an exchange system, distance is not particularly related to work expenditure and, thus, has a different connotation. Quite possibly, distance measures the effect of the cumulative number of consumers.

B. Systems Analysis

In the following systems analysis, a model is derived to provide a conceptual framework of general principles rather than an empirical model of relationships. In the model, the simultaneous effects of effective population, distance, and distance to the nearest alternative obsidian source on the exchange index are evaluated for 10 individual exchange systems.

There are three problems involved with the systems represented in Figure 1. (1) With the present overlap of the systems, the exchange index cannot be evaluated for individual systems. Fortunately, Jack (1976) identifies the percent of the individual obsidian sources present within the territories of many ethnolinguistic groups in northern and central California, which allows the isolation of individual systems. Although this data set is not well-controlled temporally, in this preliminary analysis the effects of diachronic changes in utilization are presumed to be relatively unimportant, because of the high percentage of Late Horizon sites represented in this sample. (2) With the isolation of the individual systems, the effects of overlap have to be controlled in some way. The third variable, the distance to nearest alternative obsidian source, potentially can control this variability. (3) The individual systems appear to be asymmetrical with respect to distance. A regression model may be inappropriate unless the asymmetries are controlled by the other two variables.

Ten source-specific matrices were formed for analysis using the following procedure. On the original synagraphic, 121 random points of observation were selected (Figure 1). The source-specific exchange indexes were calculated by multiplying the exchange index by the percent of obsidian of each source using the chemical characterization data presented by Jack (1976). The distances from the point of observation to the source and next nearest source were measured. The ethnographic estimates of population density (Kroeber 1925; Cook 1943, 1955a,b; Baumhoff 1963; Brown 1967) were used to calculate the effective population or number of consumers. The population within each enthnolinguistic segment was calculated by multiplying the respective population density, distance segment, and an arbitrary 10-mile width. These values were added to determine the effective population. The above procedure generated the data forming the source-specific matrices of the exchange index, source distance, effective population, and alternative source distance.

The next step in the procedure was to define the mathematical model to be analyzed. The model, described in Equation (1), assumes that the quantity of exchange item at any point is a function of the three variables, where Q is the exchange index, P is the effective population, X is the distance to the source, and Y is the distance to the next nearest obsidian source.

$$Q = Q(P, X, Y) \tag{1}$$

The multilinear regression equation was selected for analysis to evaluate the simultaneous effects of the three variables. The equation is formulated in Equation (2), where a is the general coefficient, and b, c, and d are the coefficient of effective population, distance, and distance to the next nearest obsidian source, respectively.

TABLE 1

Results of Multilinear Regression Analysis of Three Systemic Variables of the Ten Exchange Systems

	Medicine Lake	Obsidian Butte	Bodie Hills	Casa Diablo	Surprise Valley	Annadel	Fish Springs	Coso	Clear Lake	St. Helena
Multiple R	0.8659	0.9385	0.7359	0.8337	0.8895	0.8305	0.5386	0.8512	0.6597	0.4395
Degrees of freedom	3/18	2/19	3/24	3/32	3/20	3/8	3/9	3/18	3/21	3/25
F ratio	17.977	70.157	9.452	24.308	25.254	5.928	1.226	15.777	5.395	1.931
P (tail)	0.00001	0.0000	0.00026	0.00000	0.00000	0.01976	0.35575	0.00003	0.00653	0.14051
Sample size	22	22	28	36	24	12	13	22	25	29
Correlation										
Q-P	−0.3780	−0.7130	−0.5972	−0.4083	−0.7993	−0.6387	−0.4142	−0.5035	−0.6287	−0.2069
Q-X	−0.7561	−0.9363	−0.6737	−0.7655	−0.8433	−0.8290	−0.2717	−0.8361	−0.6447	−0.0371
Q-Y	−0.1893	nd	0.4159	−0.1098	−0.2885	−0.8182	−0.2585	−0.3333	−0.4471	0.1894
P-X	0.7887	0.8020	0.8698	0.7163	0.7132	0.7290	0.0635	0.6511	0.8689	0.8837
Coefficients										
a	57.9321	82.3712	40.7956	77.7533	64.3954	32.8587	18.6332	64.3318	49.9648	29.2515
b	0.014	0.008	0.002	0.001	−0.023	−0.001	−0.007	0.001	−0.004	−0.009
c	−0.929	−0.789	−0.388	−0.649	−0.238	−0.386	−0.146	−0.667	−0.324	0.122
d	0.396	nd	0.180	0.346	−0.016	0.029	0.140	0.089	0.037	0.367

$$Q = a + bP + cX + dY \tag{2}$$

Each "source-specific" matrix was analyzed by multilinear regression analysis, using the computer program BMDP1R (Jackson and Douglas 1975). The results are presented in Table 1.

Even though the systems are relatively asymmetrical, the general linear model holds for most of the sources (i.e., most of the variability of the data is explained by the three variables and the model). The notable exceptions are Fish Springs, Clear Lake, and St. Helena. Among the three variables, distance has the greatest power of prediction. Although important, effective population was less significant than first expected. This result is probably due to errors of the original population estimates. Generally, there was a high correlation between effective population and distance. The distance to the next nearest obsidian source appears to be an insignificant variable except for the Annadel system. A further evaluation of the data is made by Ericson (1977).

One final note: Stepwise regression analysis (Jackson 1975) was applied to the ten matrices in order to determine three regression equations. The simultaneous solution of these equations provided a means to calculate the basic properties of each system. The catchment and estimated total population or potential number of consumers within each system, whose boundary was set at $Q = 10\%$, is presented for a comparison in Table 2.

VI. CONCLUSIONS

California offers an ideal setting in which to study the development and organization of egalitarian exchange systems, which are defined in this paper by the use of particular sources of obsidian. The proposed three-dimensional

TABLE 2

THE CHARACTERISTICS OF THE TEN EQUALITARIAN EXCHANGE SYSTEMS
IN CALIFORNIA AT $Q = 10\%$ BASED ON STEPWISE REGRESSION ANALYSIS

System	Radius of catchment (km)	Estimated total population
Annadel	98	29870
St. Helena	206	391750
Borax Lake	138	109963
Medicine Lake	209	31171
Surprise Valley	241	35663
Bodie Hills	226	98274
Casa Diablo	256	354056
Fish Springs	68	17091
Coso	162	74133
Obsidian Butte	159	21333

approach, which overcomes some of the basic limitations of former methodology, is applied to archaeological data of the Late Horizon of California.

Synagraphic mapping of the obsidian data describes the spatial patterning of its utilization. Ten relatively asymmetric and overlapping systems are presented (Figure 1).

The qualitative results of the analysis of three variables are quite interesting. The presence and location of alternative lithic materials determine the extent and symmetry of individual systems. The correspondence between the major trails and gradients of the systems suggests that the trails served as lines for exchange. The observed lack of correspondence between the anomalies within the systems and the location of ethnolinguistic boundaries suggests that the model of reciprocity, proposed by Sahlins (1972), may require modification.

The significance of distance as a measure and variable is not clearly understood. It is suggested that the significance of distance depends upon the mode of acquisition of specific items and their local importance. A further examination of its significance is warranted.

A general multiple linear model best describes the variability of the exchange data. The variables (distance, effective population or potential number of consumers, and distance to next nearest obsidian source) are evaluated by multilinear regression analysis for each of the ten exchange systems. Although distance is the most predictive variable, the effect of population, or an equivalent archaeological measurement, on diminishing supply within a system should not be neglected in subsequent analysis. Even though the location of alternative lithic (nonobsidian) materials is a definite factor, the distance to the next nearest obsidian source appears to be an insignificant variable in this study.

The characteristic properties of each system, such as its catchment and total population, suggest that the modes of production and general organization are basically different.

Finally, it is hoped that the conditions and factors favoring the development, maintenance, and stability of exchange systems among hunter-gatherer economies will be eventually isolated.

Acknowledgments

The author would like to thank Dwight Read for his continued support and helpful comments on the numerous versions of this paper, and Frank Findlow for his efforts in computer analysis. Also, the author is grateful to the personnel of the UCLA Computer Network Center for their special effort in printing the synagraphic map. Supporting data of this study are presented in the dissertation (Ericson 1977).

References

Baumhoff, M. A.
  1963 Ecological determinants of aboriginal California population. *University of California Publications in American Archaeology and Ethnology* **49**:231.
Brown, A. K.
  1967 The aboriginal population of the Santa Barbara Channel. *University of California Archaeological Survey Report* **69**:1.
Cook, S. F.
  1943 The conflict between the California Indian and white civilization: I. The Indian versus the Spanish mission. *University of California Publication, Ibero-Americana* **21**: Appendix.
  1955a The aboriginal population of the San Joaquin Valley, California. *University of California Anthropological Records* **16**:1.
  1955b The aboriginal population of the north coast of California. *University of California Anthropological Records* **16**:127.
Davis, J. T.
  1961 Trade routes and economic exchange among the Indians of California. *University of California Archaeological Survey Report* **54**:1–71.
Ericson, J. E.
  1975 New results in obsidian hydration dating. *World Archaeology* **7**:151–159.
  1977 Evolution of prehistoric exchange systems: results of obsidian dating and tracing. Unpublished Ph.D. dissertation. University of California, Los Angeles, Department of Anthropology.
Ericson, J. E., and T. A. Hagan
  n.d. The establishment of an archaeological data bank for California. Archaeological Survey Manuscript File, University of California, Los Angeles.
Ericson, J. E., and J. Kimberlin
  n.d. The chemical characterization of obsidian sources in California, Oregon, and Nevada by instrumental neutron activation analysis (manuscript in preparation).
Ericson, J. E., A. Makishima, J. D. MacKenzie, and R. Berger
  1975 Chemical and physical properties of obsidian: a naturally-occurring glass. *Journal of Non-Crystalline Solids* **17**:129–142.
Ericson, J. E., T. A. Hagan, and C. W. Chesterman
  1976 Prehistoric obsidian sources in California I: geological and geographical aspects. In *Advances in obsidian glass studies: archaeological and geochemical perspectives*, edited by R. E. Taylor. Park Ridge, New Jersey: Noyes Press (forthcoming).
Fisher, H. T.
  1963 SYMAP 1. *Laboratory for Computer Graphics and Spatial Analysis, Harvard University* **1**:1.
Hodder, I.
  1974 Regression analysis of some trade and marketing patterns. *World Archaeology* **6**:172–189.
Jack, R. N.
  1976 Prehistoric obsidian sources in California II: archaeological aspects. In *Advances in obsidian glass studies: archaeological and geochemical perspectives*, edited by R. E. Taylor. Park Ridge, New Jersey: Noyes Press, (forthcoming).
Jack, R. N., and I. S. E. Carmichael
  1969 The chemical "fingerprinting" of acid volcanic rocks. *California Division of Mines and Geology, Special Report* **100**:17–32.

Jackson, D.
  1975   Stepwise regression: BMDP2R. In *Biomedical computer programs,* edited by W. J.
         Dixon, pp. 491–439. Los Angeles: University of California Press.
Jackson, D., and J. Douglas
  1975   Multiple linear regression: BMDP1R. In *Biomedical computer programs,* edited by
         W. J. Dixon, pp. 453–489. Los Angeles: University of California Press.
Jackson, T. L.
  1974   The economics of obsidian in central California prehistory: applications of X-ray
         fluorescence spectography in archaeology. Unpublished M. A. thesis. Department of
         Anthropology, California State University, San Francisco.
Kroeber, A. L.
  1925   Handbook of the Indians of California. *Bureau of American Ethnology Bulletin* **78**:1–
         995.
Krumbein, W. C., and F. A. Graybill
  1965   *An introduction to statistical models in geology.* New York: McGraw-Hill.
Lankford, P.
  1974   *A guide to SUPERMAP.* Classnotes, University of California, Los Angeles.
Renfrew, C., J. E. Dixon, and J. R. Cann
  1968   Further analysis of Near Eastern obsidians. *Proceedings of Prehistoric Society, Series
         2* **34**:319–331.
Sahlins, M.
  1972   Stone age economics. Chicago: Aldine-Atherton.
United States Department of Commerce
  1954   Plane coordinate intersection tables (2½ minute) for California. *Special Publication,
         U.S. Department of Commerce* **327**:1–75. Washington, D.C.: U.S. Government Print-
         ing Office (out of print).

Chapter 7

MODELING ECONOMIC EXCHANGE

FRED PLOG

I. INTRODUCTION

During the last several years, archaeologists' awareness of and interest in models of economic exchange has increased substantially. Some reasons for this growing interest are discussed in the introductory chapter of this volume. Results obtained to date suggest both the feasibility of studying prehistoric exchange and the considerable insight into the organization of prehistoric societies that can be gained from such studies.

This essay, however, will raise a number of questions concerning the adequacy of the efforts that archaeologists are undertaking. I do not raise the questions because of any disenchantment with the line of investigation, but because of two problems that have arisen in past attempts by archaeologists to understand prehistoric social organization: (1) a tendency to borrow uncritically models from other subdisciplines of anthropology and other social sciences and (2) a tendency to focus research on one or a few key variables that are assumed to provide insights into organizational variation without either adequately arguing the relevance of the key variables to the organizational phenomena or considering other nonorganizational, even noncultural, causes for the variation in question. Therefore, I intend to concentrate on the problem of developing a descriptively adequate model of exchange relationships in the broadest sense.

II. ELEMENTS OF MODELS

Two of the most useful literatures bearing on exchange relations are those of network analysis and locational geography. Locational analysis is now familiar to archaeologists, and the network approach is discussed in the paper by Irwin-Williams in this volume. For this discussion, I will not focus on more formal network concepts nor advocate the use of "network theory" *per se*. I will use the concept of a network—a series of elements linked by specified exchanges of goods, behavior, and information—as a key concept for building exchange models. In archaeological research, the elements of such models are not individuals or groups but loci: sites, rooms on a site, activity areas on a site, etc. The relationships are transfers of raw materials, finished products, and items in various stages of manufacture between these loci.

At a descriptive level, an investigator's interest is primarily in defining the existence of such a network. Sites are located by survey or rooms are excavated. The nature of the activities carried out at each locus is established by collecting samples, from the surface or the ground, and analyzing the materials in an appropriate fashion. Using appropriate techniques to establish that exchanges of goods have occurred is a final step.

Many of the papers in this symposium cover such aspects of describing exchange. I intend to add little to this discussion at present save for noting that understanding the organization of an exchange network will ultimately require a very thorough understanding of sites within the subject area. Hit and miss—a site here, a site there—approaches leave too many variables and too much intervening territory uncontrolled; such data are inappropriate for discussing networks, exchange, or any other organizational phenomena. I will return to such considerations later in the paper.

At this point, I want to turn from questions concerning data pertinent to exchange networks to the issues that will be the focus of the paper—describing the organization of exchange networks and explaining organizational variation.

III. CHARACTERISTICS OF
EXCHANGE NETWORKS

Let us assume that we have defined an exchange network—identified a number of loci and materials that appear to have been exchanged between them. On the basis of a variety of analyses that have been performed, it is known that a series of sites were inhabited by participants in an exchange network. What should one try to learn of the organization of this network? I suggest that the following variables are critical.

(1) What is the *content* of the network? The content of a network is the range of materials that are being exchanged: raw materials, finished goods, partially finished goods, and/or money items are relevant alternatives. If one knows that an exchange network existed, it should be possible to specify what items were being exchanged. There is, however, clearly a problem as to how far we will be able to go in describing the role of perishable goods in most prehistoric exchange networks.

(2) What is the *magnitude* of the network? Magnitude refers to the quantity of goods that are being exchanged.

(3) What is the *diversity* of materials that were exchanged? In some exchange networks, materials were relatively homogenous—only one or a few items were involved. But, others are diverse—many different kinds of items were exchanged.

(4) What is the *size* of the exchange network, the territory over which it extended?

(5) What was the temporal duration of the network? For what period or periods of time did it exist?

(6) What is the *directionality* of the exchange? A network may involve the flow of goods from locus A to locus B, from locus B to locus A, or in both directions.

(7) What is the *symmetry* of the exchange? Directionality is only a presence/absence measure of the flow of goods. Even if goods are flowing in both directions, the flow from locus A to locus B may be substantially greater than that from B to A and vice versa.

(8) To what extent is the network *centralized?* A centralized pattern is one in which substantially greater quantities of the resources in question occur at some few loci.

(9) How *complex* is the network? Complexity refers to variation in symmetry, directionality, centralization, and diversity over the territory covered by the network. If distinctly different patterns of exchange link the loci in the network, it is complex. Simple networks are characterized by more uniform patterns of exchange.

IV. ORGANIZATION, UNDERSTANDING, AND EXPLANATION

In discussing the preceding characteristics, I am not attempting to describe a number of attributes of exchange networks that I think it would be "nice to know about." Nor would I agree that the particular characteristics, which given investigators will chose to employ in their research, will vary with the problem that they are investigating. These are critical structural characteristics; critical because (1) it is unlikely an investigator can accurately model exchange networks without attention to the characteristics, (2) these are the characteristics that will define patterns of variation space and time on which efforts to explain variation in the organization of networks can focus, and (3) comparing two or more networks requires a list of attributes such as these. Let us consider points one and three since, if they are accepted, two follows.

First, knowing these network attributes is critical to understanding the organization of an exchange network. The characteristic, magnitude, is an example. If one is defining a network on the basis of a few pieces of obsidian, there is a high risk that there is no network at all. There are many ways short of recurrent exchanges that a few objects might have been moved to a series of loci, even very distant loci. Similarly, it would be foolhardy to conclude that we are dealing with centralization if five pieces of obsidian are found at one locus and one at each of a number of other loci. Such a distribution could have arisen from behavior that has little to do with exchange. Duration is equally critical. If an investigator cannot demonstrate that the loci said to participate in the exchange network are contemporaneous, there is no reason to believe that a network existed at all. And, although exchange networks need not involve week to week or month to month exchanges to be important, the difference between exchanges that occur once in a decade and ones that occur once in a month is evident.

What if an investigator should fail to consider centralization? The risk of missing information that some exchange items were produced or processed at a single locus or a few loci within the network would be high. Alternatively, information that exchange objects entered the region from some outside source, came first to some central site, and were distributed to other loci would be missed. It is not possible to claim to understand the organization of prehistoric exchange without such information.

What might we miss if we do not know of the directionality of exchange? If resources are moving only from A to B, if the exchange is not mutual, then, in all probability, we are dealing with a situation in which either B had some command over the resources of A or exchange items whose presence we have not yet discovered were moving in the opposite direction.

But directionality gives us only a presence/absence measure of the mutuality of exchange, and the relative magnitude of the goods moving in different directions (symmetry) is equally important. If more resources are inferred to have moved from A to B than from B to A, either B had some command over A's resources or we are failing to detect other goods that were involved in the exchange network.

In short, (1) each of these characteristics has important organizational implications, (2) we may not be able to make sound inferences about one characteristic without knowing something of the others, and (3) it is from common configurations of these characteristics that we will ultimately be able to identify "types" of networks, if we so wish.

Moreover, it is these same characteristics that will identify critical patterns of spatial and temporal variation in the organization of networks that will be the topic of our efforts to explain organizational variation. I assume that in seeking explanations for variability in the organization of exchange networks we are looking for aspects of the social and natural environment, past and present, of a network, that "cover" the observed variation. I suggest that each of these characteristics can be the subject of such an explanation. This is not to deny that explanation could focus on some types defined by combinations of attributes. But each attribute can be used for constructing a continuous variable, and if variation in that variable is observed, it can be the topic of explanation.

Centralization is an example. A number of papers in this volume deal with variation in the degree of centralization of networks (cf. Renfrew, Chapter 4; Sidrys, Chapter 5). While centralization is an important characteristic of an exchange network, many different phenomena may account for variation in the extent of centralization of particular networks. This variation may simply reflect the presence of a large population at one site in a sample of sites. Where there were more people, there were more artifacts. Our "explanation" might be no more complex than this statement. But it may be much more complex. Centralization could reflect the operation of natural environmental factors. If a prehistoric trade route passed through a narrow mountain pass, it would not be surprising to find large quantities of exchange items located at a nearby site. Following relatively simple locational principles, such a locus would have been a convenient meeting place for populations on either side of the pass. But the centralization of exchange could also reflect a more pervasive centralization of organization. It is far more likely that centralized networks existed in states or chiefdoms than among bands or tribes. (As I will argue later, it is dangerous to assume that centralization as a characteristic of a population of exchange items can be automatically equated with centralized organization of a society.)

Directionality is a second example. Suppose that a relationship appears to go only from A to B. Such a situation might come about if the environment of B did not contain any of the material in question. Similarly, the social environment could have been a factor. If exchange goods were in fact moving in only a single direction, then this may have been the case because B exercised some control over A. Such a situation would more likely have occurred in a chiefdom or a state than in a band or a tribe. In short, each of these characteristics may be tied to a variety of natural and cultural phenomena in order to aid us in understanding why particular networks are similar to or different from others.

V. EMPIRICAL CONSIDERATIONS

To this point, I have focused on conceptual aspects of studies of exchange. It should be clear, however, that studying exchange in the suggested manner demands relatively sophisticated techniques of data collection and relatively complete sets of data. Of primary importance are the needs for sophisticated intra- and inter-site sampling techniques and a regional approach to research design. Without either, it is unlikely that any of the characteristics of exchange networks can be adequately described.

Let us first consider the issue of sampling as it pertains to the collection of data from particular sites. Unless a sampling strategy is employed in collecting data from the surface of a site or in selecting areas of a site for excavation, problems such as the following are likely to arise.

(1) The content of the network cannot be adequately assessed. Given that different activities are carried out in discrete areas of a site, a surface collection is unlikely to tap the full range of goods involved in the network unless it is based on a probability sample. Collections made in restricted areas of a site are unlikely to reflect the range of diversity in materials found on the site, and selective surface collections of artifacts are notorious for overrepresenting particular artifact categories and underrepresenting or completely missing others. These same problems exist when excavation is concentrated in particular loci or where only particular features are considered excavated.

(2) The magnitude of the network cannot be adequately assessed. Nonprobability samples provide no reliable basis for estimating the relative magnitudes of goods that are on a site as a result of exchange and goods that were produced there.

(3) The diversity of materials cannot be accurately assessed when selective or nonrepresentative data collection techniques are used because of the problems discussed under (1) above.

(4) Given problems in assessing content, magnitude, and diversity, it is impossible to accurately measure the directionality or the symmetry of the exchanges in question.

Thus, reconstructions based on the selective recovery of artifacts from a site must be suspect. The probability that evidence recovered in this manner will reflect only a segment of the activities and, therefore, exchanges in question is simply too high and the need for speculation as to the overall definition of the network too great.

Secondly, there are a number of problems that arise when a regional perspective and regional sampling are not associated with exchange studies. In particular, low intensity site surveys that focus on the larger sites within a region, and therefore fail to reflect the diversity of sites, create immense problems. Specifically:

(1) The size or territory of a network cannot be assessed by a hit-and-miss survey or one that focuses on only the larger sites within a region. The probability of missing important boundaries is increased when the full range

of sites is not studied. And the inhabitants of larger sites within a region may well have participated in exchange relationships that did not affect the inhabitants of smaller sites in any meaningful way.

(2) Similarly, the duration of the network will be unknown or incorrectly estimated if the focus is not on the full range of sites. Again the difference between ephemeral and enduring exchange relationships is critical to our understanding of this organizational phenomenon.

(3) One is in a poor position to discuss either the centralization or complexity of an exchange network if the data base is composed largely or exclusively of larger sites. In essence, the data have been biased by selecting for the likely central places and more complex organizational forms. The relevance of an exchange network to smaller settlements in hinterland areas cannot be known from excavations at larger sites alone. Certainly, selective data on exchange can be obtained, but our ability to relate these data to an ongoing settlement system is severely limited.

Admittedly, none of these problems arise if our only interest is in showing that prehistoric exchange existed. But the problems are inherent in efforts to understand the organization of exchange and/or its relationship to other organizational phenomena.

VI. AN ILLUSTRATION

Some of the potential insights as well as some of the potential difficulties of the approach that I suggest may be clarified by applying the approach to a specific set of data. I will use materials collected by the Chevelon Archaeological Research Project directed by myself, James N. Hill, and Dwight Read. The Chevelon drainage is in east central Arizona to the south and east of Winslow, Arizona. It is a triangular area of roughly 2000 square kilometers with its base along the Mogollon Rim and its apex at the confluence of Chevelon Creek and the Little Colorado River. During the summer of 1971, a survey of the area was done employing a probability sample. Transects .1 kilometer wide and quadrats 1 kilometer square were surveyed at locations dispersed over the drainage. The overall sample of the drainage was approximately 1%. Three hundred and fifty prehistoric sites were located covering a time range from approximately 8000 to approximately 700 BP. Materials from 85 of those sites with sufficient ceramic materials to permit dating will be discussed. Obviously, these sites provide less than an ideal sample. At the same time, they are broadly reflective of the site types, site sizes, site locations, and periods of occupation represented in the sample as a whole. Compared with surveys done in surrounding areas, they represent a relatively high density of sites, a substantial diversity of site types, and a relatively small average site size. And they provide a data base encompassing more sites than has been used in many exchange studies.

An initial indication that exchange relationships existed between the prehistoric inhabitants of the drainage and those of other areas came from an analysis of obsidian flakes (Findlow et al., in press). This analysis showed that 20 obsidian flakes recovered during the 1971 survey were from sources near Flagstaff, Arizona, some sixty miles to the northwest. Chipped stome artifacts recovered during the 1971 survey have been analyzed by Green (1975). She broke the artifacts into four raw material categories: volcanic (predominantly basalt), quartzite, vitreous chert, and chalky chert. Studies by Findlow (personal communication) of basalt sources in the area indicate that the basalt used in making the artifacts was brought into the drainage from sources between Chevelon and Flagstaff. The other raw materials are indigenous to the drainage. While sources of these materials are somewhat localized, they are required to determine to what extent intra-drainage exchanges of these materials may have occurred. Recent petrographic studies of Little Colorado White Ware sherds suggest that they may also have been a part of the exchange network. Small, distinctive volcanic inclusions likely to have been a part of the clay used in manufacturing the vessels occur in Chevelon sherds as well as sherds from an area exceeding 10,000 square kilometers around Chevelon. The inclusions are sufficiently distinctive as to suggest a quite restricted clay source. Therefore, exchange of either vessels or raw materials probably occurred. The source of clays is not currently known, and further studies are required to clarify this situation and to determine if other ceramic wares may have been as broadly exchanged.

I will consider each of the network characteristics defined earlier.

(1) *Content.* Initially, the content of the exchange network was only 20 obsidian artifacts. On the basis of these artifacts it was clear that either (1) the prehistoric inhabitants of Chevelon were traveling outside of the drainage to obtain the resources from inhabitants of nearby areas, (2) inhabitants of these nearby areas were traveling to Chevelon and bringing the materials, or (3) rights of access to raw materials were being exchanged. The analysis of the chipped stone raw materials showed that basalt was also included in the exchange network. Clearly, many additional raw materials may have been involved. It is unlikely for this project, and I suspect most projects, that any significant understanding of the role perishable materials played in such exchanges can be determined. But a few flakes of obsidian are only the crudest suggestion of exchange, and investigations of at least the full range of nonperishable artifacts must be undertaken if the content of the network is to be understood.

(2) *Magnitude.* From this point on, I will focus on chipped stone materials alone, relying heavily on Green's data (1975). The difficulty of reconstructing the magnitude of the network is evident from a comparison of the conclusions

that would be reached on the basis of obsidian artifacts as opposed to basalt artifacts. The two dozen or so obsidian artifacts collected during the first summer represent roughly 0.3% of the 7400 artifacts analyzed by Green. There were, however, 591 basalt artifacts, or roughly 8% of the sample. And for one time period (ca. A.D. 1200 – 275) roughly 21% of the artifacts were made of basalt. Clearly, whether 0.3% or 21% of the artifacts were being obtained through exchange or made of materials obtained through exchange makes a critical difference to our understanding of the importance of the exchange networks in the local economy and technology. Again, as few artifacts as were recovered in the case of obsidian say little about recurrent and patterned exchange behavior. As many artifacts as were made of basalt suggest a far more substantial and recurrent pattern of exchanges.

(3) *Diversity*. Without a more comprehensive understanding of the range of nonperishable materials involved in the exchange network, measures of the relative diversity of materials at different times and places is pointless. Yet information on the diversity of materials exchanged is essential for a full understanding of the importance of the exchange network to local populations and its potential impact on other organizational phenomena (cf. Irwin-Williams, Chapter 8).

(4) *Duration*. The earliest site from which obsidian artifacts were recovered dates to A.D. 850–1050 and the latest to the abandonment of the drainage between A.D. 1400 and 1500. Basalt artifacts were obtained from sites that are at least as early as A.D. 700 and probably date to the earlier preceramic period. Thus, the addition of basalt raw materials to the data base adds considerable longevity to the network. On the basis of the obsidian, the network appears to be associated with the Pueblo stage, while the basalt clearly indicates an earlier origin.

Using obsidian alone, there are too few sites to accurately reconstruct variation in the magnitude of the network over time. Yet using the basalt artifacts, important changes are evident. Between A.D. 700 and 850, about 6% of the artifacts were made of basalt. By about A.D. 1200, this figure had increased to 9% and was about 21% from A.D. 1200 to A.D. 1275, when all but the northernmost portion of the drainage was abandoned. Clearly the magnitude, potentially the importance of the network, grew over time.

(5) *Size*. Again, the obsidian alone is insufficient for estimating the territory encompassed by the network. When the basalt artifacts are included, important spatial patterns and important changes in these patterns through time are evident. First, only 0.5% of the artifacts in the southwestern corner of the drainage were made of basalt. This figure is not higher than 0.5% in any time period. Thus, populations living in this area seem not to have participated or participated only insignificantly in the exchange network. For the whole occupation of the drainage, the highest concentrations of basalt artifacts were found in the central (19%) and southeastern (27%) areas of the drainage. thus, the basalt artifacts appear to be distributed in a band from

the west central to the southeastern edges of the drainage. The center of this line is a single stream system that has its mouth on the western edge and its headwaters in the southeastern corner. Finally, the percentages for the central area are highest between A.D. 800 and 1125, and the percentages in the southeast are highest between A.D. 1125 and 1275, when nearly one third of chipped stone artifacts were made of basalt. Thus, the importance of the exchange network varies from one area to another and through time. Populations living in some sectors of the drainage seem not to have been involved in the exchange network, while populations living as little as 16 kilometers away were involved in a major way.

(6) *Directionality and symmetry.* Neither the known range of materials involved in the exchange network nor the nature of the survey data permit a meaningful understanding of directionality or symmetry. First, because the data are from sample units, spatial discontinuity militates against such studies. While transect or other survey techniques employing isolated sample units are clearly useful for some purposes, they do not provide an adequate data base for studying the relative quantities of different materials at nearby sites. Second, the discussion to this point indicates in a variety of different ways that studies of symmetry and directionality could only be undertaken with data from outside Chevelon. Distributions of materials in the Flagstaff and intervening areas would be critical to our understanding of these characteristics. Finally, knowledge of a much more substantial array of nonperishable materials would be required.

(7) *Centralization.* Centralization, like symmetry and directionality, is best studied using intensive survey data from a continuous region where fall-off rates and characteristics of the settlement system can be examined in detail. When data are drawn from dispersed sample units, the reconstruction of the settlement system *per se* is close to impossible and measures of fall-off rates highly problematical because there are a large number of intervening sites that might drastically change conclusions.

Nevertheless, some sense of the importance of centralization can be obtained from the Chevelon data. For example, we may ask if basalt tends to be concentrated on a few sites or relatively evenly distributed over the majority of sites. Concretely, what percentage of the basalt is accounted for by the 20% of sites having the greatest concentration of basalt artifacts? For the entire occupation of the drainage the figure is 70%—the 20% of sites with the greatest number of basalt artifacts has 70% of the artifacts. Between A.D. 850 and 1050 roughly 80% of the artifacts occur on the 20% of sites with the most artifacts, roughly 70% between A.D. 1050 and 1125, and roughly 60% from A.D. 1125 until the abandonment of the drainage. Thus, although a few sites account for the majority of the artifacts in all time periods, the degree of centralization of the distribution decreases over time. It is also important to note that variance is high for all time periods—that the mean figure is not particularly representative, but an average of a few relatively high and many relatively small site totals. When one examines the relationship of centralization in the distribution of basalt artifacts to centralization in settlements, the picture is extremely complex. Only between A.D. 850 and 1050 is one of the sites with a large number of artifacts also a member of the class of largest settlement. In the remaining time periods, none of the sites with a large number of basalt artifacts is either a site with a large number of habitation rooms or a large number of habitation rooms and a great kiva, the typical "central" sites in the area. While this information lends credence to the notion of decreasing centralization through time, it does not suggest an easy fit between centralization in the exchange system and centralization in the settlement system as a whole. Moreover, five of the twelve sites with the greatest number of obsidian artifacts are artifact scatters, sites without any habitation or ceremonial structures at all. This information should be a warning to those who suggest that centralization as measured by variables such as fall-off rates is a reflection of an overall pattern of centralization. Yet the pattern observed is not meaningless—the nonhabitation sites may have been loci at which periodic exchanges occurred, for example.

(8) *Complexity*. Too many underlying variables have now been left undefined to allow any meaningful discussion of variation in the complexity of the exchange network.

Admittedly, the data employed in this illustration are not ideal for the purposes for which I have used them. The sampling strategy was designed for another purpose entirely. Nevertheless, the kind of data employed made a substantial difference in the understanding of the exchange system obtained. Specifically, whether exotic materials (obsidian) or mundane materials (basalt) were used drastically affected understanding of the content, magnitude, duration, and size of the exchange network. Whether an exchange network that involved 0.3% or 30% of the raw materials that a prehistoric population used in making chipped stone artifacts is critical to any assessment of the importance of the exchange network. Whether the system grew or decreased in magnitude and size and became more or less centralized are equally important. The characteristics of networks identified early in the paper show important patterns of space–time variation that merit explanation.

VII. SUMMARY AND CONCLUSIONS

Is it realistic to undertake an examination of prehistoric exchange relationships that is going to involve so much work? I do not doubt for a monent that the work required to pursue the understanding of exchange networks in the fashion described here is substantial. Nor do I doubt the necessity of such a pursuit. Nor, ultimately, do I doubt our ability to succeed in such an effort. Analyses of networks and of exchange by archaeologists have already shown that much of the information that I have discussed can be obtained. In cases where techniques for obtaining the necessary information are not yet available, they must be developed. Where would this volume be if the difficulties of applying trace-element analyses to the past had prevented archaeologists from employing and improving this technique?

My plea is simply for doing a thorough, original, and appropriate job of designing an approach, a set of models for understanding exchange, that is usable for understanding the past because it is sensitive to archaeological data. In the past, our first impulse has been to borrow the conceptual tools and models of other disciplines. But, in the past, borrowing has often led us from rather than toward an understanding of the phenomena that we wished to understand. As a result of this borrowing, our discipline has a very large bag of magic wands—magic ecological wands, magic philosophy of science wands, and so on. Such "wands" carry the impression that by the application of a few key concepts a true understanding of the prehistoric record can be obtained. But such is never the case. It is for this reason that I have chosen to use network only as a concept rather than applying the variables and theories of networks developed for other contexts and other data.

Moreover, I do not wish to argue that the specific attributes of networks I have emphasized taken individually or together are completely adequate. There is much need for experimentation and debate before an adequate approach is devised.

In attempting to develop a descriptively adequate model of exchange networks, I believe that it is essential to pay careful attention to the nature of our data and the kinds of inferences that can be made from them. First, it will be necessary to be judicious in regard to some of the loftier claims archaeologists have made concerning our ability to reconstruct the past. I do not doubt that it would be nice to be able to infer that Joe Chevelon made two trips each year to the Flagstaff area to exchange raw materials with Charlie Sinagua to whom he was linked by longstanding ties of reciprocity. Similarly, it would be nice to know that Site 145 was a location at which Joe and his kinsmen met with Charlie and his kinsmen or with traveling traders from Wupatki. But I believe that our data will not support such inferences—even to the point of indicating whether inhabitants of Chevelon were exchanging goods with inhabitants of other areas or whether the rights of access to territory were in fact the item exchanged. But either is exchange, either has material consequents, and either is important. It is for this reason that in this paper and an earlier one (Plog 1974), I have argued for "limited inferences" based on characteristics of artifact and site distributions rather than more complex inferences that claim to identify specific behavioral correlates of the patterns. Clearly, the attributes I have identified are sterile from the perspective of reconstructing "what prehistoric people were doing" in the nitty-grittiest sense of reconstructing the past. But the attributes can be and were used to provide insights into patterns of behavioral variation at a more abstract level, at a level of detail our data base will support.

Second, I believe it is important to avoid the use of concepts developed for purposes that require data archaeologists do not have and that are insensitive to sociocultural variation that is characteristic of human behavioral patterns. Reciprocity, redistribution, and marketing, for example, are, on the one hand, concepts that refer to cognitive as well as behavioral phenomena, and, on the other, far short of water-tight categories. The boundaries of these categories are unclear, and day-to-day exchanges involve highly complex admixtures of the three. Band, tribe, chiefdom, and state are highly idealized concepts that are useful in introductory texts and global syntheses. But a relative minority of cultural systems fall conveniently within these pigeonholes, rendering them inadequate for detailed analyses of organizational variation. Harris (1968) warned of many such problems, and Kushner (1970) has amplified the discussion. Many archaeologists have not been quick to heed their warning.

Finally, I have argued elsewhere (1973) that the data with which we deal are records of change to a great degree and records of the day-to-day operation of stable societies to only a limited degree. It is for this reason that I have focused on network characteristics that can be represented and analyzed as continuous variables and continuous patterns of change and argued for avoiding efforts to formulate types of networks and correlate them with types of social organization, an approach that obscures rather than elucidates the nature of prehistoric change.

Acknowledgments

The Chevelon Archaeological Project was supported by funds from the National Science Foundation. This support is gratefully acknowledged.

References

Findlow, F., S. D'Atley, and L. Hudson
    n. d.   Source analysis of obsidian artifacts from the Chevelon drainage. In *Chevelon Archaeological Monographs,* No. 1, edited by F. Plog, J. Hill, and D. Read. Los Angeles: UCLA Archeological Survey (in press).
Green, M.
    1975   Patterns of variation in chipped stone raw materials from the Chevelon drainage. Unpublished M. A. thesis. Binghamton, New York: State University of New York.
Harris, M.
    1968   Discussion. *New perspectives in archaeology,* edited by L. Binford and S. Binford, pp. 359–361. Chicago: Aldine.

Kushner, G.
  1970 A consideration of some precessual designs for archaeology as anthropology. *American Antiquity* **35**:125–132.
Plog, F.
  1973 Diachronic anthropology. In *Research and theory in current archaeology,* edited by C. Redman, pp. 181–198. New York: Wiley.
  1974 Settlement patterns and social history. In *Frontiers of anthropology,* edited by M. Leaf, pp. 68–91. New York: Van Nostrand Reinhold.

Chapter 8

A NETWORK MODEL FOR
THE ANALYSIS OF PREHISTORIC TRADE

CYNTHIA IRWIN-WILLIAMS

I. THE PROBLEM

The exchange of material goods and services is the subject of a large body of literature in anthropology, economics, geography, and sociology. The treatment of the subject, especially in archaeology, has tended to be broadly programmatic or simply descriptive and has suffered from an absence of a coherent quantitative methodology for applying large-scale theory to field and laboratory data. For example, methods for quantifying the archaeological equivalent to reciprocity and redistribution and for defining quantitatively the place of exchange centers in the growth of urban society are generally lacking. Accordingly, attention is focused here on outlining appropriate techniques, on deriving network models, and on suggesting some of the more general problems to which these may apply.

To date three major areas of concern have served as foci for consideration: (1) the material objects involved in exchange, through source identification, distributional studies, etc. (e.g., Renfrew et al. 1966); (2) the specific economic function of trade and its diachronic and synchronic relations to the function of other cultural subsystems, particularly the evolution of other institutions such as urban society, the state, etc. (Renfrew 1969; Rathje 1971; Tourtellot and Sabloff 1972); and (3) exchange as a symbolic medium and as a focus for patterns of social interaction (e.g., Sahlins 1965).

II. THE NETWORK MODEL

The model developed here is not designed to provide the sole methodology for an anlysis of prehistoric trade. As previously stated (Irwin-Williams 1971), the most efficient approach to the construction of models lies in the derivation of as wide a range as possible of theoretical structures so as to produce the fullest explanation of the data. The current model has its origin largely in the concept of social exchange as used in economic anthropology, of sociometric network theory as applied in ethnology, sociology, and human geography, and movement theory as developed in economic geography. The particular constructs discussed are currently being applied in studies of Pueblo prehistory of the Puerco River and in the San Juan Basin of northwestern New Mexico.

In brief, exchange is considered here to be a form of interaction that creates and reflects specific socioeconomic linkages between individuals, groups, societies, regions, states, etc., in short, biological and social systems over a wide range of size and complexity. These linkages make up a network differing in content but not in structure from networks considered in other fields. In archaeology it is made up of settlements, the network points or vertices, and exchange relations, the edges or links, and is subject to a variety of analytic approaches. The raw materials of archaeology lend themselves well to these analyses because they present a permanent "fossilized," though incomplete, record of prehistoric exchange patterns. Several of the requirements, problems, and parameters for measurement are considered briefly below.

Initially, in order to deal with networked exchange relationships, it is necessary to establish approximate contemporaneity of points and links within the pattern. This essential point is too often overlooked. However, any consideration of exchange or other interaction between members or elements of a cultural system *must assume* that these members existed at roughly the same time or else the exchange could not take place. It is realized that this is often difficult to accomplish in archaeology, but as far as possible it must be attempted. Where archaeological time units are unavoidably long (more than a few hundred years at most), this and all other methodologies that make assumptions of contemporaneity should be used with great caution or not at all.

Once a degree of contemporaneity has been established, network linkages may be measured in several ways and at several levels of detail. For example, the linkages may be measured in terms of the following: (1) within assemblages from a given settlement, the presence or absence of objects originating at another point; (2) the proportion of specific exchange goods from a particular origin to local goods of the same class; (3) the proportion of goods of the same class originating at various different points; (4) the directional dominance of the flow of goods, that is, the import–export ratio between settlement points; (5) the number of classes of objects exchanged between points; (6) the kinds of classes of objects exchanged between points.

If the objects cannot be localized with sufficient accuracy to points within a region, it may be necessary to resort to *similarity indices*. Similarity indices may be established by a variety of quantitative techniques, which simply measure the degree of similarity of one artifact class or assemblage to another in terms of attributes, stylistic parallels, typologic representation, or other features (King 1969; Krumbein and Graybill 1965). However, if similarity indices are used in this way, it must be understood that while these probably do reflect total social communication between points, they do *not* necessarily reflect exchange patterns. Accordingly, not all of the following analyses will be relevant.

Some difficulty arises inescapably from the use of material culture objects as indicators of linkage between localities. Even after contemporaneity has been established, it is recognized that the only relationship definitely identified is that between the point of origin of the goods and the final point of their consumption. Accordingly, it is not usually possible to examine specific exchange events by this method. Rather the aim is to identify and analyse the *pattern* produced by repeated exchange events. Some degree of uncertainty must exist over whether the goods were directly or indirectly received from their point of origin. However, several specific tests may be applied to permit an objective assessment. For example, consistent distinction should be made between (1) pairs of localities that are joined by a two-way flow of objects and those whose linkage is unidirectional, (2) paired localities that exhibit multiple classes of mutually originating imported objects and those linked by only a single class of objects (see item E in Section III), and (3) localities at which a relatively large proportion of the goods in a specific class are imported from linked localities and those at which these imports play a small part. These and other relevant parameters can be quantitatively expressed to reflect probability of direct as opposed to indirect linkage.

III. SPECIFIC ANALYTIC APPROACHES

With this background, it is impossible to consider specific analytic approaches. Each of these approaches can be expected to yield information on specific kinds of exchange, human interaction patterns, and social and economic dynamics within and between cultural systems. As a whole the method provides both the means for testing hypotheses derived from other sources and may itself serve as a source for the development of further hypotheses. The particular approaches outlined here have been chosen because they seem best adapted to reflect a variety of interaction patterns.

A. Exchange networks can be considered from three points of view. First, the "global" approach views the whole network (or as much of it as is visible) but concentrates on only one or two types of relationship. In the archaeological context, such as approach might, for example, focus specifically on the maximum distribution patterns for certain pottery styles and other material culture elements would be excluded from the discussion. This would yield information on the *specific* well-defined types of interaction involved over a relatively wide area. Second, a "zonal" approach separates out a specific zone within the whole network for concentrated attention. In the archaeological context, a zone may be selected on the basis of spatial, environmental, cultural, or other reasons, and all visible indications of socioeconomic interaction within it will be considered. It will produce maximum information on several levels and kinds of human interaction and will permit the exploration of elements of group identity, social boundaries, and related phenomena. Third, the "anchored" approach focuses on a central anchorage point, equivalent to "ego" in kinship analysis, and its specific links with a large network. From this, for example, the specific position of a single settlement can be examined within the larger social universe (see the Southwestern example, Section V).

B. Network exchange relationships can be represented in a variety of formats, including graphs and matrices such as Figure 1, reflecting the existence of exchange connects or "connectivity" between a series of points. The significance of connectivity to the understanding of prehistoric socioeconomic systems cannot be overestimated. The use of graphs and matrices representing connectivity permits the conversion of ordinary archaeological data into a simple quantitative form amenable to relatively sophisticated manipulation. So, for example, even simple potsherd type-counts can yield information on interregional trade that can be expressed in matrix form. More detailed analysis of ceramic, lithic, and other attributes can be expected to produce data on smaller scale intraregional exchange patterns.

The total "connectivity" of the exchange network is measured by converting the graph of linkages between points into a symmetrical connectivity matrix, which will reflect different levels of exchange-related interaction within differently structured societies. For such a matrix the connectivity of any single point will be found by a sum of rows and/or columns of the matrix. From this it should be possible to construct a hierarchy of settlements in terms of their connective significance within the regional pattern. Transformations of this matrix (such as powers and use of factor analysis) make it possible to detect elements of localization, which may then be correlated or interpreted in terms on contextual factors of geography, resource availability, and system trajectory (Haggett and Chorley 1969). If information on the dominance of points within the regional flow pattern is available, the result is a digraph (directed graph, indicating flow direction) and an asymmetrical

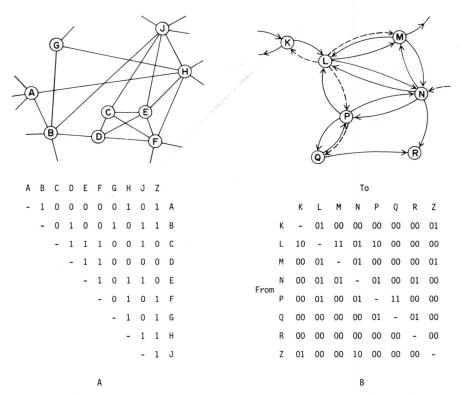

	A	B	C	D	E	F	G	H	J	Z	
	-	1	0	0	0	0	0	1	0	1	A
		-	0	1	0	0	1	0	1	1	B
			-	1	1	1	0	0	1	0	C
				-	1	1	0	0	0	0	D
					-	1	0	1	1	0	E
						-	0	1	0	1	F
							-	1	0	1	G
								-	1	1	H
									-	1	J

A

		To							
		K	L	M	N	P	Q	R	Z
	K	-	01	00	00	00	00	00	01
	L	10	-	11	01	10	00	00	00
	M	00	01	-	01	00	00	00	01
From	N	00	01	01	-	01	00	01	00
	P	00	01	00	01	-	11	00	00
	Q	00	00	00	00	01	-	01	00
	R	00	00	00	00	00	00	-	00
	Z	01	00	00	10	00	00	00	-

B

Figure 1 Two networks and derivative matrices describing (A) the simplest links between nodes (sites, persons, etc.) in a social network and (B) directional linkages (reflecting flow dominance, action initiation, etc.). Although these illustrations are only presence/absence type formation, in many situations numerical entries are possible. From J. A. Barnes, SOCIAL NETWORKS copyright © 1972 Cummings Publishing Company, Inc., Menlo Park, California.

matrix that will further qualify the relations between regional communities (Figure 1; Harary et al. 1965).

C. The density of connections for a given zone is found as the dividend of the number of actual zonal links divided by the total number of possible links (Haggett and Chorley 1969; Mitchell 1969). The relative span or exchange-integration levels of various zones may be measured in terms of the ratio of their relative densities. In addition, variation in exchange density in a previously little known context will provide information on social boundaries and the degree of integration that characterizes social systemic units.

D. Most excavation-based archaeology concentrates on one or a few sites within a regional or supra regional universe of the kind described. In addition, in studies of urbanization and centralization, one or a few loci may become increasingly dominant and their precise function within the interaction network may need to be specified. Using a site of this kind as an "anchorage," the network of all points with which the anchorage maintains contact has been termed the "first order star" of the points (Barnes 1972). The total of all the relations between all the members of this star is then the "first order zone." A measure of the significance of the principal settlement within this zone is found by taking the difference between the connectivity of the whole first order zone minus that of the anchorage based star itself. In addition to clarifying the specific nature of the intrazonal relationships involved, this also permits comparison of the dominance patterns of zones of differing size, composition, and level of complexity.

E. Member elements in an exchange network may circulate goods of one or more classes, which Kapferer's multiplexity concept enables us to evaluate (Kapferer 1971). Single channel, uniplex relations, involving the exchange of one class of objects (e.g., painted pottery bowls), are more limited and less binding than multiplex links involving the exchange of several classes of goods. Linkages may be ranked accordingly and settlements ranked in terms of the number and degree of their multiplex relationships. The significance of this may be viewed as the result of involving differential numbers of subsystems within the large society in the exchange networks. The quantity or proportion of goods in each class serves as an indicator of the size of the channels (uniplex or multiplex) and likewise will vary with the strength and directness of the relationship.

F. Employing the concepts of relative density and multiplexity, it is possible to differentiate zones with maximum internal linkage bounded by zones of relative low density and few multiplex relations (Kapferer 1971). On a larger scale, these *boundaries* may serve to differentiate discrete social systems, regional enclaves, and areal spheres of influence.

G. Epstein (1971) has distinguished between *effective* and *extended* networks, which have their equivalent in the larger regional interaction pattern. The effective network here will be characterized by large channels, multiplex linkages, and relatively great density. Relations within the extended network will be more attenuated and probably more specialized.

IV. EXCHANGE SYSTEMS AND SOCIAL SYSTEMS

It may be readily seen that prehistoric exchange–interaction network of the kind described provide an entrée into other areas of social–systemic analysis as well. Although these cannot be discussed at length, it is possible to indicate a few specific directions currently being followed in the southwestern Pueblo research already mentioned.

The first of these concerns differential distribution of classes of goods.

Initial indications from the data suggest that exchanged goods do not travel uniformly through space. Concepts from statistical geography provide limited but useful models in this sphere. Durer (in Haggett 1965) defines the *specific value* as the value of the object divided by its weight. He proposes, following Zipf's law of least effort, that objects of low specific value will move shorter distances than those of higher value, other things being equal. The ideal geometric field generated by this principle is a cone or a circle with the center at the object's source. Alternatively, following a gravity-flow model, the quantity of movement between points should be proportional to the product of their populations divided by the square of the distance between them. In contrast to these optimal distributions, actual patterns are widely distorted by geographic–topographic features and by the action of prehistoric social systems. Accordingly, it is possible to simulate a model reflecting random distribution, distribution around a point of origin, distribution as a function of distance between population centers, distribution as a function of bounded interaction zones, distance as a function of class of goods, etc. The essential nature of these models is to compare and contrast real space, economic–ideal space, and social space.

A second area for investigation concerns the central but poorly understood concept of class of goods. Binford (1962) has defined three major classes of artifacts in general in terms of their systemic function: ecotechnic, sociotechnic, and ideotechnic. However, difficulties arise in objectively defining the memberships of these classes. Differential distribution of object classes is a key to this kind of analysis. For example, in northwestern New Mexico, corrugated Pueblo culinary ware seems to have been exchanged in a manner distinct from that of painted bowls and mugs. The different patterns probably reflect distinct primary uses—large-scale container for food and water as opposed to small-scale decorated eating utensil. Likewise luxury goods, "wealth" ("primitive valuables" in Dalton's terms), and other ideotechnic items may be expected to move in distinctive patterns. Unquestionably, however, analysis of the differential distances, directions, zones, and networks reflected by the distribution of exchange items is central to the understanding of the operation of the systems involved.

Sahlins (1965) has distinguished two essential types of primitive exchange: reciprocity and redistribution. Redistribution involves the central collection of goods from members of the group and to some degree the redivision within this group. The alternative form of exchange is reciprocity. Reciprocity varies in form from general reciprocity involving small-scale, frequent, and informal generous reciprocity among relations and coresidents, through balanced reciprocity, fuller but more formal exchange between members of a larger social system or systems that desire to establish permanent relations, to negative reciprocity involving careful exchanges and sharp dealings between remote contacts and strangers.

Employing the methods reviewed above, it is possible to formulate predictions for the various exchange patterns and to test them in the field. Thus, if redistribution centers are present and are the commonest model of exchange, there should occur within the sample occasional settlement nodes displaying the following characteristics: dense multiplex connections to numerous linked dependents; large first order zone and high order dominance in their formation; domination of the network flow in terms of import–export relations; a large effective network; relatively well-defined boundaries between first order star zones; concentration of a maximum diversity of goods, particularly valuable goods, at the central point. In contrast, reciprocal exchange systems should be characterized by relatively equally functioning settlement nodes throughout; each node should display multiplex dense relationships within a small first order zone, and there should be relatively little domination of this zone by the first order star or any other node; there will be less domination of network flow patterns and more even two-directional flow; any node will have a relatively small effective network, characterized by the exchange of low value items (such as food), although its extended uniplex network may be of considerable size; the boundaries between first order star zones will be relatively weaker; distribution of goods will be relatively more even.

V. A SOUTHWESTERN EXAMPLE

As already noted, the network model is currently being employed in investigations of ancient Puebloan society on the Puerco River and on the San Juan River in northwestern New Mexico. This research is still in progress, and it is not possible to deal with it in detail here. However, a few examples may serve to illustrate elements of the discussion.

In the middle Puerco River valley several hundred sites belonging to the Basketmaker III–Pueblo III phases (ca. A.D. 700–1300) are under investigation. Geological and paleobotanical evidence indicates that this was a period of considerable climatic fluctuation, which apparently had marked effects on the Puebloan population. Throughout this time period most of the indigenous population of the region was dispersed in small groups of pithouse structures or 3–20 room simple masonry dwellings and never aggregated into larger towns. However, the size range and distribution of these hamlets varies considerably with time and in response to climatic change. There are two exceptions to this dispersed settlement pattern. One is a large well-constructed town built in the late eleventh century apparently by intrusive population elements from the Chaco Canyon 45 miles to the north. The other is a single, loosely aggregated "town" built in the thirteenth century adjacent to a large irrigation complex.

It may readily be seen that elements of the network approach outlined above will provide useful information on a variety of specific questions in this research situation. If ceramic and other analyses are able to demonstrate localized production of goods, the full range of techniques noted in items A–G (Section III) comes into play. It is not possible to consider all of the possibilities, but two areas of research interest will suffice as illustrations.

1. *The identity and integration of units within the larger socioeconomic system.* The research area comprises a well-defined zone corresponding to certain spatial and environmental parameters. Within this zone it is desirable to measure the connectivity between settlements as reflected by the exchange of goods. Methods suggested in B above may be used to indicate the degree of overall interaction, the position of individual settlements within the total zone, and to identify clustering of sites in terms of exchange patterns. This information can then be entered into equations relating to the position of natural resources, the effects of climatic change, the relationship of site clustering to geographic distance, and the relation of degree of connection to population size and other elements.

The density of exchange connection within and between clusters within the larger zone (C and F above) will permit the identification of clusters of settlements that functioned at least to some degree as "communities," and the establishment of boundary areas (less dense interaction). Here also the affects of resource location, geographic distance, population size, and other factors may be measured in terms of their effects on interaction patterns.

Within the larger zone it should be possible to compare and contrast the relative distribution of different classes of goods in relation to distance and social unit (E above). It is possible to test whether certain classes of goods are exchanged entirely within the units of maximum exchange interaction already defined or simply vary as a function of distance or other phenomena. In the same way the overall size of exchange channels (multiplexity) may vary along these lines.

2. *The position of towns within the Puerco River socioeconomic universe.* Two settlements of a size greatly exceeding the norm for the area have been identified: one, the intrusive Chaco town, apparently reflecting the character of the densely aggregated and sophisticated Chaco centers to the north; the second, apparently indigenous in origin, probably reflecting the exigencies of climatic deterioration and the requirements of a large-scale irrigation system. It is highly desirable that these be compared and contrasted in order to understand their essential organizational principles. Some important distinctions between the two will be visible in terms of their local and regional relationships and interaction patterns.

The relative position of the two towns within the regional exchange system may be considered using concepts such as the direction of goods flow (B above) and the degree of dominance of their first order zones by their first order stars (D above). The possibility of either town acting as a focal point for regional exchange or a redistribution center can be explored in terms of flow dominance (B above), degree of multiplexity (E above), the size and degree of integration of their effective networks (G above), the size and dominance of their first order stars (D above), and the degree of their boundary definitions (F above). All of these and other attainable relationships can then be considered within the framework of climatic alteration, population size change, etc.

This by no means exhausts the possibilities, but it is evident that a number of critical problems concerning the cultural systems of the Puerco River can be approached in terms of the network model and methods suggested.

References

Barnes, J. A.
    1972   Social networks. *Addison-Wesley module in anthropology,* No. 26.
Beschers, J. M., and E. O. Lauman
    1967   Social distance: a network approach. *American Sociology Review* **32**:225–236.
Binford, L. R.
    1962   Archaeology as anthropology. *American Antiquity* **28**:217–225.
Boissevain, J., and J. C. Mitchell (Eds.)
    1972   *Network analysis: studies in human interaction.* The Hague: Mouton.
Bott, E. J.
    1971   *Family and social network.* London: Tavistock.
Epstein, A. L.
    1971   Gossip, norms and social network. In *Social networks in urban situations,* edited by
           J. C. Mitchell. Manchester: Manchester University Press.
Haggett, P.
    1965   *Locational analysis and human geography.* New York: St. Martin's Press.
Haggett, P., and R. J. Chorley
    1969   *Network analysis and geography.* London: Edward Arnold.
Harary, G., R. Z. Norman, and D. Cartwright
    1965   *Structural models: an introduction to the theory of directed graphs.* New York: Wiley.
Irwin-Willaims, C.
    1971   *Models for reconstructing the economy of early hunters.* Paper for the 36th annual
           meeting of the Society for American Archaeology.
Kapferer, B.
    1971   Norms and the manipulation of relationships in a work context. In *Social networks in
           urban situations,* edited by J. C. Mitchell. Manchester: Manchester University Press.
King, L. J.
    1969   *Statistical analysis in geography.* Englewood Cliffs, New Jersey: Prentice-Hall.
Krumbein, W. C., and F. A. Graybill
    1965   *An introduction to statistical models in geography.* New York: McGraw-Hill.
Mitchell, J. D. (ed.)
    1971   *Social networks in urban situations.* Manchester: Manchester University Press.
Mitchell, J. C.
    1973   Norms, networks and institutions. In *Network analysis studies in human interaction,*
           edited by J. Boissevain and J. C. Mitchell. The Hague: Mouton.
Price, W. L.
    1971   *Graphs and networks.* New York: Butterworth.

Rathje, W. L.
  1971   The origin and development of classic Maya civilization. *American Antiquity* **36**:275–286.
Renfrew, A. C.
  1969   Trade and cultural process in European prehistory. *Current Anthropology* **10**:151–169.
Renfrew, A. C., J. E. Dixon, and J. R. Cann
  1966   Obsidian and early culture contact in the Near East. *Proceedings of the Prehistoric Society* **32**.
Sahlins, M.
  1965   The sociology of primitive exchange. In *The relevance of models for social anthropology,* edited by M. Blanton. London: Tavistock.
Tourtellot, G., and J. A. Sabloff.
  1972   Exchange systems among the ancient Maya. *American Antiquity* **37**:126–135.
Wolfe, A. W.
  1970   On structural comparisons of networks. *Canadian Review of Anthropology and Sociology* **7**:226–234.

Chapter 9

IDENTIFICATION OF PREHISTORIC INTRASETTLEMENT EXCHANGE

GLEN D. DEGARMO

I. INTRODUCTION

Webster's defines "exchange" as "a reciprocal giving; [a] giving and receiving." Although material and nonmaterial things can be given and received by the participants in an interaction, students of prehistory are concerned with different human activities preserved in different kinds and distributions of material goods. Accordingly, in the following discussion the term "exchange" will be restricted to mean a reciprocal giving and receiving of material objects only. As an economic phenomenon, exchange minimally can result in a regularized movement of materials between participants, and it provides one form (in some cases the only form) of integration between them.

On the basis of ethnographic analogies, it seems probable that prehistoric exchange could have been important at three geographical cum sociocultural levels—interregional, intersettlement (intraregional), and intrasettlement. The several exchanges occurring within each of the levels can be conceptualized as a network in which the different participants in the interactions are the network nodes and the exchanges are the links between them (cf. Haggett 1965:61–79; Haggett and Chorley 1969; Irwin-Williams, Chapter 8; Plog, Chapter 7). Although ethnographic studies of network phenomena tend to focus upon interactions between individuals (Mitchell 1974), it is at least very difficult to identify individuals in archaeological materials, and it seems probable that investigations of prehistoric exchange networks will depend upon an ability to archaeologically identify social *groups* as the participants in exchange. Thus, the analysis of network characteristics begins with two complementary tasks: identification of prehistoric social groups and identification of the exchange links that integrated them.

At the interregional and intersettlement levels, social groups can be identified with little difficulty, because the populations of different settlements each represent a social group of some kind. Several papers in this volume illustrate the emerging strategies for demonstrating exchange links between such settlement groups. Within settlements, however, the two analytical tasks are not so easily performed. In many cases it can be safely assumed that the residents of a settlement were organized into distinct social groups and that these groups were integrated by exchange; yet the archaeological identification of these phenomena rarely has been accomplished.

The following discussion summarizes an attempt to demonstrate prehistoric exchange at the intrasettlement level. The data were recovered from Coyote Creek, Site 01—a 30-room pueblo in east central Arizona.[1] The discussion is divided into two sections in which the identification of social groups and of exchange links between them are considered separately. Each of the sections also is divided into two parts. In the first part of a section earlier studies of southwestern archaeology that focus specifically upon the intrasettlement problem are reviewed, and in the second part the preliminary results from Site 01 are summarized.

A concern with the adequacy of archaeological measures for sociocultural phenomena is expressed throughout the discussion.

II. IDENTIFICATION OF INTRASETTLEMENT SOCIAL GROUPS

A. Prior Research

There is little modern archaeological literature for the American southwest that is explicitly concerned with recognizing social units smaller than the archaeological "culture" or the site (cf. Wilcox 1975). Two of the more recent studies are those of Longacre (1964, 1970) on Carter Ranch pueblo

---

[1] The discussion in this paper is a brief summary of some aspects of my Ph.D. dissertation (DeGarmo 1975). Readers interested in the data and supportive arguments that underlie the summary should consult the dissertation.

and of Hill (1966, 1970) on Broken K pueblo. Both Longacre and Hill statistically defined spatial differences in intrasettlement distributions of painted decorative elements observed on pottery fragments. They both use these results to argue that they have identified several matrilocal social groups.

Although the interpretations of data formulated by Longacre and Hill have been criticized (Allen and Richardson 1971; Stanislawski 1969), their work represents an important methodological landmark in studies of southwestern prehistory. Both investigators assumed first that variability in archaeological materials resulted from variability in *behaviors*. Second, they formulated deductive arguments about prehistoric social behavior, which they then tested against variability in archaeological data (Watson et al. 1971; Woodall 1972).

Two additional recent reports on prehistoric pueblos (Dean 1969; Rohn 1971) contain valuable suggestions for the study of intrasettlement social organization. In the first, Rohn (cf. Rohn 1965) uses architectural data from Mug House on Mesa Verde to identify units he calls "suites." Suites are defined by differences in the ease of interaction between rooms: "Throughout the ruin, doorways tend to connect clusters of rooms and outdoor areas around one large nuclear space" (Rohn 1971:31). Rohn then uses additional architectural data to identify higher order groupings—suites are combined into "courtyard units," which are themselves grouped into two larger units that represent a binary partitioning of the entire structure.

Minimally, the archaeological data provided by Rohn show that the residents of Mug House were organized into a hierarchy of groups defined architecturally by differences in the ease of intrasettlement interaction. Other characteristics of these interactional groups are rather uncertain. The suite is thought to contain both habitation and storage rooms, and its occupants are inferred to have been a "household," defined as "any group of individuals who share the economic workload and occupy jointly one house or a cluster of contiguous spaces that are well demarcated and into which outsiders do not freely intrude . . ." (Rohn 1971:31). The social and economic features of the other Mug House interactional groups are not specified. However, since courtyard units are associated with rooms defined as ceremonial rooms called kivas (Rohn 1971:37–39), these units may represent ceremonial groups.

Dean (1969, 1970) has identified architectural units he calls "room clusters" and "courtyard complexes" found in Tsegi Phase pueblos of northeastern Arizona. These units, particularly at the pueblos of Betatakin and Kiet Siel, are similar to the suites and courtyard units at Mug House. Dean believes that both room clusters and courtyard complexes "represent but one type of household, the extended family type" (1969:37, 1970:163). Dean goes considerably farther than Rohn in his inferential suggestions about the organizational characteristics of social groups at these pueblos. He suggests that extended families may have practiced matrilocal residence, and he even suggests that they may have been "grouped into matrilineal lineages and clans, neither of which was localized within the village" (Dean 1970:169).

Both Rohn and Dean used variability in architecture as a reliable (and by no means trivial) archaeological measure of variability in intrasettlement interaction. It clearly was easier for the occupants of two or more adjacent rooms to interact when walls between them had doorways than when they did not—they must have interacted almost continually. Since one of the behavioral criteria for social group formation and maintenance is regular interaction between group members (Barth 1969:10–11; Homans 1950; Levy 1952:380–381), both Rohn and Dean have identified one criterion for recognizing prehistoric interactional cum social groups.

While the above studies have useful methodological features, they also have two related problems. First, they represent a narrow view of the possible organizational characteristics of the settlements' residents. Because of the fact that there has been little obvious change in the material remains from prehistoric pueblo populations to their modern descendents, it is common to accept modern pueblos as the model for prehistoric pueblo organization (e.g., Gjessing 1975:324; cf. the cited publications of Dean, Hill, Longacre, and Rohn). One consequence of this narrow view is that interpretations of prehistoric pueblo social organization do not account for the considerable variability in architecture between the pueblos analyzed. For example, in Mug House, Betatakin, and Kiet Siel room clusters (suites) were common, but there is great variability in the association of suites with kivas and in the clustering of suites into courtyard units. Kivas are sometimes plentiful and sometimes virtually absent. In contrast, neither room clusters nor courtyard units are reported at Carter Ranch and Broken K. There are comparatively few kivas at these two settlements (at least in comparison to Mug House), and Carter Ranch is the only pueblo with a Great Kiva. Assuming that this architectural variability is correlated with variability in social organization, it seems improbable that the residents of these five settlements had the same organizational properties.

Second, given the apparent similarity between prehistoric and historic pueblo remains, it is quite common to interpret prehistoric materials by analogy to *emic* social units found in modern Pueblo society. There is, however, a fundamental weakness inherent in this interpretative analogy. For example, extended families, nonlocalized lineages, and clans are emic kinship units that have not been translated into specific behaviors that would result in characteristic patterning in material remains recoverable by an archaeologist. That is, there are no *archaeological* measures for the inferred phenomena (Binford 1967).

The studies of Longacre and Hill use a more rigorous methodology, but they fail to exclude alternative sociocultural phenomena that could have produced the observed pottery design variability (cf. DeGarmo 1975:66–70).

B. Coyote Creek, Site 01

The following discussion of the materials from Coyote Creek, Site 01 attempts to improve upon and to extend the above analyses. I use archaeological data to show that two social groups occupied the settlement and that intrasettlement exchange may have linked the groups.

Coyote Creek, Site 01 is a pueblo structure located in east central Arizona (Figure 1) in the interface zone between two archaeological cultures—the Anasazi and the Mogollon. The structure was occupied during the middle of the thirteenth century A.D.

The analysis of the Site 01 materials has sidestepped the question of the degree to which emic groups in prehistoric and historic Pueblo society can be said to be the same, and the following interpretive description concentrates upon discovering prehistoric social groups defined with reference to *archaeological* measures of variability in behavior. The analysis makes use of the archaeological implications of the criteria for recognizing the enthnographically ubiquitous "domestic group" (Goody 1972).

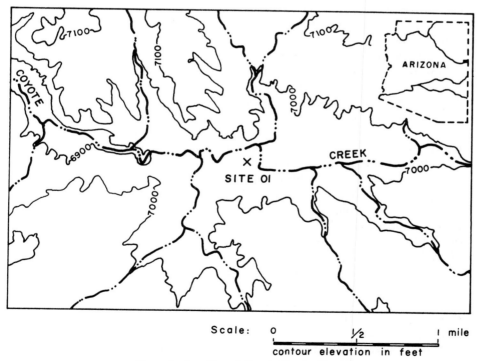

Figure 1   Location of Coyote Creek, Site 01.

A domestic group is behaviorally defined as a minimal, localized residential group principally responsible for performing its own subsistance and maintenance activities. Although difficult to test archaeologically, a domestic group usually includes both males and females and all age grades found in the society to which the group belongs. Ethnographically, a domestic group may be an entire hunting and gathering camp, part of a village or town, or simply a conjugal family. The definitional criteria for a domestic group permit formulation of the following *archaeological* proposition:

PROPOSITION

If Site 01 housed more than one domestic group, then there should be evidence of two or more localized residential areas in the structure. Further, each of these residential areas should contain evidence for domestic group activities, and these activities should represent both males and females.

To test the above proposition, the structure at Site 01 was examined for architectural evidence of two or more residential areas. The pueblo was found to be divided into three separate units or roomblocks (Figure 2). Each roomblock is an interactional unit composed of several rooms most of which are connected by open doorways, and the roomblocks are separated from each other by walls without connecting openings. The roomblock units are similar to the suites and room clusters in Mug House, Betatakin, and Kiet Siel.

The roomblocks were shown to have been contemporaneously occupied on the basis of trash levels, distributions of traditionally defined pottery types, and (especially) interroom and interroomblock distributions of bone from two individual *Bison* and fragments from many individual ceramic containers (DeGarmo 1975:110–135).

Preliminary support for interpreting the roomblocks as domestic residential areas is provided by distributions of space devoted to different room uses. Rooms in the structure have a bimodal distribution with respect to floor area, and firepits, mealing bins, and compacted dirt floors are both individually and as a group significantly associated with the larger but not the smaller rooms. From the distributions of these features, it is inferred that rooms of the larger and smaller size mode were used, respectively, as habitation and storage rooms. The three roomblocks have no statistically significant differences in their proportions of space devoted to the two room uses. Assuming that separate residential areas in the pueblo would have both habitation and storage rooms and that the proportionate amounts of space devoted to these two room uses would have been similar in each area, these distributional data suggest that each of the three roomblocks could have been a residential unit.

Additionally, in order to conclude that the three roomblocks were used as residential areas for domestic groups, it was necessary to show that domestic activities were represented in each. The procedure involved several steps.

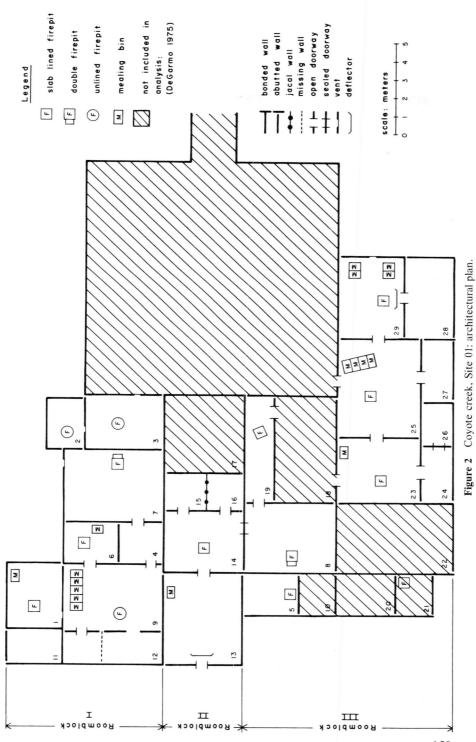

Figure 2 Coyote creek, Site 01: architectural plan.

Legend

F	slab lined firepit
F	double firepit
(F)	unlined firepit
M	mealing bin
▨	not included in analysis: (DeGarmo 1975)

bonded wall
abutted wall
jacal wall
missing wall
open doorway
sealed doorway
vent
deflector

scale: meters
0 1 2 3 4 5

159

First, justification for concluding that domestic activities occurred at Site 01 was provided by determining the probable former uses of ceramic containers and of nonceramic artifacts. The determinations were heavily dependent upon evidence of macroscopic and microscopic wear. Variations in the artifacts' wear, morphology, and material provided the primary information about different activities performed by the residents of the pueblo. Interpretations of these variations permit several conclusions: First, most of the activities represented at the structure are domestic activities that were predictable on the basis of ethnographic reports about the Western Pueblo Indians. Second, the activities include some probably performed by males and others probably performed by females (Table 1; cf. Murdock 1937). Third, the inventory of artifacts is quite similar to inventories from other prehistoric settlements in the region; thus, there is no preliminary evidence of any major intersettlement economic specialization, and it seems probable that the residents of Site 01 were economically generalized and largely self-sufficient.

TABLE 1

DISTRIBUTIONAL SUMMARY OF ACTIVITIES AT SITE 01.

	Sex	Activity	Kind or number of artifacts	Quantity in room block		
				I	II	III
A	f	Cooking, storage (solid chunks)	Wide-mouth jar	0	0	0
	m/f	Storage (liquids, powders)	Necked, narrow-mouth jar	0	0	0
	m/f	Mixing, eating food	Bowl	0	—	0
	m/f	Stirring, serving food	Ladle	0	—	0
B	m	Woodworking	Eight different tools	0	0	0
	?	General purpose cutting and scraping	Seven different tools	0	0	0
	?	General purpose rubbing and pounding	Six different tools	0	0	0
	f	Basketmaking	Two different tools	0	0	0
	f	Potterymaking	Start: muller and turntable	0	—	0
			Finish: smoothing pebble	0	+	0
	f	Seed grinding	Metate	0	0	0
			Mano: short	0	+	0
			Mano: long	0	—	0
			Corn sheller	0	—	0
	m/f	Ornament	Bone, marine shell	0	—	0
	m	Preform manufacture	Three different techniques	0	+	0
	m	Arrowmaking	Three different tools	+	0	—
	m	Stoneworking	Flaking hammerstone	0	0	0
			Pecking hammerstone	—	0	+
			Core	—	0	+

Symbols: 0, relatively expectable quantity; +, relatively too many; —, relatively too few; m, male; f, female.

Second, in order to learn how the various activities were distributed between the roomblocks, the quantity of artifacts representing each activity in each roomblock was tested with the Binomial Probability Distribution (Siegel 1956:36–42). This statistical test permits calculation of the probability of obtaining the observed frequency of an artifact (activity) for each of the roomblocks (given the total number of that artifact in the settlement). The test requires a statement of the relative probability that any artifact will be found in each of the sample units. This probability was defined for each roomblock, and it was specified to be the proportion of the structure's total habitation room floor area contained in a roomblock.

The Binomial Probability Distribution was used, initially, to test the interroomblock frequencies of each of four principal shapes of domestic, ceramic containers recovered from Site 01 (De Garmo 1975:177–178). The test results show (Table 1-A) that each kind of container occurs with relatively expectable frequencies in roomblocks I and III (see Figure 2), but there are too few bowls and ladles in roomblock II. Bowls and ladles have been interpreted to have had important uses in a residential area—the mixing, serving, and eating of food. Assuming that all of the activities represented by the different containers usually would be performed in a domestic group residential area (especially those activities represented by bowls and ladles), the test results strongly suggest that roomblock II was not being used as a residential area by the occupants of the pueblo.

Third, the relative roomblock frequencies of the different activities represented by the nonceramic artifacts were tested, and these test results (Table 1-B) demonstrated convincingly that roomblocks I and III, but not roomblock II, probably were used as residential areas.

Note that *all* activities except arrowmaking and certain stoneworking tasks occur with relatively expectable frequencies in roomblocks I and III. In contrast, many of these same activities occur rarely in roomblock II, or they are heavily concentrated in that part of the structure. The patterning in the presence and absence of activities in roomblock II can be interpreted in at least two ways: The roomblock either was abandoned and subsequently used as a salvage area, or it was being used as an interior work space (De-Garmo 1975:289–291). Choosing between these two alternatives is unnecessary for present purposes, for the critical implication of the patterning is that roomblock II was *not* being used as a residential area.

Fourth, the remaining distributional data importantly enter into the discussion of possible intrasettlement exchange in the following section, for these data (Table 1-B) show that males in the settlement were divided into two activity groupings. Males of roomblock I were involved in arrowmaking tasks to a significantly greater degree than males in roomblock III. These tasks are represented by antler pressure flakers, arrowpoints, and limestone shaftstraighteners. In contrast, the males of roomblock III concentrated upon other stoneworking activities as shown by the significantly high frequencies of two sizes of angular, pecking hammerstones that were used for a crumbling form of stoneworking (e.g., Pond 1930) and of two sizes of cores. Note, however, that although these different activities were *relatively* concentrated in one of the residential areas, none of them were *absent* in the other area.

In summary, the architectural characteristics of Site 01 and the patterning in the location of different activities between the structure's three roomblocks strongly suggest that two domestic groups occupied the settlement. The residents of roomblocks I and III represent two interactional groups (Levy 1952:380–381), since they occupied two different areas each comprised of several rooms connected by open doorways. Interactions between these two areas were restricted both by masonary walls with no openings and by roomblock II, an interior workspace or abandoned area. Both interactional groups also represent activity groups (Nadel 1957:14), for they both regularly performed the full range of related activities identified at Site 01. These related activities were concerned with subsistance and maintenance, and since they also represent both males and females, the two groups were domestic groups by definition. Additionally, since males of the two domestic groups were further differentiated by arrowmaking and other stoneworking tasks, they represent two subgroups within the population. This latter phenomenon increases the complexity of the social groups that occupied Site 01, but it does not alter the underlying domestic group characteristics of the residents of the pueblo.

Ethnographic data indicate that domestic groups' membership criteria normally are phrased in a cognitive idiom of kinship relations of some kind. I do not know of any archaeological data with which to demonstrate whether kinship relations were present at Site 01 or, if present, what they might have been. The archaeological variability merely demonstrates that two domestic groups probably occupied the settlement.

The two domestic groups may have formed nodes in an exchange network. Some of the possible characteristics of this network are investigated in the following section.

III. INTRASETTLEMENT EXCHANGE

A. Prior Research

The requirements for demonstrating intrasettlement exchange are the same as for intersettlement and interregional exchange. It must be shown that there probably was a reciprocal movement of goods between social groups said to have been part of an exchange network. In intersettlement and interregional studies, exchange can be inferred by patterning in declining quantities of goods from a source location as distance from the location increases (Renfrew, Chapter 4). In intrasettlement studies demonstration of such declining patterns may be impossible. Instead, exchange links between social groups are indicated by data that show products manufactured by one or more social groups were *consumed* by other social units of the settlement. Ideally, a reciprocal production–consumption relationship should be demonstrated; but, frequently, nondurable goods (e.g., food) enter into an exchange, and the reciprocal relationship may be preserved archaeologically only by evidence for a one-way movement of goods.

In the southwestern archaeological literature, studies of intrasettlement exchange are virtually nonexistent. The principal exception is Longacre's (1966) discussion of the distributions of tools at Broken K pueblo. He divides the settlement in half—one half characterized by a high frequency of shaftstraighteners and the other half by high frequencies of gravers, blades, saws, and antler flakers. Longacre (1966:100) suggests that the residents of the two areas were linked by "reciprocal exchange." Curiously, however, both of these areas crosscut other intrasettlement areas previously identified by Hill (e.g., 1970:59, 65) as residential units occupied by *different* matrilocal social groups.

B. Coyote Creek, Site 01

At Site 01 the different distributions of tools used for the production of arrows and of other stone tools indicate that males of the two domestic groups were partially specialized by manufacturing activities. This finding may suggest but it does not itself demonstrate exchange between the residents of the two residential areas. Indeed, there are at least three interpretive possibilities relative to the consumption of the manufactured products:

1. The products were differentially consumed by the domestic groups that manufactured them—semispecialized production *and* consumption: no exchange.
2. Although semispecialized production activities separated the two domestic groups, the resulting products were exchanged between them, and there was no differential consumption by the two groups—intrasettlement exchange.
3. The products were exchanged for goods produced at other settlements—intersettlement or interregional exchange.

These three possible utilization practices will be examined with the relevant data from Site 01.

1. *Differential domestic group consumption.* Testing, first, whether or not products made in roomblock III also were principally consumed there, note that both cores and pecking hammerstones are significantly concentrated in

roomblock III. This locational pattern is interpreted to mean that most of the flake tools as well as most of the objects made by the pecking technique of stoneworking were manufactured in this residential area. If these two classes of products were used principally by the domestic group that produced them, then one would predict that they also should be concentrated in roomblock III. Contrary to this prediction, it was found that the two residential units have almost identical quantities of flake tools—roomblock I (excluding arrowpoints), 403 items; roomblock III, 401 items. Likewise, the roomblock totals for axe and maul heads, manos, and metates (all objects made by the pecking process) are not significantly different—roomblock I (excluding shaftstraighteners, which formed part of the arrowmaking tool kit), 203 items; roomblock III, 191 items. Thus, there is no evidence of differential domestic group consumption of these two classes of manufactured goods.

Continuing with the above logic, note that the greater concentration of arrowmaking equipment in roomblock I would suggest a higher frequency of hunting and, consequently, a greater consumption of game animals for the residents of this residential unit. It should be possible to infer (a) a higher incidence of hunting by a concentration of arrowpoints having worn edges (Ahler 1971) and (b) a more frequent consumption of game from a greater quantity of animal bone.

Contradicting these expectations, the quantities of worn arrowpoints are not significantly different in the two roomblocks (DeGarmo 1975:260), and the amounts of fragmented, unidentifiable animal bone also are quite similar—roomblock I, 1398 grams; roomblock III, 1301 grams. Additionally, while the identifiable animal bones are not yet completely analyzed, the preliminary counts of the minimum numbers of large and small game animals in the two roomblocks (Table 2) are not very different.

TABLE 2

MINIMUM ANIMAL COUNTS, ROOMBLOCKS I AND III.

Animal name		Quantity in roomblock	
		I	III
Large size:			
Antilocapra	(antelope)	3	4
Odocoileus	(deer)	6	4
Bison	(adult)	1	1
Bison	(infant)	1	1
Small size:			
Sylvilagus	(rabbit)	66	49
Lepus	(rabbit)	10	12
Cynomys	(prairie dog)	22	19
Thomomys	(gopher)	17	14

Generally, none of the data summarized in the preceding paragraphs demonstrate that the products of arrowmaking and other stoneworking tasks were differentially consumed by the domestic groups that performed those tasks. Accordingly, the first of the three above propositions is rejected.

2. *Intrasettlement exchange.* Next, I examine the evidence that products made by one domestic group may have been consumed by the other. Note that since there were no significant intrasettlement differences in the consumption of the products resulting from the kinds of manufacturing activities that divided males of the Site 01 settlement, it might be inferred that exchange linked the domestic groups residing in roomblocks I and III. The inference would be greatly strengthened, however, if it could be shown that individual artifacts recovered from one roomblock were manufactured in the other residential area. The possibility that artifacts in roomblock I were made in roomblock III is explored first.

All of the more complex artifacts made from flakes (arrowpoints, drills, and bifacial knives) found in roomblock I were compared visually with cores and flaking debris in roomblock III. It was thought that it might be possible to match raw material characteristics of the finished product with manufacturing debris in roomblock III.

The attempt to match stone characteristics was not successful. But this apparently negative evidence may not be significant, for it seems unreasonable to think that the considerable waste resulting from the production of flake tools would be tolerated in the residential areas—that is, most production may have occurred *outside* of the structure. Since no excavations have been conducted around the Site 01 structure, the attempt to match stone characteristics remains inconclusive.

Attempts to match roomblock I's artifacts shaped by the pecking process with manufacturing debris and raw materials in roomblock III also remain inconclusive for the present. These artifacts were made from sandstone, vesicular basalt, and nodules of limestone. Although experimental shaping of these materials by the pecking technique produces small bits of angular waste, such small bits of debris were not recognized during the excavation of Site 01.

Chunks of raw materials stored for later use in production by the pecking technique were also not found during the excavation of the settlement. However, such materials probably would have been kept outside of the structure prior to their use. Planned excavations around the periphery of the building may uncover stored materials and perhaps a workshop area associated with roomblock III, and it might then be possible to match stone characteristics between the two residential areas.

Next, the possibility that materials in roomblock III were related to the concentration of arrowmaking equipment in roomblock I was explored. Note that the distributions of large and small game animal bone suggest similar consumption of game in the two residential units. Although the concentration of arrowmaking tools in roomblock I might, then, suggest that game was exchanged into roomblock III from roomblock I, the evidence for different production patterns does not itself demonstrate that game was hunted principally by males residing in roomblock I. Ethnographic reports, however, often refer to a prescription that specific animal parts be given to individuals having particular social relationships with a successful hunter(s). Since there probably were intergroup social relationships of some kind between the residents of the two roomblocks, the distributions of large animal bone were examined to learn if members of complementary sets of bone (i.e., left and right, front and rear) differently characterized the two roomblocks. Nothing even remotely suggestive of differential distributions emerged from this test.

To summarize the above findings, intrasettlement exchange is suggested by the different production but similar consumption practices that have been found to characterize the two domestic groups at Site 01, but it cannot now be conclusively demonstrated.

3. *Intersettlement and interregional exchange.* In addition to intrasettlement exchange, it is conceivable that the products of the manufacturing activities that partitioned males at Site 01 may have been distributed to consumers via exchange with other settlements located in the Coyote Creek and Upper Little Colorado River drainage. Adequate documentation of intersettlement exchange is not yet possible, but there are limited data that suggest that the residents of Site 01 exchanged their stone tools for horticultural products grown at nearby settlements (DeGarmo 1975:378–380).

The postulated intersettlement exchange links may, in turn, have connected Site 01 into an interregional network such that the whole formed an interactional sphere (e.g., Struever and Houart 1972). An interregional network apparently is documented by marine shell from the Gulf of California and by obsidian perhaps obtained from an area close to Flagstaff, Arizona—both of which were recovered from the settlement.

The suggested possibility of intersettlement and interregional exchange does not mean that the probability of intrasettlement exchange is now lessened. Rather, I suspect that the residents of Site 01 participated in exchange at all three levels. An analytical problem for future investigation, thus, is the determination of the relative importance of these various exchange links.

Interestingly, investigation of intersettlement and interregional exchange could produce results suggestive of an increased probability of intrasettlement exchange at Site 01. For example, the limited quantities of marine shell and obsidian recovered from Site 01 can be inferred to mean that importation of these exotic materials was not a major activity at the settlement—it was not sufficiently important to require semispecialized production of goods to be exchanged for those materials. Thus, if intersettlement exchange eventually is eliminated as the principal method of consumption for the products differentially manufactured by males at Site 01, intrasettlement exchange will be shown to be more likely even in the absence of additional confirming data from the settlement itself.

IV. CONCLUSIONS

The various conclusions made at various points in the analysis as well as the emphasis upon archaeological measures for behaviors have been sufficiently stressed to make a summary of these points unnecessary. Instead, it is more useful to identify four other aspects of this study.

1. The analysis of Site 01 uses the fortunate fact that the structure was divided into interactional areas represented by the three roomblocks. When such obvious architecturally defined units are not found, the preliminary identification of different residential areas will be quite difficult and sometimes impossible [see Wilcox (1975) for another approach using variability in the construction of corners formed by room walls].

When architectural data cannot be used to define different residential areas, it may be possible to detect social group boundaries by analysis of the distributions of stylistic attributes of craft goods. Since social groups are boundary maintaining units, some intrasettlement production of craft products may have been accomplished by work units whose members were all from the same residential and social group. Peer group pressure in such work units could result in the emergence of partitions in design variability corresponding to interactional boundaries between the members of different social groups. Definition of stylistic variability purported to be representative of prehistorically real social groups is, however, an extremely tricky business. It is not an archaeological excercise that I think ought to be attempted given the contemporary lack both of an extensive knowledge about what constitutes stylistic attributes and an understanding of the sociocultural determinants of variability in such attributes (cf. Brothwell 1970). For the present, I suggest that such phenomena are more profitably studied with ethnographic data.

2. The preceding discussion of intrasettlement exchange at Site 01 is heavily dependent upon interpretations of the probable former uses of various artifacts (including the structure itself). The interpretations, in fact, are critical components of the discovery that two, not three, domestic groups occupied the settlement. During the interpretive analysis it was found that there were artifacts with the same gross morphology but different uses, artifacts with dissimilar morphologies but identical uses, and artifacts with uses other than those suggested by their gross morphologies (e.g., De Garmo 1975:402). These findings have important implications with respect to archaeological taxonomy. Archaeological typologies frequently are not designed to produce units representative of prehistoric phenomena. Many typologies are formulated with taxonomic reference to differences in gross morphological attributes of artifacts, and the criteria for making taxonomic choices from among the numerous available attributes often are unstated and seemingly quite arbitrary. The resulting types probably would not be useful for analyses of prehistoric intrasettlement exchange.

3. The excavation of Site 01 has been acknowledged to have been deficient in at least one respect: the lack of excavation outside of the structure makes it impossible to satisfactorily pursue the investigation of intrasettlement exchange with currently available data. Anticipated further excavations at Site 01 will be planned to correct this lack—In fairness, however, I should report that this deficiency was a function of limited time and manpower for more adequate fieldwork.

4. The discussion of the possible relative importances of interregional and intersettlement exchange at Site 01 highlights an important analytical point: an understanding of the human population that once occupied a settlement depends upon an ability to fit that settlement into a regional system of interacting settlement populations.

In summary, the preceding discussion of Site 01 demonstrates clearly that studies of intrasettlement exchange are merely one of a group of archaeological endeavors that can be profitably pursued only within a framework of research designed to maximize the recovery of data pertaining to prehistoric *behavioral variability* both within and between contemporaneous settlements of a region.

Acknowledgments

The excavation of Coyote Creek, Site 01 was made possible by a Dissertation Research Grant (GS-90093) awarded by the National Science Foundation and by additional grants awarded by the Museum of Northern Arizona and by the UCLA Friends of Archaeology. This support is greatfully acknowledged.

References

Ahler, S. A.
1971 Projectile point form and function at Rodgers Shelter, Missouri. *Missouri Archaeological Society, Research Series*, No. 8.

Allen, W. L., and J. B. Richardson, III
1971 The reconstruction of kinship from archaeological data: the concepts, the methods, and the feasibility. *American Antiquity* 36:41–53.

Barth, F.
1969 *Ethnic groups and boundaries: the social organization of cultural difference*. London: Gorge Allen & Unwin.

Binford, L. R.
1967 Smudge pits and hide smoking: the use of analogy in archaeological reasoning. *American Antiquity* 32:1–12.

Brothwell, D.
1970 Stones, pots and people: a plea for statistical caution. In *Science in archaeology: a survey of progress and research,* edited by D. Brothwell and E. Higgs, pp. 699–679. New York: Praeger.

Dean, J. S.
1969 Chronological analysis of Tsegi Phase sites in northeastern Arizona. *Papers of the*

Laboratory for Tree-Ring Research, No. 3. Tucson, Arizona: The University of Arizona Press.

1970 Aspects of Tsegi Phase social organization: a trial reconstruction. In *Reconstructing prehistoric pueblo societies,* edited by W. A. Longacre, pp. 140–174. Albuquerque, New Mexico: University of New Mexico Press.

DeGarmo, G. D.

1975 Coyote Creek, Site 01: a methodological study of a prehistoric pueblo population. Ph.D. dissertation, Department of Anthropology, University of California, Los Angeles. Ann Arbor, Michigan: University Microfilms.

Goody, J.

1972 Domestic groups. *Addison-Wesley Modular Publications,* No. 28. Reading, Massachusetts: Addison-Wesley.

Gjessing, G.

1975 Socio-archaeology. *Current Anthropology* 16:323–341.

Haggett, P.

1965 *Locational analysis in human geography.* London: Edward Arnold.

Haggett, P., and R. J. Chorley

1969 *Network analysis in geography.* London: Edward Arnold.

Hill, J. N.

1966 A prehistoric community in eastern Arizona. *Southwestern Journal of Anthropology* 22:9–30.

1970 Broken K Pueblo: prehistoric social organization in the American Southwest. *Anthropological Papers of the University of Arizona,* No. 18.

Homans, G.

1950 *The human group.* New York: Harcourt.

Levy, M. J., Jr.

1952 *The structure of society.* Princeton, New Jersey: Princeton University Press.

Longacre, W. A.

1964 Archaeology as anthropology: a case study. Unpublished Ph.D. dissertation. Department of Anthropology, University of Chicago.

1966 Changing patterns of social integration: a prehistoric example from the American Southwest. *American Anthropologist* 68:94–102.

1970 Archaeology as anthropology: a case study. *Anthropological Papers of the University of Arizona,* No. 17.

Mitchell, J. C.

1974 Social networks. In *Annual Review of Anthropology,* Vol. 4, edited by B. Siegel, pp. 279–299. Palo Alto, California: Annual Reviews Inc.

Murdock, G. P.

1937 Comparative data on the division of labor by sex. *Social Forces* 15:551–553.

Nadel, S. S.

1957 *The theory of social structure.* New York: The Free Press of Glencoe, Crowell-Collier.

Pond, A. W.

1930 Primitive methods of working stone, based upon the experiments by Halvor L. Skavlem. *Logan Museum Bulletin* 2. Beloit, Wisconsin: Beloit College.

Rohn, A. H.

1965 Postulation of socio-economic groups from archaeological evidence. In *Contributions of the Wetherill Mesa Archaeological Project,* assembled by D. Osborne, pp. 65–69. *Memoirs of the Society for American Archaeology,* No. 19.

1971 Wetherill Mesa excavations: Mug House, Mesa Verde National Park, Colorado. *National Park Service, Archaeological Research Series,* No. 7-D. Washington, D.C.: U.S. Department of the Interior.

Siegel, S.
1965 *Nonparametric statistics for the behaviorial sciences*. New York: McGraw-Hill.
Stanislawski, M. B.
1969 The ethno-archaeology of Hopi pottery making. *Plateau* **42**:27–33.
Struever, S., and G. L. Houart
1972 An analysis of the Hopewell interaction sphere. In *Social exchange and interaction*, edited by E. Wilmsen, pp. 47–79. *Museum of Anthropology, University of Michigan, Anthropological Papers*, No. 46.
Watson, P. J., S. LeBlanc, and C. Redman
1971 *Explanation in archaeology: an explicitely scientific approach*. New York: Columbia University Press.
Wilcox, D. R.
1975 A strategy for perceiving social groups in puebloan sites. In *Chapters in the prehistory of eastern Arizona, IV,* edited by P. Martin, E. Zubrow, D. Bowman, D. Gregory, J. Hanson, M. Schiffer, and D. Wilcox, pp. 120–159. *Fielddiana, Anthropology,* Vol. 65,
Woodall, J. N.
1972 *An introduction to modern archaeology*. Cambridge, Massachusetts: Schenkman.

Chapter 10

QUARRY ANALYSIS AT BODIE HILLS, MONO COUNTY, CALIFORNIA: A CASE STUDY

CLAY A. SINGER AND JONATHON E. ERICSON

I. INTRODUCTION

Studies of prehistoric trade systems have usually attempted to reconstruct the pattern of distribution for a raw material from data on its final disposition in archaeological sites. Such studies are becoming more frequent in archaeology (Wright 1969; Cann et al. 1970; Hogg 1971; Cobean et al. 1971; Hodder 1974), and their potential is generally recognized (cf Cann et al. 1970:590). Because such studies require careful collection of samples from many sites and natural sources, as well as chemical characterization of samples, they tend to be both time consuming and very costly. As an alternative, analysis of production at quarry sources offers a relatively inexpensive and comprehensive means to investigate prehistoric trade. Production analysis at the quarry source is intended to focus on artifact manufacture and diachronic trends in production. The results of production analysis are used to estimate the quantities of items produced for export as a function of time and to complement information gained through the analysis of product consumption in the surrounding region.

Quarry production analysis is designed to provide both qualitative and quantitative data on artifact production. Measurements of artifact density taken at set intervals along linear transects provide the data for quantitative estimates of total artifact production and for the identification of workshop

171

areas. Special samples are collected to gain additional information on lithic materials and technology and to verify quantitative estimates of artifact production. No source characterization of individual artifacts is required, if the assumption is made that all obsidian materials come from the source under investigation. Hydration dating of selected obsidian artifacts provides the temporal framework within which a diachronic model of production modes and manufactured products can be constructed.

The Bodie Hills quarry analysis project required 16 man-days of fieldwork and 40 man-days of laboratory analysis to establish the data base for this report. The total cash expenditure was less than $500.00. Specifically, project preparation began in the spring of 1974, and fieldwork was carried out between 28 June and 2 July of the same year. Laboratory analyses were completed in December 1975. The Bodie Hills notes and collection are stored at the UCLA Department of Anthropology Museum, Los Angeles, California (Accession No. 567).

II. THE BODIE HILLS SITE

Bodie Hills is one of several, large deposits of glassy obsidian located on the eastern side of the Sierra Nevada Mountains in east-central California near the Nevada state line (Ericson et al. 1976). This source, first located and characterized by Jack and Carmichael (1969), is situated north of Mono Lake on the western margin of the Great Basin within the territory occupied by Paiute Peoples in late prehistoric and historic times (Meighan 1955; Davis 1964). The site is located some 12 kilometers east of the town of Bridgeport (on the East Walker River) at elevations around 2500 meters in an area characterized by sparse, high desert scrub vegetation. The site consists of a more or less continuous area where obsidian flakes and other artifact forms are scattered on the hillsides and adjacent ridges (Figure 1).

Worked obsidian material covers a total area of approximately eight square kilometers varying in density from an isolated flake every few meters on the valley floor, to a solid pavement of cores, flakes, blades, bifaces, and other worked and unworked pieces near the primary outcrops and other locations. The density of worked material at and around these three outcrops far exceeds the site's average density of 50 flakes per square meter, with the overall density dropping off as one moves away from the primary sources.

Natural obsidian occurs in two distinct forms: primary terrace outcrops of angular material, and secondary ridge deposits of cobbles. Figure 2 shows the three primary terrace outcrops (T_1, T_2, and T_3), located on the high flanks of the 2649 meter mountain, along with the location and direction of the transects and special collection areas. The primary outcrop deposits consist of solid pavements of obsidian that form small terraces with fan-shaped talus slopes composed of angular chunks, broken blocks, and worked artifacts.

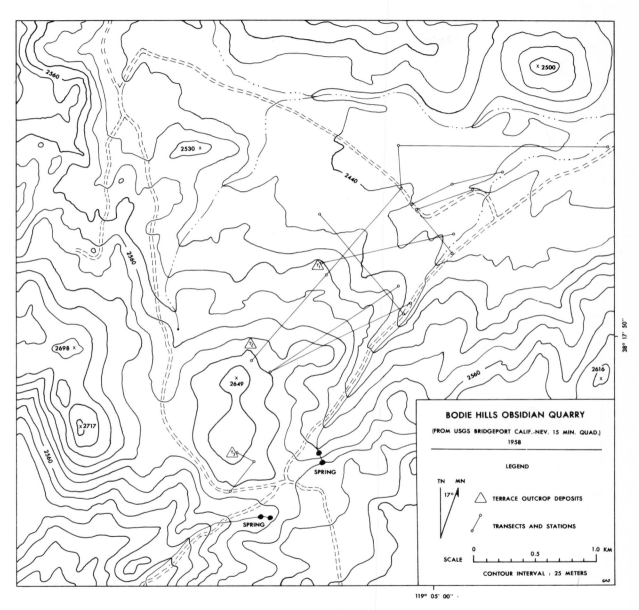

Figure 1 Map of Bodie Hills obsidian quarry.

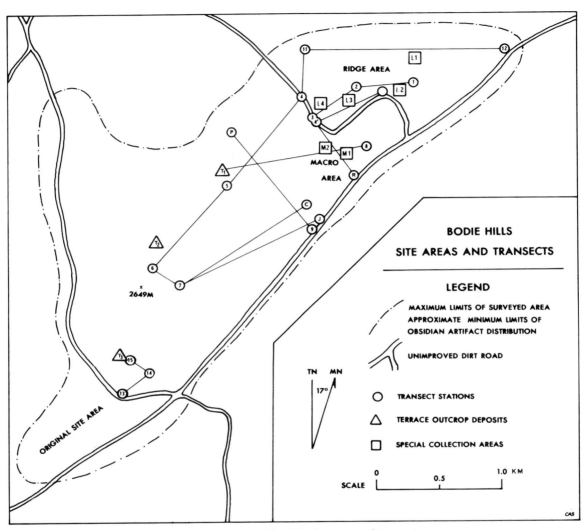

Figure 2   Map of Bodie Hills site areas and transects.

The depth of these deposits are unknown, but the total volume of material must be immense; for example, the T_1 deposit has a surface area of over 2000 square meters of solid obsidian. Secondary deposits (such as Macro Areas 1 and 2 and the Ridge Area near Stations 3, 4, and 4′) occur on a number of ridges and spurs that project out from the main slopes onto the valley floor. Weathered spherical nodules up to 20 cm diameter are found on ridge surfaces downslope from the primary deposits, but nodule size decreases as a function of distance from the three primary outcrops. Several kinds of obsidian can be distinguished visually including clear-gray, banded, and dense black varieties, occasional pieces of mottled reddish-brown and black ("mahogany obsidian"), and a clear variety with crystalline inclusions from outcrop T_2. With a site of such size and material volume, one is immediately beset with the problem of where to begin and how to adequately record and collect data. Therefore, a rigorously controlled sampling procedure was designed and used to overcome these problems.

III. SAMPLING PROCEDURES AND AREAS

Two kinds of field data were collected: (1) artifact descriptions and distributional data, and (2) artifact samples for hydration and technological analyses. A combination of measured linear transects and special area collections were used to provide the data base for this study.

Each transect consisted of walking between designated stations and recording the following information at specified 60 meter intervals:

1. Artifact density recorded as flakes per square meter—this count considered flakes and other artifact forms over 1 cm in diameter only.
2. Types of artifacts present with their relative frequencies.
3. Approximate sizes of artifacts.
4. Presence (or absence) of natural obsidian material including size and form.
5. Description of any nonobsidian materials—both natural and artifactual.
6. General description of topography and proximity to natural outcrops.

A total of 14 transects were walked, with a combined linear distance in excess of 11,300 meters. Artifact distributions, density measurements, and other data were recorded at 230 different points along the transects, which comprise about 4% of the total site area.

Samples of individual artifact types and any naturally occurring materials were collected at each recording point on most transects. All projectile points were collected, since these artifacts have been shown to be excellent time markers (Hester 1973; O'Connell 1967).

In addition, a series of special collections were made in three areas—the Macro Area, the Ridge Area, and the Original Site Area (Figure 2), all of which presented unique situations or materials relevant to our analyses of artifact production. The first area collections were made in Macro Areas 1 and 2, where concentrations of large and medium-size biface fragments and core preforms were observed. A one square meter surface sample within Macro Area 2 was also recovered by removing all material to a depth of 15 cm and screening with 1 mm square mesh, nylon window screen. Approximately 25 kg of retained material was returned to the laboratory for subsequent analysis. The Ridge Area samples consist of four small collections made at points along the northeast–southwest axis of the continuous low ridge that forms the principal feature in the northeast section of the site. Collections L_1, L_2, L_3, and L_4 were made at locations where obsidian and chert blades, chert flakes, and small obsidian bifaces appeared to concentrate. The last special collection was made in the large area southwest of outcrop T_3, designated as the Original Site Area.

Sampling procedures were designed in part to minimize the number of artifacts collected, thus reducing transport and storage problems and analysis time. A total of 816 individually catalogued artifacts and other lithic samples were collected and analyzed. It must be remembered that the artifacts observed and collected represent only materials left behind and not

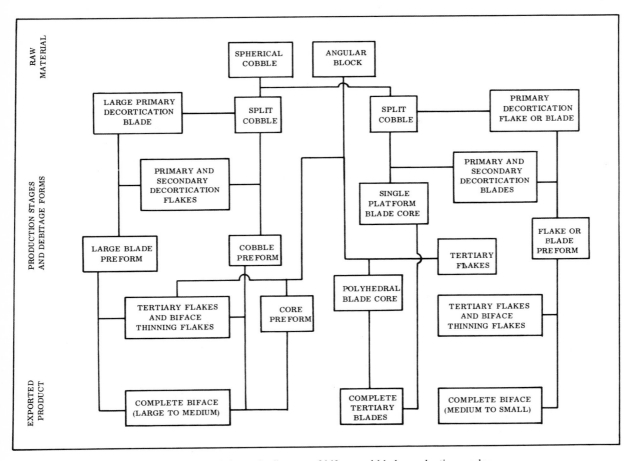

Figure 3 Schematic diagram of biface and blade production modes.

exported and should thus be thought of as rejected, broken, unfinished, or lost items. In this sense they are probably atypical of export products.

IV. ANALYTICAL RESULTS

Our analyses have shown that two distinct artifact forms were produced for export: (1) prismatic blades, and (2) partially finished bifaces. The production modes for these two forms are schematized in Figure 3. Prismatic blades (Figure 4) ranging from 3 to 15 cm in length were recovered from all site areas, but larger and thicker examples were found most often in areas where large and medium-size bifaces were also produced. Smaller, thinner

Figure 4 Blades and projectile points: (1) large secondary decortication blade preform; (2) large tertiary blade; (3) thick tertiary blade utilized as side scraper, all from transect 4-5; (4) tertiary blade; (5) secondary decortication blade; (6) small tertiary blade, all from Area L_2; (7) projectile point fragment with ribbon flaking, 3.0 microns, Area L_4; (8) Elko-eared point, 4.0 microns, Ridge Area; (9) Elko-eared point, 2.5 microns, Area L_2; (10) Silver Lake point, 9.2 microns, Area L_4.

blades (3 to 7 cm long) were found most often in the Ridge Area, north and west of stations 3, 4, and 4′, as were all three complete projectile points. Unfinished core preforms and broken or unfinished bifaces were the *most abundant* and noticeable artifacts on the site (Figure 5). A broad range of biface forms and sizes were produced (Figure 6). There appears to be a correlation between the morphology of the biface and the time when it was produced. For analytical purposes, core preforms, broken, and unfinished bifaces were classified according to the estimated size of whole specimens (large = over 10 cm long; medium = 7 to 10 cm; small = under 7 cm) and their basal configuration (convex, pointed, or straight). Large and medium-size bifaces occurred primarily in areas north and west of stations 3, 4, and 4′, while medium and small bifaces with convex or straight bases were found mainly in the Ridge and Original Site Areas.

Complete, finished artifacts and retouched or utilized tools were particularly scarce, although examples were collected in all site areas. The vast

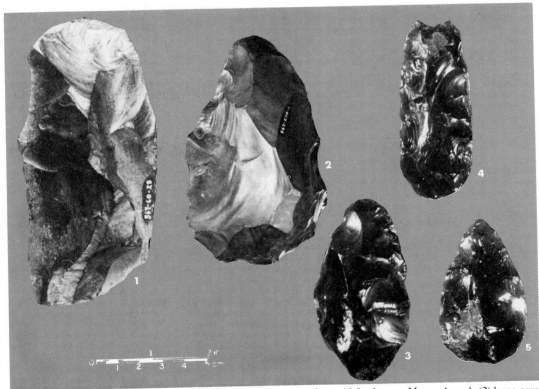

Figure 5 Biface preforms: (1) large core preform, 16.0 microns, Macro Area 1; (2) large core preform, 7.0 microns, transect P-9; (3) medium-size core preform, 7.0 microns, transect P-9 near station 9; (4) medium-size blade preform, Original Site Area; (5) small flake preform, Original Site Area.

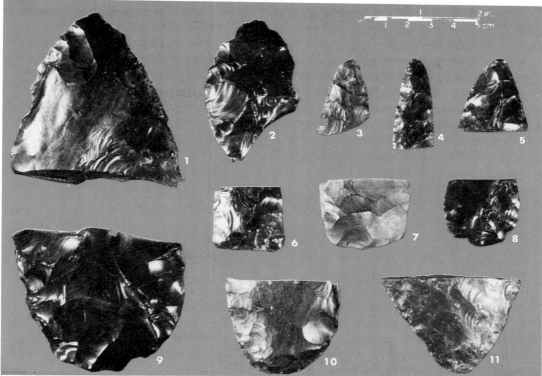

Figure 6 Broken bifaces: (1) large biface fragment, 4.5 microns, transect 4-5; (2) small biface fragment, 4.2 microns, transect 4-5; (3) small biface fragment, 3.8 microns, Area L_1; (4) small biface fragment, Area L_1; (5) small (?) biface fragment, 2.8 microns, Area L_1; (6) small biface fragment, 2.9 microns, Area L_3; (7) small (?) biface fragment, 4.9 microns, Area L_4; (8) small biface fragment, Area L_2; (9) large biface fragment, 7.8 microns, Macro Area 2; (10) medium-size biface fragment, 6.0 microns, Area L_2; (11) medium-size biface fragment, transect 4-5.

majority of unretouched flakes and blades show no regular wear patterns resulting from systematic utilization. A combination of severe weathering and natural edge damage on many specimens increased the difficulty of assessing the true amount of flake and blade utilization without retouch; none the less, fewer than 5% of the collected flakes and blades showed signs of use as either scrapers or knives.

The two most abundant forms of retouched tools were scrapers and perforating tools. Scrapers were usually produced by modifying secondary decortication or tertiary flakes, while perforators were made by utilizing or creating an acute point on the end of a blade or flake.

With the exception of one small (173.5 grams) battered obsidian core, collected in the Original Site Area, no hammerstones of any material were found. Initial percussion for decortication or core preparation was accomplished using a direct block-on-block or cobble-to-cobble technique.

This was followed by soft hammer (billet) percussion for shaping and thinning of bifaces and blade removal. Most blades, including the thinner examples, have low but prominent bulbs of percussion indicating removal by direct rather than indirect percussion. Although no direct evidence exists, we may infer that antler billets, and possibly wood billets and small imported hammerstones, were used. It should be noted that local nonobsidian rocks are very sparse and are generally not suitable for use as hammerstones. Evidence of pressure flaking was seen only in low flake density areas, taking the form of occasional, partially finished small biface fragments or a few small ribbon flakes. Finishing of bifaces by pressure flaking was not a major activity at Bodie Hills. Examples of each of the principal retouched tool forms collected are shown in Figure 7.

Nonobsidian stone materials are rare at Bodie Hills. However, flakes, blades, or small cores of white, beige, gray, and pink cherts, chalcedony,

Figure 7   Principle tool forms: (1) side scraper on large tertiary blade fragment, 4.3 microns, transect 11-12; (2) side scraper on secondary decortication flake, transect 4-5; (3) notched beak on tertiary flake fragment, Macro Area 2; (4) perforator on tertiary blade, 4.0 microns, transect 4-5; (5) knife on blade fragment, transect 11-12; (6) perforator on tertiary flake, Macro Area 2; (7) multiple notched side scraper on secondary decortication flake, transect 10-4'; (8) pebble with retouched edge (retoucher?), transect 4-5; (9) end scraper on secondary decortication blade fragment, 5.8 microns, transect 11-12; (10) perforator on secondary decortication flake, transect 11-12.

petrified wood, red and yellow jasper, and fine-grained volcanics—all imported materials—and locally occurring gray andesite and red rhyolite were observed in Areas L_1, L_2, L_3, and L_4, the Original Site Area, and at several points on the Ridge Area transects. Only three nonobsidian bifaces, one fragment each of red and white chert and one unfinished felsite example, were recovered.

The above evidence suggests that Bodie Hills was a single activity site devoted exclusively to the production of bifaces and blades for export. This conclusion is also supported by the apparent total absence of any habitation refuse, organic debris or charcoal, food processing implements (e.g., grinding equipment), or structural remains.

Without organic material for radiocarbon dating, the temporal framework necessary for diachronic production analysis had to be constructed using the obsidian hydration dating technique. A diachronic production curve for the site (Figure 8), which shows the frequency and temporal distribution of 98 obsidian hydration values reported in Meighan and Bennett (1976), was established using a source-specific hydration rate of 650 years per micron (Eric-

Bodie Hills Obsidian Production Curve

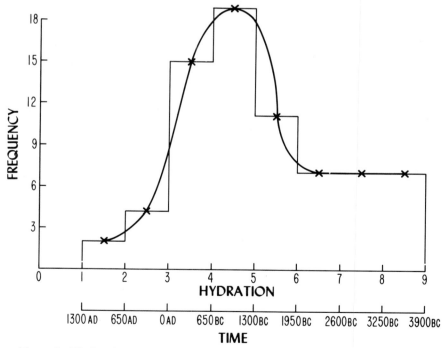

Figure 8 Diachronic production curve for Bodie Hills based on 98 hydration values.

son 1975). The curve shows initial production commencing around 6000 years ago, increasing to a maximum about 2500 years ago, and decreasing abruptly around 1500 years ago.

The bracketing dates are well supported by typological analysis and hydration dating of two nearly complete Elko-eared points (1625 years B.P. and 2600 years B.P.) and one complete Silver Lake point (5980 years B. P.). These points are considered ''Archaic'' forms typical of the Middle Horizon of California prehistory (Hester 1973; O'Connell 1967). In addition, the ab-

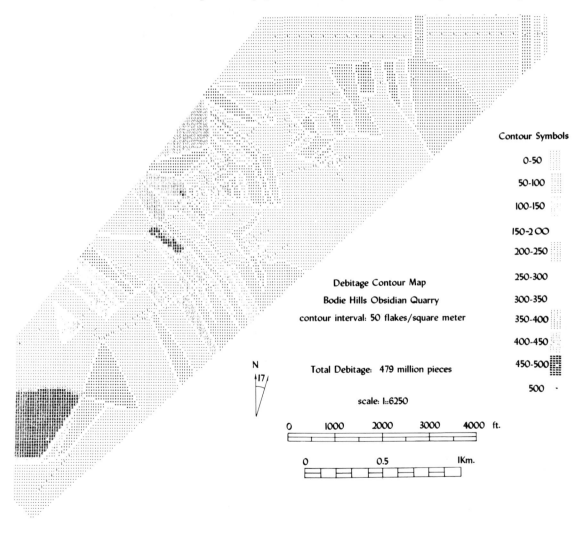

Figure 9 Synagraphic map of debitage distribution at Bodie Hills.

sence of Late Horizon projectile points, and artifacts with less than 1.6 microns of hydration, indicates that production at the Bodie Hills workshops underwent a marked decline before 500 A.D. and was probably utilized only by the "late" populations that occupied the immediate area.

Diachronic production during the period of extensive site use (approximately 5000 years) was assessed by calculating the total debitage on the site analyzing its distribution with the aid of the SYMAP computer program (cf. Ericson, Chapter 6). Using obsidian density estimates recorded at 240 transect points, the total debitage was calculated to be 479 million pieces. The distribution of this material is displayed by the SYMAP (Figure 9). Several features are apparent upon examination of this map. Artifact densities are highly variable in space, indicating the locations of workshop areas. The highest densities correspond with outcrops T_1 and T_3 (T_2 not displayed), while other high density areas correspond to discreet workshop loci usually located on secondary deposits. When artifacts from workshop areas, including the Macro Area, were dated, the majority of readings fell within the period of maximum exploitation between 2250 and 5000 B.P. (~3.5 to 7.5 microns). The relatively late readings from the two sampled outcrops (T_1 and T_3) may well reflect sampling error, or they may mean that secondary deposits, such as Macro Areas 1 and 2, where readings range from 5.2 to 16.0 microns (3300 to 14,000 B.P.), were exploited before the primary outcrop deposits. Dated bifaces from various workshops show that larger, bipointed forms tend to occur nearer the outcrops and are generally older than the medium to small forms with straight or convex bases, which occur away from the outcrops. Obsidian artifacts found south and west of an arbitrary line drawn between stations 8 and 11 are generally older than material found north and east of the line. In general, artifact density and hydration values decrease as a function of distance from the primary outcrops.

With the determination of the total quantity of on-site debitage, a temporal framework, and some space-time trends related to artifact distribution, it was then possible to make quantitative estimates of artifact production. As bifaces were the most predominant artifact, a quantitative assessment of biface production was undertaken. It was necessary to determine (1) the amount of debitage resulting from the manufacture of each biface and (2) the proportion of biface debitage, as opposed to blade debitage, on the site. Quantitative assessment of individual biface manufacture was done by comparing the materials collected from a one meter square sample area in Macro Area 2 with debitage statistics resulting from experimental manufacture of "thick handaxes" [i.e., percussion flaked biface preforms (Newcomer 1971)]. The entire contents of the one square meter sample unit was washed, sorted, and analyzed, and the total lithic contents of this unit are presented in Table 1. The 427 unutilized flakes and blades in category (H), Table 1, were then analyzed to determine tha relative frequencies of biface and blade production debitage (cf. Binford and Quimby 1963; Crabtree 1970; Newcomer

TABLE 1

TOTAL LITHIC MATERIAL FROM 1 BY 1 METER SAMPLE UNIT
IN MACRO AREA 2

Category	Material description	Size (diameter in cm)	Weight (in gm)	Frequency (pieces)
[A]	Natural obsidian nodules[a]	>1.0	9019.0	960
[B]	Natural obsidian nodules	0.2–1.0	4596.0	~10000
[C]	Natural nonobsidian rock[b]	>1.0	239.0	30
[D]	Natural nonobsidian rock	0.2–1.0	420.0	~4500
[E]	Mixed natural obsidian and non-obsidian rock	<0.2	89.0	~7650
[F]	Obsidian flakes	<0.2	25.5	~2400
[G]	Obsidian flakes[c]	0.2–1.0	944.0	4850
[H]	Obsidian flakes[d]	>1.0	3678.0	459
[I]	Obsidian biface preforms[e]	>1.0	75.0	4
[J]	Obsidian cores and core preforms	>1.0	3426.0	11
[K]	Natural obsidian pebbles with steeply retouched edge[f]	>1.0	41.5	2
		Totals	22553.0	30855

[a] Unmodified material, largest piece 236.0 gm.
[b] Unmodified material, largest piece 29.0 gm.
[c] Includes 3 utilized pieces (retouched tools).
[d] Includes 29 utilized pieces (retouched tools).
[e] Fragmentary specimens.
[f] Possible pressure flaking tools(?).

1971). Table 2 shows that biface production debitage (categories 2, 3, 4, and 8) outnumbers blades (categories 5, 6, and 7) by a ratio of about 9 to 1, and at least five distinct forms of biface thinning and trimming flakes (BTF's) were identified.

Newcomer (1971:90–93) estimates that between 35 and 70 blows with both hard and soft hammers are necessary to produce one complete biface (hand-axe), with an average of 50 flakes larger than 2 cm produced in each of his four experiments. If Newcomer's figure of 50 flakes per biface is applied to the debitage larger than 1 cm from the one square meter sample unit (Table 2), and allowing that only 90% of the debitage resulted from biface production, an estimate of the total number of bifaces produced in this unit can be made.

$$\frac{90\% \text{ (unutilized flakes} > 1.0 \text{ cm)}}{50 \text{ flakes per biface}} = \frac{0.9(427)}{50} = \frac{384.3}{50} = 7.69 \text{ bifaces}$$

The four biface fragments from the unit may account for approximately half the debitage, and we may assume that four more bifaces were finished, removed from the area, and exported from the site. Similar production esti-

TABLE 2

BREAKDOWN OF UNUTILIZED MATERIAL IN CATEGORY [H], TABLE 1

Category	Debitage description	Frequency (pieces)	Weight (gm)
[1]	Core fragments and chunky flakes	22	416.1
[2]	Primary decortication flakes	55	603.4
[3]	Secondary decortication flakes	145	1120.6
[4]	Tertiary flakes (without BTF's)	118	498.8
[5]	Primary decortication blades	2	23.1
[6]	Secondary decortication blades	12	97.5
[7]	Tertiary blades	26	189.1
[8]	Biface thinning and shaping flakes (BTF's)	47	303.4
	Totals	427	3252.0

mates can be made for all the high flake density areas designated as workshops, but not for the relatively low density areas where biface production debitage and broken bifaces are often equaled or outnumbered by thin, prepared platform prismatic blades and associated debitage. Blade cores were seldom seen in older site areas, and the blades recovered in these areas tended to be thicker and more irregular than the examples collected in the younger areas.

An estimate of the total number of bifaces produced at the Bodie Hills site can be calculated using the following equation:

$$B = d(D)/F \tag{1}$$

where B is the total number of bifaces produced, d is the percent of total debitage resulting from biface production; D is the total quantity of debitage at site, and F is the number of flakes larger than 1 cm resulting from the production of one biface preform. Inserting the estimated values into Equation (1) yields the following figures:

$$B = \frac{(0.5 - 0.9) \times (4.79 \times 10^8)}{(5 \times 10)} = 4.79 - 8.62 \times 10^6 \text{ bifaces}$$

Thus, somewhere between 4.79 and 8.62 million bifaces of all shapes and sizes were produced over a span of about 5000 years, between circa 4500 B.C. and 500 A.D. The annual production rate for 5000 years is estimated at 960 to 1725 bifaces per year. Considering that approximately 20 bifaces could easily be produced by a single knapper in one day, something like 48 to 86 mandays per year would have been required to accomplish this output. It is likely that small groups of people (probably stoneworking specialists) spent several weeks or longer at the site during the summer months (June to September) and carried their semifinished products away to various trading localities.

These people may have lived along the East Walker River, or they may have come from considerable distances, perhaps even from villages in central and southern California on the western side of the Sierra Nevada Mountains.

V. DISCUSSION AND CONCLUSIONS

Archaeologists working in the coastal and inland valley areas of central and southern California have often noted that obsidian artifacts recovered from Late Horizon contexts (500–1800 A.D.) are nearly always smaller than pieces found in earlier Middle Horizon contexts (2000 B.C.–500 A.D.) and that artifacts from later sites are often reworked pieces or utilized fragments of larger bifacially flaked implements. The artifact forms recovered from Middle and Early Horizon sites are most often various types of large and medium-size dart or lance points, biface knives, and occasional blade tools. Cores are exceedingly rare, and many artifacts are recovered from burials (Ragir 1972).

Analysis of the Bodie Hills collections verifies that export of obsidian material into central and southern California began well before 2000 B.C. (cf. Heizer 1974:195) and was substantially reduced around 500 A.D. Partially finished bifaces and complete unmodified prismatic blades were products carried away from the quarry–workshops and distributed within consumer areas, since no evidence exists that these artifacts were utilized at the production site. Large bipointed and convex-base bifaces were the first items produced at Bodie Hills, followed by medium-size and small bifaces with convex or straight bases. Large and medium-size bifaces were "roughed-out" by direct hard and soft hammer percussion and never finished by pressure retouching, while smaller bifaces were sometimes retouched along their margins and/or base. Since no unfinished projectile points were found, it seems probable that smaller, partially completed bifaces were exported to various groups of consumers who subsequently modified them into finished projectile points. This same situation may apply to some of the unmodified blades produced at and exported from the workshops. The question of where projectile points were made will have to be resolved by debitage analysis at consumer sites. As mentioned earlier, blades produced during the earlier phases of exploitation tended to be larger, thicker in cross section, and less regular in shape than those from the later phases, and the frequency of blade production of small bifaces.

Although the actual number of complete bifaces and blades exported from the Bodie Hills workshops is unknown (breakage and rejection may be 50% of total production), two types of relevant information have been generated by this study. The diachronic production curve (Figure 8) suggests a fluctuating rate of production through time with the period of maximum production and export occurring between 300 B.C. and 2200 B.C. (57 of 98 hydration values from 3.5 to 6.5 μm). In terms of bifaces, this means that about 60% of all biface production and export occurred during the Middle Horizon of California prehistory. Secondly, an annual average biface production rate of 960 to 1725 pieces has been made based on our estimates of total site debitage (479 million pieces) biface production debitage (50 flakes per biface), and the 5000 year duration of production activities. We interpret these results to mean than production activities were casual and seasonal, requiring only 48 to 86 man-days per year. We have at present no quantitative data from which to estimate total blade production for export, although we believe that blades became increasingly more important as time went on. Blade production probably reached its peak during the terminal phase of site exploitation between 2000 B.C. and 500 A.D.

Still unresolved are a number of questions concerning the precise configuration of the site and the distribution of materials in various site areas. Additional studies will be necessary at Bodie Hills if we are to assess adequately the nature of the changes in biface forms and the production of blades throught time. More importantly, we are still in the process of determining the size and scope of the consumer region served by the Bodie Hills workshops and the nature of the stimuli that regulated production at this and other sources. What remains to be seen is if the rate of consumption at sites away from the quarry–workshops correlates with our production estimates, a subject currently under study (Ericson 1977). The apparent decline in use of this source may eventually be explained by a series of factors related to Late Horizon population expansions and movements in both California and the Great Basin, coupled with increased utilization of alternative obsidian sources and other lithic materials.

We believe that our site sampling and analytical procedures have proven quite successful in providing an overall picture of the products and production modes at this extensive quarry–workshop site. The data collection and analytical techniques are relatively simple and easily replicable and should be applied to similar sites.

Acknowledgments

The authors would like to express their appreciation to Professors Clement W. Meighan and Rainer Berger for their continuous support and encouragement, to Ms. V. C. Bennett for preparing and reading the obsidian hydration samples, and to Mrs. Lynne F. Singer and Ms. Cheryl Burke for their assistance in the field. We also gratefully acknowledge the kind permission of Mr. Baron Hilton, Flying M Ranch, who allowed us to conduct archaeological research on his property. This project was supported in part by a Student Field Research Award from the UCLA Department of Anthropology.

References

Binford, L. R., and G. I. Quimby
  1963   Indian sites and chipped stone materials in the northern Lake Michigan area. *Fieldiana—Anthropology* **36**:277–307.

Cann, J. R., J. E. Dixon, and C. Renfrew
   1970   Obsidian analysis and the obsidian trade. In *Science in archeology,* edited by D.
            Brothwell and E. Higgs, pp. 578–591. New York: Praeger.
Cobean, R. H., M. D. Coe, E. A. Perry Jr., K. K. Turekian, and D. P. Kharkar
   1971   Obsidian trade at San Lorenzo Tenochtitlan, Mexico. *Science* **174:**666–671.
Crabtree, D. E.
   1970   Flaking stone with wooden implements. *Science* **169:**146–153.
Davis, E. L.
   1964   An archaeological survey of the Mono Lake Basin and excavations of two rockshel-
            ters, Mono County, California. *UCLA Archaeological Survey Annual Report*
            6:251–392.
Ericson, J. E.
   1975   New results in obsidian hydration dating. *World Archaeology* **7:**151–159.
   1977   The evolution of prehistoric exchange systems in California: results of tracing and
            dating techniques. Unpublished Ph.D. dissertation, Department of Anthropology,
            University of California, Los Angeles.
Ericson, J. E., T. A. Hagan, and C. W. Chesterman
   1976   Prehistoric obsidian sources in California I: geological and geochemical aspects. In
            Advances in obsidian glass studies: archaeological and geochemical perspectives,
            edited by R. E. Taylor. Park Ridge, New Jersey: Noyes Press (forthcoming).
Heizer, R. F.
   1974   Studing the Windmiller culture. In *Archaeological researches in retrospect,* edited by
            G. R. Willey, pp. 177–204. Cambridge, Massachusetts: Winthrop.
Hester, T. R.
   1973   Chronological ordering of Great Basin prehistory. *Contributions of the University of
            California Archaeological Research Facility* **17.**
Hodder, I.
   1974   Regression analysis of some trade and marketing patterns. *World Archaeology*
            6:172–189.
Hogg, A. H. A.
   1971   Some applications of surface fieldwork. In *The Iron Age and its Hillforts,* edited by M.
            Jesson and D. Hill.Southampton: University of Southampton Press.
Jack, R. N., and I. S. E. Carmichael
   1969   The chemical "fingerprinting" of acid volcanic rocks. *California Division of Mines and
            Geology, Special Report* **100:**17–32.
Meighan, C. W.
   1955   Notes on the archaeology of Mono County, California. *Reports of the University of
            California Archaeological Survey* **28:**6–28.
Meighan, C. W., and V. C. Bennett
   1976   Obsidian dates II: a compendium of the obsidian determinants made at the UCLA
            Obsidian Hydration Laboratory. UCLA Institute of Archaeology Monograph 6
            (forthcoming).
Newcomer, M. H.
   1971   Some quantitative experiments in handaxe manufacture. *World Archaeology* **3:**85–94.
O'Connell, J. F.
   1967   Elko-eared/Elko corner-notched projectile points as time markers in the Great Basin.
            Reports of the University of California Archaeological Survey **70:**129–140.
Ragir, S.
   1972   The Early Horizon in central California prehistory. *Contribution of the University of
            California Archaeological Research Facility* **15.**
Wright, G. A.
   1969   Obsidian analysis and prehistoric Near Eastern trade: 7500 to 3500 B.C. *University of
            Michigan Museum of Anthropology Anthropological Paper* **37.**

Part IV

The Use of Ethnography and Ethnohistory

Chapter 11

ABORIGINAL ECONOMIES IN STATELESS SOCIETIES

GEORGE DALTON

. . . whenever peace was made between tribes of equal strength, it would be prudent to preserve it carefully with return gifts, the essential tokens of its permanence. What was "peace" for the author of *Beowulf* but the prospect of exchanging gifts between peoples! The risky policy of alternating raids was being replaced by a regular round of mutual offerings [G. Duby, *The Early Growth of the European Economy*].

One of the primary effects of a system of gift exchange is that it provides a concrete means of social linkage [R. Firth, *We, the Tikopia*].

Economic exchanges and trade relationships symbolized political alliances [R. M. Berndt, "Warfare in the New Guinea Highlands"].

I. INTRODUCTION

Recent fieldwork in New Guinea and recent reanalysis of early writings on the northwest coast of America allow one to construct a model of those aboriginal economies in stateless societies that employed ceremonial exchanges (potlatch, kula, moka, abutu). This paper constructs such a model, emphasizing the importance of relations of alliance and hostility and the

191

special role of primitive valuables in political transactions in stateless societies.

I begin by singling out those institutions and activities and those ecological and demographic conditions that had the following attributes: They were widely shared, that is, common to all the aboriginal societies employing ceremonial exchanges; they were related to one another, not independent attributes (see Figure 1); and they led to the formation of four sorts of alliance relations between corporate descent groups, alliances that were *simultaneously* political, economic, and social. I want to explain particularly the material elements, that is, the role of foodstuffs and valuables, and I want to emphasize that I am concerned here with these economies and societies as they were organized before European colonial incursion.

A. Small Scale

These were small groups of hunters, gatherers, fishermen, and swidden agriculturalists organized into lineages, lineage clusters, and clans of varying size. Their access to food and natural resources also varied. Typically, population densities were low and the size of cohesive political units very small. The total population of the Trobriands was 8,000 people, only a fraction of whom Malinowski studied in villages in the northern part of the main island.

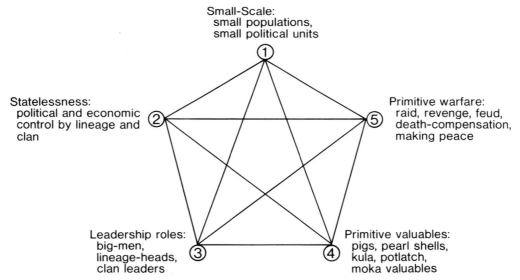

Figure 1 Interdependent attributes making for alliances. The arrows are meant to indicate functional interdependence among the five features, as would be apparent from arranging them in a circle, or as in Douglas (1962). On such functional interdependence, see also Myrdal (1957:Chapters 1–3).

Firth's seven books on Tikopia are about a small island—three miles by one and a half miles—whose population in 1929 was just under 1,300 organized into four clans comprising some 30 lineages. There were 10,000 Yanomamö occupying such a large area that the population density came to only 28 people per 100 square miles (Chagnon 1968a:116). It is estimated that the Kwakiutl in 1830, just before the hundred-year decline in their numbers from disease and other causes, numbered some 23,000 persons. And, of course, it was not the "tribe of all the Kwakiutl" that was the functioning, cohesive society, the operative political and economic unit, but much smaller groupings, Kwakiutl lineages or subclans comprising clusters of related lineages. A useful political demarcation for such societies is the maximum segment within which lethal fighting is prohibited. Such a political unit usually varied from a few dozen to a few hundred persons (see Bulmer 1960:2).

Unusually small clan segments were politically vulnerable in the sense of being militarily weak, and so needed allies for defense when attacked and for successful raiding or retaliation for revenge; they also needed allies for refuge when they were overrun and had to flee their home areas: ". . . small, militarily vulnerable villages tend to be located close to their staunchest ally, to which they turn to refuge in case of war" (Chagnon 1968a:117). "While certain groups have expanded through success in warfare, others have shrunk and have either become linked to larger groups as their protectors or have occupied areas peripheral to the territories of the stronger groups" (Strathern 1971:16; see also p. 152).

Clan segments that were poor in natural resources were economically vulnerable; that is, they needed allies to provide emergency food for them in times of drought, flood, and other disaster, and they needed allies for trade or gift access to special goods not locally available [e.g., salt, stone (see Heider 1969)]. *Sporadic hunger, sporadic warfare, and external trade* were very common in precolonial times. Ceremonial exchange partners, other allies, and primitive valuables were all used in emergency to get food and refuge. Giving women in marriage and giving valuables were ways of contracting alliances, which, once formed, could be used for a variety of purposes. Very unfortunate lineages and clans, those that were militarily weak or very poor, or both weak and poor, tried to marry their girls "upward" to stronger and richer lineages and clans: ". . . a major aim in arranging a marriage was to secure strong affinal kindred and thereby the friendship of powerful sibs from other [tribes or clans]" (Berndt 1964:196).

B. Lineages and Clans

I prefer to use the term "stateless" rather than "acephalous" because it makes explicit the absence of a state. The importance of corporate descent groups in stateless societies is considered very fully in anthropological writings: exogamy and rules of preferential marriage and residence, unilineal descent, lineages, lineage clusters or sub-clans, clans, clan-pairs—in short, "tribal segments." These, of course, were the operative political and economic units; the whole "tribe" was not (see Hallpike 1973). Kwakiutl killed those other Kwakiutl who were not their allies as readily as they killed non-Kwakiutl who were not their allies. The maximum political unit was the corporate group within which only nonlethal fighting and nonlethal dispute settlement was permissible. The tribal segment was the defense and war-making unit, the adult male members of which also had joint responsibility in paying bridewealth and bloodwealth compensation for lineage- or clan-mates (Middleton and Tait 1958:6). Through their control over bridewealth valuables, the lineage leaders controlled the marriage alliances that their junior clansmen were to make, and, of course, they also controlled the marriages to be made by their girls.

Corporate descent groups also owned real property such as garden land and fishing sites, and intangible property, such as magic, crests, names, and dances (see Drucker and Heizer 1967:11). Here are some quotations describing how generally dependent persons were on their lineage and clan affiliations in precolonial times:

> . . . in a crisis a person [in the New Guinea Highlands] could rely with certainty only on members of his own clan, and ultimately only on those of his own lineage [Berndt 1964:188].

> [Among the Tlingit and Haida of the northwest coast] It is the localized kin unit which we shall call the lineage, that consists of one or more houses and that has rights to territories for hunting and fishing, cemetery areas, house sites, trade routes, as well as the use of crests, personal names, house names, and secret society rites. This is the unit with corporate and legal functions which conducts warfare and participates in feuds, and which makes alliances through marriage . . . [Rosman and Rubel 1971:35].

Individual persons depended on their lineage and clan affiliations and superiors for land, brides, husbands (i.e., deciding which external group to marry into), physical safety, and protection—in short, for material livelihood and political security. How exactly dependence relationships are structured is important in all societies. In these stateless societies, a person's dependence on his lineage and clan was remarkably comprehensive because there were no *alternative means of livelihood and protection* (as there came to be with European colonial peace, government, cash, and markets).

The corporate descent group was also a cohesive religious unit: common clan ancestors, heroic clan founders, special divine spirits and supernatural beings who mythically aided clan ancestors and founders, decided victory or defeat in warfare, material abundance or famine, health or sickness. Aborigines were not at all Marxian. The Kwakiutl and Trobrianders believed rather strongly in the supernatural determination of economic and noneconomic happenings, the supernatural determination of joyful events and of catastrophe. Theirs were also idiosyncratic ancestors, gods, and spirits, special to each corporate descent group (unlike the "world religion" of Catholic and Moslem peasantries). Here, too, a person's dependence was structured in the descent group, dependence on a common set of ancestors and supernatural beings for welfare in the here and now, ancestors and divine spirits who must be beseeched by ritual formulae and incantations known to lineage heads, elders, or ritual specialists, and thanked and placated by sacrificial offerings—gifts to the gods—made seasonally (as with first fruits) and in time of crisis (see Firth 1940 for an excellent and detailed example).

On the northwest coast of America and in New Guinea there were no states, no centrally organized kingdoms within the orbit of interaction of the clans and lineage clusters we are concerned with. Clans and clan segments had to deal only with other clans and clan segments. In parts of Africa this was not the case, for example, with the stateless Tallensi who were within the orbit of powerful states, such as Mamprusi. This made a difference to the aboriginal military situation, to the network of hostile relations, and, therefore, to precolonial alliance formation and to whether or not ceremonial exchanges were employed. There were almost certainly *several* reasons why groups like the Tallensi did not employ ceremonial exchange like the potlatch or kula, one of which was the presence of kingdom-states. Other reasons included the Great Festivals (Fortes 1936), the existence of *permanent* alliances between clan segments (Fortes 1940), and the unusually effective power to settle disputes exercised by "privileged intermediaries."

On the northwest coast and in New Guinea, external relations with major and minor allies and enemies, therefore, were horizontal; that is, fluctuating coalitions and enmities between culturally homogeneous groups all organized in similar stateless fashion, not vertical, as between satellite clans as subordinates paying tribute upward to neighboring kingdom-states of greater size and power. Very frequently the culturally homogeneous clan segments were not equal in size, property, or power, but were socially stratified as dominant and subordinate lineages, which, I think, misled Malinowski into using the political terminology of traditional European kingdom-states in calling the big-men leading dominant lineages in the Trobriands "chiefs," and calling materially poorer and politically weaker lineages "vassals," and payments to brothers-in-law who were big-men lineage leaders "tribute."

C. Big-men, Lineage-heads, and Clan Leaders

The word "chief" is conventionally used by anthropologists for leadership positions in quite different sorts of polities: The head of a lineage, lineage cluster, or clan in stateless societies such as the Trobriands and the potlatching groups of the northwest coast is called a "chief" (and so too religious specialists in such societies, e.g., "leopard-skin chief"). And the petty leader of a local kinship or territorial grouping within a state is also called a "chief." I shall avoid calling any political, religious, or warrior leader in a stateless society "chief" so as to avoid the word's association with central government. Leadership in stateless societies entailed internal and external roles, and political leaders particularly had superior access to ordinary goods (foodstuffs), women (through polygamy), and valuables (through ceremonial exchanges). Leadership, of course, conferred superior power but also special responsibilities toward corporate juniors.

Where leadership was not inflexibly fixed by primogeniture, where leadership was achieved rather than determined by birth, where leadership careers were open to talent, rivalry for leadership positions existed between lineage- or clan-mates equally eligible. In such cases, leadership positions were won by demonstrating superior ability, achievement, and luck—in oratory, dispute-settlement, war-prowess, peace negotiation, and success in ceremonial exchange. In New Guinea, for example, leadership positions were open to talent to an unusual extent. Those who became big-men demonstrated their effectiveness in entrepreneurial roles: the planner of group policy, the settler of private disputes, the peace-maker in war, the arranger of death compensations, the generous provider of food, the leader who secures strong allies in warfare and pays for their services with valuables, the organizer of moka ceremonial exchanges.

> War and the Moka were the two widest fields in which individuals achieved their [leadership] positions. A man's exchange partners outside his clan and his net of supporters and partners inside it were necessarily complementary. Really important operators in the Moka have to be members of large powerful clans. Men who are outstanding in the Moka are renowned over a wide area, as were successful war-leaders in pre-contact days, who also had to be members of powerful clans. It is hard now to reconstruct precisely how Moka leadership and war leadership were related, but it seems that a man's most stable and valued Moka partnerships were with members of groups whom he could hope to mobilize when necessary in the shifting inter-clan alliances which characterized Kyaka war-making. Further war allies outside the clan were mobilized both by stressing obligations of kinship and affinity as such, and by promises of substantial material reward for assistance [Bulmer 1960:12].

Quite frequently access to clan leadership positions was constrained by lineage, only members of dominant lineages being eligible, as in Malinowski's Trobriands (Powell 1956, 1960). One of Uberoi's (1962) contributions was to show how success in the kula abroad enhanced one's political position at home; to which I might add that success in the kula abroad also meant acquiring valuables that could be used at home as payments in political and social transactions (see Dalton 1971a).

Finally, successful activities carried out by leaders—success in warfare, ceremonial exchange, etc.—always had a double effect: to enhance the position of the successful leader and to enhance the reputation and the power of his descent group or entourage of followers on whose behalf he was acting (see Strathern 1971:13).

D. Primitive Valuables

The meaning and usage of primitive valuables in aboriginal economies without central government is, perhaps, the least well understood of the institutions and situations I am here singling out for their special importance. Examples of such valuables are kula shell necklaces and bracelets, pigs, pearlshells, and, on the northwest coast of America in pre-European times, slaves and fur robes. Like leadership, these too had internal and external political roles. To acquire and disburse valuables in political or social transactions was usually the exclusive prerogative of leaders; or else the valuables were permissibly acquired by leaders in greater quantity or in superior quality than permissibly acquired by small men: ". . . status requisites were imposed on the accumulation and use of valuables such that possession in quantity and certain display uses were restricted to big-men—the leaders of men's clubhouses" (Harding 1967:226). (See also Malinowski 1922:504–505.)

There are several reasons why the roles of primitive valuables are difficult to understand, why we do not have in economic anthropology a persuasive "theory of primitive money."

There is a semantic/conceptual ambiguity of unusual tenacity—the various meanings of "money"—that goes back to the earliest modern anthropological analyses of the money-like stuff found in stateless tribes. Malinowski (1921) and Firth (1929) posed the question: Are primitive valuables, such as kula shell bracelets, really "money"? By "money," of course, they meant British sterling, what I now prefer to call "cash" (to avoid the word "money"). Malinowski and Firth concluded that primitive valuables were not really "money" (cash):

> The tokens of wealth [*vaygua:* ceremonial stone axe blades, kula shell necklaces and arm bracelets] have often been called 'money.' It is at first sight evident that 'money' in our sense [British sterling] cannot exist among the Trobrianders. . . . Any article which can be classed as 'money' or 'currency' must fulfill certain essential conditions; it must function as a medium of exchange and as a common measure of value, it must be the instrument of condensing wealth, the means by which value can be accumulated. Money also, as a rule, serves as the standard of deferred payments. . . . We cannot think of *vaygua* in terms of 'money' [Malinowski 1921:13–14].

> But according to precise terminology, such objects [strings of shell discs] can hardly be correctly described as currency or money. In any economic system, however primitive, an article can only be regarded as true money when it acts as a definite and common medium of exchange, as a convenient stepping stone in obtaining one type of goods for another. Moreover in so doing it serves as a measure of values. . . . Again, it is a standard of value . . . [Firth 1929:881].

Of course primitive valuables were not cash. Kula bracelets were not means of commercial exchange because Trobriand economy had only a very petty market sector *(gimwali);* nor did the Trobriands have a state. Cash—British sterling, coined money of any sort—exists only in states. After saying they were not cash it is necessary to say what primitive valuables were, what they did, and why they were in some sense important. The Trobrianders, after all, risked their lives to fetch them, traveling in canoes hundreds of miles over open seas. The kula valuables were more than sentimental symbols or tokens, like crown jewels or sports trophies. They were spent, transacted, paid out, but in noncommercial ways, that is, in political and social ways, such as death compensation, bridewealth, and war alliance formation (for a listing, see Dalton 1971a). Only in aboriginal stateless societies do we find valuables used in such political transactions.

The second reason why we do not have a persuasive theory of "primitive money" is that we do not have a clear-cut set of distinctions between "primitive" (or "tribal") and "peasant" economies (see Dalton 1972). The literature of primitive money lumps together three sorts of money-like things, calling them all "primitive money" (Einzig 1948 is the best example because he attempts to draw analytical conclusions). Some of these things are found only in aboriginal stateless tribes without market-place exchange (e.g., pearlshells before the Europeans arrived in Highland New Guinea), some in aboriginal tribes having petty market-place exchanges (e.g., cowries, twists of wire in Africa), and some in traditional peasantries within kingdom-states (e.g., cowries and also coined money in ancient China and coins in medieval Europe; see Swann 1950 and Bloch 1967).

To understand money-like things in aboriginal tribes and traditional peasantries, it is necessary to separate these three monetary things, to give different names to them, and to explain in which sort of society which sort of money-thing appeared, and how exactly each sort was used in that kind of society.

Primitive valuables, such as kula bracelets in the Trobriands and pearlshells in the Highlands, are of most interest to us because they were intimately connected to statelessness, to ceremonial exchanges, and to alliance formation; in short, they were the most important sort of money-like thing in aboriginal economies in stateless societies employing ceremonial exchange. It was primitive valuables that were used by big-men and lineage leaders for important political and social transactions: death compensation, payments to allies, bridewealth, and, occasionally, for "emergency conversion" (Bohannan and Dalton 1962), as when the precolonial Trobrianders traded off kula valuables for seed yams in time of famine.

It was primitive valuables (and women) that were the necessary means of reciprocal, noncommercial payment in warfare and peace-making: "We have cassowaries, young nubile women, fat pigs and pearl shells [to pay an assassin willing to poison an enemy big-man]" (Strathern 1971:85). In pre-

European times, primitive valuables never entered ordinary market place transactions of ordinary goods, such as foodstuffs. Nor, of course, was coinage minted in stateless societies.

By *primitive money,* I mean what economists used to call "commodity money" (Quiggin 1949:316), uniform things such as twists of wire, strips of cloth, and bars of salt (and cigarettes in prisoner-of-war camps in the Second World War). Like cash today these were used as means of commercial exchange in aboriginal tribal economies and some very early peasantries that had marketplace transactions of produce, or, less frequently, market transactions of land or labor. The word "money" is appropriate here precisely because of the commercial (market) usages of primitive money. The word "primitive" is also appropriate to mark off the cowries and slabs of salt from modern sterling or francs (cash) used in states. Primitive money transacted marketplace purchases and sales in aboriginal economies having only small market sectors and petty or peripheral market exchange.

Some of the best-known primitive monies, such as cowries in Africa, were introduced before European colonial times by earlier commercial intrusion:

Cowries were introduced to the country [Buganda] by the Arabs and were at first principally a medium of foreign trade. They came to be used in all transactions, but they did not replace barter. They never became the sole medium of exchange or a standard in terms of which every other commodity could be valued; and they differed also from money [cash, i.e., British sterling] in that their use was not solely that of a means of exchange, but they were also used to decorate various valued objects [Mair 1934:131].

The third thing called "primitive money" is *early coinage.* In traditional peasantries, such as those in Europe, Japan, and China, what I shall call *early cash* (coined money) was present as was the state that invented early coinage. And cash, of course, was used for payment of political obligations such as taxes and fines as well as for ordinary market transactions.

The third reason why we do not have a satisfactory theory of "primitive money" is because of the very special monetary complications that came about during the colonial period, which made it very difficult for anthropologists to disentangle aboriginal from colonial monetary usages. A good deal of fieldwork was done late in the colonial period when francs or sterling were present side by side with either aboriginal primitive valuables (pigs, pearlshells, and kula valuables) or precolonial primitive monies (cowries) (see Bohannan 1955; Douglas 1958, 1962, 1967).

By the time Bohannan and Douglas did their fieldwork among the Tiv and Lele in the late 1940s, colonial sterling and francs had displaced some—but not all—the uses to which the primitive valuables or primitive money had been put in precolonial times. For example, bridewealth was paid in sterling or francs. As will be explained in a later paper (Dalton 1978), European colonial presence introduced other factors (peace, enhanced safety in traveling, enlarged production for market sale, European goods, reduced frequency of famine) that changed decisively both the aboriginal alliance systems and the traditional usages of primitive valuables and primitive monies.

E. Primitive Warfare

Malinowski (1920) wrote an article about aboriginal warfare in the Trobriands telling us the last raids occurred in 1899, but warfare did not figure prominently in his large books (see Malinowski 1922:6,67,69; Uberoi 1962:23–24). Unlike Chagnon (1968a), warfare was not something that Malinowski himself could observe during his fieldwork. Among the aboriginal stateless societies with ceremonial exchange, warfare, raiding, and lethal fighting were *always* present—an important prevailing situation—before colonial peace came, and so political and marriage alliances for purposes of enhanced military strength were important.

Warfare, trade, and marriage meant external relationships of hostility and alliance, relations of antagonism and dependence, the opposite of isolation and self-sufficiency. These societies composed of lineage clusters lived in networks or interaction spheres with other lineage clusters. There were war parties and peaceful excursions. War parties went forth to kill, to abduct women, capture weapons, and sometimes capture slaves, crests, and land. Peaceful expeditions went forth to visit and feast, conduct ceremonial exchange, trade, arrange marriages, and to use the natural resources of external groups with whom peaceful relationships existed, with, of course, their hosts' permission (see, e.g., Drucker and Heizer 1967:41).

Within lineages and clans and between most (but not all) allied groups, it was only *lethal* fighting—killing—that was prohibited. Nonlethal fighting with fists and clubs, and contests, duels, and rivalries expressed nonlethally (dart games, chest-thumping, competitive food displays) were not forbidden; indeed, they were essential as ways to settle disputes without breaking off mutually advantageous relationships and alliances, as killing most certainly would have done: ". . . members of villages that stand in trading relationships with each other occasionally have duels with either fists or clubs, and suspect the other group of plotting to abduct women" (Chagnon 1968a:122).

> In warfare sub-clans of a clan were expected automatically to aid each other against outside attackers. Internally, fist-fighting is expected within them from time to time, since, as Hageners say, 'brothers are jealous,' but it is disapproved of. Sub-clans may on occasion corporately attack each other with sticks, but they usually avoid causing deaths in these melees. Fighting within the clan with shield and spear in the fashion of warfare would be greeted with horror by clansmen not immediately involved, as it sometimes was in the past between men of paired clans. Individual sub-clan mates who begin a fight are separated by their fellows, and lengthy discussions on the dispute follow. Big-men are again likely to be prominent in this process.
>
> From these remarks it can be seen that a good deal of animosity can arise within sub-clans, but it is not regularly allowed to develop into dangerous physical action [Strathern 1971:26].

With colonial peace lethal fighting stopped, but nonlethal fighting, contests, and rivalries, which aboriginally were confined exclusively to clansmen, affines, trade partners, and other allies, were now extended to former major enemies, whom one killed before the European colonial peacemakers came and with whom, traditionally, one did *not* conduct ceremonial exchanges. This is one of *several* reasons why potlatch and moka intensified with colonial peace. They were indeed "fighting with property" because the colonial authorities would no longer allow them to kill enemies. But fighting major *enemies* with property was a new thing, a colonial change, and it sometimes took on frenetic intensity, as in the rampant potlatch, that was not the case in precolonial times.

One reason why ordinary commercial marketplace purchase and sale was absent, infrequent, or possible only under very special conditions before colonial peace came was that hostile relations prevailed, making it impossible for persons from different lineages and clans—who were not allies—to mingle peacefully in a marketplace. Here, Malinowski is especially illuminating. He describes two sorts of petty market exchange, both occurring only under very special conditions. "Pariah" woodcarvers, with whom no alliance of any sort was desirable and whose infertile land could not support them, hawked their wooden bowls in exchange for yams. The name for this sort of petty market exchange was *gimwali,* which the Kirwinians sharply distinguished from kula (Malinowski 1922:95–96). The second sort took place abroad under the peace and protection guaranteed by kula partnerships (Uberoi 1962:140, Chapter 8). It was what Malinowski described as trade in utilitarian (not kula) goods, carried out with the clanmates of one's kula partners (but not with kula partners themselves), while abroad on kula-valuable collecting expeditions (Malinowski 1922:361–363; 1935:456). Here too, colonial peace caused deep change in modes of transaction by making it generally safe to travel without the protection of special alliance relationships. Thus ordinary market trade expanded when colonial peace came. And with the diminished need for aboriginal alliances, market trade also displaced reciprocity—gift giving trade—in the transaction of ordinary goods.

It is clear that in these aboriginal stateless societies, warfare, raiding, revenge, and feud were a "major preoccupation," a prevailing condition affecting everyday life and everyday movement. But victory in a raid did not entail political incorporation or permanent subjection of the defeated, although it did sometimes entail extermination of lineages, capturing women and children, and, on the northwest coast, capturing men as slaves. The land of the defeated was sometimes taken over, the losers having to disperse individually as refugees seeking sanctuary with kin or other allies, or regrouping their émigré lineages at a new site: "[In the New Guinea Highlands] Refugees lived with relatives or affines until they became strong again, or until peace-making ceremonies permitted them to return; or they acquired land from their hosts in exchange for one or more brides" (Berndt 1964:196; see Strathern 1971: Chapter 4).

F. Summary

1. Relations of alliance established peace between corporate descent groups. Only nonlethal fighting was permitted between major allies.

2. The four alliance networks were (i) warfare, raiding, revenge, feud, peacemaking, and death compensation; (ii) marriage, bridewealth, and the life-long reciprocal transactions following the establishment of affinal relationships: payments, gifts, etc. (e.g., Malinowski's *urigubu*); (iii) ceremonial-delayed-reciprocal exchanges of primitive valuables (potlatch, kula, moka); (iv) nonceremonial trade (either by reciprocity or commercial market trade) and visiting friendly parties to use the resources of allies.

3. All four networks involved transactions: exchanges or payments of material goods (food, luxuries, salt, stone, tools, weapons, primitive valuables).

4. Marriage, of course, always involved transfer of women; what was returned as bridewealth varied, primitive valuables (e.g., kula bracelets) being frequently necessary as bridewealth. Political alliance for warfare and for cermonial exchange sometimes also involved transfers of women in marriage. With polygamy, more women were always desirable, especially for those who occupied leadership roles.

5. Big-men or lineage leaders occupied entrepreneurial roles; that is, they had power to initiate transactions transferring goods and women in all four interaction spheres.

6. Quite commonly, two allied descent groups had two or more sorts of alliance simultaneously—hence "networks"—and also alliance relationships and transactions with several other descent groups simultaneously.

7. Once formed for any of these four principal purposes, the peaceful relationship of alliance now created could be used for emergency purposes such as emergency access to food and emergency refuge.

8. Most frequently, the mode of transaction used in all four networks was reciprocity, two-way transactions (of goods and/or women) as the necessary part of a specific social relationship. Occasionally, market exchange was used in external trade of ordinary goods (e.g., Malinowski's utilitarian trade accompanying the kula).

The four alliance networks listed in Table 1 and the summary statements above are meant to convey the following: Where institutions of central government were not present, what we ordinarily think of as internal and external "political" activities had to be carried out nevertheless, and political leadership roles assumed in some fashion by some persons, activities and roles such as dispute settlement within the small community and making war and military alliances with external groups of enemies and allies. The institutions through which political activities were carried out were quite special in stateless societies. The clan segments and their leaders made direct use of

TABLE I

TRANSACTIONS AND ALLIANCES

Women and things transacted between allies	Alliances
Valuables/Women	Warfare/Raiding/Revenge/Peacemaking/ Death Compensation
Women/Valuables/Ordinary Goods	Marriage/Bridewealth/Life-long Transactions between Affines
Valuables/Foodstuffs	Ceremonial Exchanges: Kula/Potlatch/Moka + Feasting
Anything moveable not locally available/ allies visit to use natural resources	Ordinary external trade, via reciprocity or market exchange; or, allies come to fish in host's waters, quarry their stone, etc.

marriage and of several other alliances created and sustained through transactions of food and valuables: "But the Tukwaa give presents of women to all the Barkley Sound tribes and call on them to make joint war against the Ucluets. . . . The Huua'ii'a chief did not let his commoners attack because it was his brother-in-law" (Swadesh 1948:80,87).

All these relationships were simultaneously political, economic, and social, and they were created between corporate descent groups and between individual persons from different descent groups (e.g., gift-exchange "partners"). They were "relations of alliance" in Radcliffe-Brown's sense, containing elements of solidarity and hostility. All relations of alliance established peace of varying duration between military allies, between groups related to each other by marriage, between groups carrying out delayed ceremonial exchange of valuables, and between groups carrying out non-ceremonial external trade of ordinary goods, tools, or weapons (see Heider 1969; Polanyi 1975; Dalton 1975). In short, special and peaceful relationships for political, economic, and social reasons were arranged in these several ways in aboriginal stateless societies.

All relations of alliance also entailed the transaction of material goods. In this sense, "economy," "polity," and "social organization" were inextricably intertwined or embedded in each other, as were the "subsistence" (food) and "prestige" (women and valuables) spheres. Death compensation to allies who had lost men in fighting, as well as death compensation between enemies in order to end hostilities, were made by paying over primitive valuables. Marriage was created by bridewealth payments of valuables and sometimes by a composite package of valuables and ordinary goods, or by "groomservice" (e.g., Chagnon 1968b), the groom performing ordinary labor services for the parents of his bride for some time after marriage. Once the marriage took place, there frequently followed a lifetime stream of reciprocal prestations of various goods and services between the affinally related groups (see Uberoi 1962:121–122) or seasonal invitations to visit and fish or quarry stone, as well as rights of emergency access to food and protection—rights got from affines and other allies. (On seasonal invitations to fish, see Drucker and Heizer 1967:41; Vayda 1967.)

Ceremonial exchange required the transaction of valuables and the feeding of guests at feast-celebrations accompanying the potlatch, moka, etc. External trade of nonceremonial sorts, a practice that was very widespread in aboriginal times, transacted anything movable that was not locally available to some group; but even commercial trade required an alliance relationship because it required peace. The general situation was quite the opposite from that suggested by one archaeologist: "Trade implies a breakdown of absolute self-sufficiency" (Posnansky 1972:87). Trade implies nothing of the sort. It is quite rare—I know of no cases—for groups to be totally self-contained, to be absolutely self-sufficient, to live in isolation, not to trade (or make war). Marriage alone required relationships with groups external to lineages or lineage-clusters.

These four sorts of alliance relations are best regarded not as paired transactions or paired relationships, but rather as crisscrossing networks, interactions spheres, "alliance blocs," or "social fields." These are networks in two senses: A given corporate group ordinarily created these relationships and transacted the goods (and women) that sustained them with more than one external clan segment. Alliance networks, moreover, changed with events over time, the neutrals or minor enemies of yesterday becoming the major or minor allies of today.

These were networks in the sense that it was also quite common for two groups to have two or more relations of alliance simultaneously (e.g., groups related by marriage also being military allies or ceremonial exchange partners or both): ". . . they rely . . . on their affinal ties, established through marriages, for their most valuable exchange partnerships" (Strathern 1971:9). And any sort of alliance could be resorted to in emergency, as with lineage segments routed and dislodged in warfare seeking refuge:

[In the New Guinea Highlands] the vanquished would become refugees. They might return to their land later after agreement with the victors, and after payment had been made; but more generally they would seek shelter among their matrikin, wives patrikin, or sister's affines. These "centers of refuge" were kept open only by maintaining economic exchanges. In fact, the basic reason for gift-giving and for exchanges of this kind was to provide "potential refuge-giving relationships" which were often separated from political alliances [Berndt 1964:196].

II. CEREMONIAL EXCHANGES: POTLATCH, KULA, MOKA, ABUTU

Before the Europeans came, ceremonial exchanges in stateless societies were of two basic sorts and were very complicated in the sense that several things were going on simultaneously; that is, several functions, purposes, and activities were all being carried out and were influencing relations and leadership positions within clans, as well as external relations between clans. One sort of ceremonial exchange was used to establish, or, once established to keep intact, peaceful alliances between different corporate groups, as described earlier. Another sort, such as *abutu* and similar competitive food exchanges in the Trobriands—and one particular sort of potlatch—were used as devices to settle rivalries for leadership positions or settle animosities between kin, affines, or allies in nonlethal fashion. I emphasize again that neither sort of aboriginal ceremonial exchange was ever carried on with major enemies, only with kin, affines and allies, and, occasionally, minor enemies.

S In ceremonial exchanges of the first sort, to establish or maintain alliances, at least four things were happening simultaneously:

(1) Distinct corporate groups (different political entities) were establishing or reinforcing their special relationship by a peaceful gesture involving the transaction of material goods of some sort.

(2) Corporate leaders were acquiring valuable things (pigs, pearlshells) and valuable relationships (exchange partners), both the things and the relationships enhancing their positions within their own corporate groups and also in external roles and activities. They were acquiring enhanced position, enhanced power, and the material means with which to initiate community activities internally and externally.

(3) Delayed reciprocity seemed invariably to characterize ceremonial exchange; that is, those who received valuables in a particular day's kula, potlatch, or moka exchange were obliged to repay at least as much as they received in future exchanges. This ground rule was not simply a point of honor but rather a necessary condition for keeping the peaceful relationship intact. The need to repay was not simply noblesse oblige, the done thing. To fail to repay was an act of hostility, a declaration that killing may now commence between the two groups. And to fail to repay *more* than you previously recieved was a declaration of corporate poverty and weakness, incurring contempt. Delayed reciprocity created continuity in the peaceful relationship, which, remembering Radcliffe-Brown's phrase, always contained elements of hostility as well as solidarity, and so required continual reinforcement (see Strathern 1971:129–130). As long as the rule was obeyed, this ping-pong device of delayed reciprocity ensured that the peaceful alliance continued. To fail to reciprocate was to signal a hostile act that ended the alliance and ended the peace between the allies.

(4) As long as the ceremonial exchanges continued to take place assuring that peace prevailed, the linked groups could continue to carry on other mutually advantageous activities, such as trade in ordinary goods, and to use each other for emergency access to refuge or food: 'A potlatch . . . is merely

one event in a continuing series of interactions between groups" (Rosman and Rubel 1971:29).

Surely we know from looking at European marriage, or Christianity, or the celebration of Christmas, that important institutions are always doing more than one thing, especially institutions that endure (although in changed fashion) despite enormous changes in the societies in which they occur. So too, potlatch, kula, and moka.

If one asks, "what was the potlatch in *pre-European times?*," that is, before 1800, the answer is rather elaborate (see Rosman and Rubel 1971; Drucker and Heizer 1967; Piddocke 1965):

(1) A festive occasion to celebrate a rite of passage: birth, puberty, marriage, death.

(2) Succession to lineage titles, names, and property rights were made publicly. There were orations recounting past glories and a recitation of corporate property owned, to impress guest-allies with the glory, power, and eminence of hosts.

(3) Among some, but not all, northwest coast groups, the potlatch was also a nonlethal rivalry contest between lineage-mates equally eligible to succeed to higher lineage position and the prerogatives and power over lineage-mates and activities conferred by leadership position.

(4) The initiator or host-patron was entitled to give a potlatch; he was a recognized lineage-head or elder ("chief" in the unfortunate language of the first anthropologists to study the northwest coast). He was a senior person or big-man within the lineage having the necessary lineage credentials permitting him to potlatch. Potlatch initiators were big-men in dominant lineages; small-men, men who did not succeed to lineage titles, positions, prerogatives, responsibilities, and entrepreneurial functions, did not initiate potlatches. Small-men were spear carriers, so to speak, part of the entourage of followers of big-men lineage-mates, or men in subordinate lineages none of whose members potlatched, but that were clustered with dominant lineages. A small-man whose entire lineage was subordinate, or a man whose junior position within a dominant lineage did not entitle him to initiate potlatches, could not on his own initiative act in uppity fashion by attempting to give a potlatch. He would not have been able to secure the necessary potlatch goods or the cooperation of his seniors, who would punish him as well.

(5) Two kinds of corporate goods were used: foodstuffs for feasts and valuables to be given to guests (fur robes, slaves, canoes, cedarbark robes, sea shells). An entourage of small-men lineage-mates contributed goods to their senior who was initiating the potlatch, and shared with him as well the glory and renown conferred by potlatching (and shared too the goods he received when he was a potlatch guest).

(6) Guests were allied to host's descent group through marriage or

through a military alliance; that is, a political alliance that meant peace between themselves and an agreement to make raids jointly on common enemies or as paid mercenaries (payment to be in women or valuables). Clan or lineage leaders who received potlatch gifts as honored guests distributed what they received to their own lineage- and clan-mates (in accordance with the latters' ranked status).

(7) Feasts and gifts were made as lavish as possible because they demonstrated wealth, power, and well-being of hosts, and thereby demonstrated to guests the continued desirability of hosts as allies in a basic situation in which there were no permanent alliances beyond a certain kin distance.

(8) The guest-recipients not only felt obliged to reciprocate in order to demonstrate in turn their wealth, power, and desirability as allies, but *had* to reciprocate to keep the alliance in being. To fail to reciprocate was the *institutionalized way* to declare the end of alliance and the opening of hostilities, hence delayed reciprocity as the ubiquitous device used in ceremonial exchange. A lineage or clan segment whose position entitled it to give potlatches would lose allies by not giving potlatches.

(9) The aboriginal potlatches were infrequent, that is, special or contingent events to certify specific happenings.

(10) As with kula valuables, potlatch valuables were also transacted in other honorific/prestige sphere/status payment/political transactions: to indemnify allies who lost men in battle on one's behalf and to make reparation payments to enemies in order to end hostilities. The valuables were transacted within a constrained set of "prestige sphere" activities and relationships.

(11) Potlatch did not exist where central government existed. Neither were primitive valuables used as means of political payment where central government existed. Primitive monies—cowries in early China—sometimes did exist before they were superseded by coins (early cash).

The rampant aggressive potlatch of colonial times, particularly after warfare ended and after the population decline due to smallpox epidemics starting in 1830, was a markedly different institution from the precolonial potlatch. The colonial potlatch of 1900 described by Codere (1950) became an individual not a group activity, no longer done by lineage leaders on behalf of the lineage represented (see also Drucker and Heizer 1967:37,317). The colonial potlatch was an egregious variant of the aboriginal rivalry potlatch and had nothing to do with cementing alliances between groups now that warfare was over, the whites in control, and cash income for livelihood got by selling to or working for the whites.

With the coming of colonial control, potlatch (and moka) intensified. The number of participants increased, the quantity of goods entering ceremonial exchanges increased, and the frequency of ceremonial exchanges increased (see Codere 1950:97,124; Strathern 1971:Chapter 5; Dalton 1978).

III. ECONOMIC DETERMINATION

I should like to suggest that the Marxian ideas of "economic determination of social and political organization" and "economic determination of social change" are much too simple; they distort a much more complicated reality by putting all the causal weight on material motivation. To be sure, lineages and clans made alliances for material purposes (for example, to get peaceful and assured access to salt or stone not found in their home areas or to emergency foodstuffs). But, very importantly, alliances were also made to retain political autonomy, to assure that the lineage cluster or clan could continue to live on as a self-governing, autonomous, sovereign group, and not be decimated or destroyed as a distinct corporate and political entity by aggressive and hostile outsiders. Chagnon (1968a), doing fieldwork among a group still very much engaged in warfare, is very clear indeed on the strength of the Yanomomö's motive to retain sovereignty in inducing them to make alliances.

There is no way to demonstrate the primacy of economic over political motivation. It is an unprovable assertion to attribute superior importance to the economic causes since the alliance networks were doing several things simultaneously in intertwined fashion, in exactly the way Evans-Pritchard suggests in underscoring a central point of Mauss's (1954) book *The Gift:*

> It is to see social phenomena—as, indeed, Durkeim taught that they sould be seen—in their totality. 'Total' is the key word of the Essay [*The Gift*]. The exchanges of archaic societies which he examines are total social movements or activities. They are at the same time economic, juridical, moral, aesthetic, religious, mythological, and sociomorphological phenomena. Their meaning can therefore only be grasped if they are viewed as a complex concrete reality . . . (Evans-Pritchard 1954:vii).

Even what it is perhaps accurate to call the "latent" functions of alliance networks—emergency access to food and refuge—were also both economic and noneconomic.

There is a special reason, I think, why "economic determination" appears persuasive to some. Several of the most obvious and most important changes introduced by colonial authorities were economic: European cash and goods, enlarged cash-earning, and enlarged production for market sale. But even here the situations were very mixed and complicated. It is not difficult to document three sorts of colonial incursions (see Dalton 1969, 1971b,c):

(1) The most frequent, perhaps, was where economic and noneconomic innovations were introduced simultaneously; when, for example, in the first generation of colonial incursion aboriginal warfare was made to end, missionaries arrived, and European goods and cash-earning introduced.

(2) Situations in which the first European contacts—before colonial politi-

cal control—were almost exclusively economic, such as European whaling and sealing ships arriving periodically in Eskimo-land, exchanging European goods (including guns) for pelts and furs; or European cod-fishermen off the east coast of America in the sixteenth and early seventeenth centuries landing to take on wood and water and to trade with the Indians; or Arabs and Portuguese introducing cowries into sub-Saharan Africa. But such economic incursions were frequently accompanied by political change or cultural incursions, the European fishermen, for example, leaving behind infectious diseases as well as European goods, thereby decimating the populations of some clans and inducing them to rearrange their military alliances and warfare relationships in response to their weakened position. (See Vaughan 1956:Chapter 1.)

(3) There were also occasional cases where the principal incursion initially was noneconomic, as when medical missionaries were for some time the only European contact. Here the causes of change were Christianity and the consequences of improved medical care, not European economic innovations. In short, whatever of importance was *first* introduced by European contact or colonization caused important change in aboriginal societies, and what was first introduced varied greatly—cowries, guns, steel axes, Christianity, horses, an end to aboriginal warfare, smallpox.

Acknowledgments

I gave earlier versions of this paper to seminars of anthropologists and archaeologists in England and Denmark during the academic year 1973–74, at Cambridge, Southampton, Sussex, The School of Oriental and African Studies (London), Copenhagen, and Aarhus; also, at Stanford during the academic year 1974–75. I am grateful to the National Endowment for the Humanities for a Senior Fellowship which enabled me to spend the academic year 1973–74 as a Visiting Fellow at Clare Hall, Cambridge University, and to the Center for Advanced Study in the Behavioral Sciences, at Stanford, for inviting me to spend the academic year 1974–75, during which I wrote the present version of this paper for presentation at a symposium on "Economic Systems in Prehistory" at the May 1975 meetings of The Society for American Archaeology.

I could not have written this paper without the excellent works of Strathern (1971), Rosman and Rubel (1971), Chagnon (1968a,b), Uberoi (1962), and Young (1971). This paper is quite directly built on their work and the work of others I have mentioned throughout, particularly the work of Radcliffe-Brown. But I believe I have added some things of interest to what they have said, especially about the roles of primitive valuables and the specific impacts of colonization, and have demonstrated as well the analytical advantages that follow from considering aboriginal economies in stateless societies as a set, that is, in a comparative framework, especially in contrasting them with traditional peasantries of long settlement in kingdom-states (e.g., Europe, China). I am grateful to Andrew Strathern, Abraham Rosman, and Paula Rubel for reading an earlier draft of this paper and giving me their critical comments and suggestions. For the impact of colonization on aboriginal economies in stateless societies, see Dalton (1978).

References

Berndt, R. M.
  1964 Warfare in the New Guinea highlands. *American Anthropologist* **66,** No. 2, Part 2, pp. 183–203.

Bloch, M.
   1967   Natural economy or money economy: a pseudo-dilemma. In *Land and work in medieval Europe*. New York: Harper Torchbooks.
Bohannan, P.
   1955   Some principles of exchange and investment among the Tiv. *American Anthropologist* **57**:60–70.
Bohannan, P., and G. Dalton
   1962   Introduction. In *Markets in Africa*, edited by P. Bohannan and G. Dalton. Evanston, Illinois: Northwestern University Press.
Bulmer, R.
   1960   Political aspects of the moka ceremonial exchange system among the Kyaka people of the western highlands of New Guinea. *Oceania* **31**:1–13.
Chagnon, N. A.
   1968a Yanomamö social organization and warfare. In *War: the anthropology of armed conflict and aggression*, edited by M. Fried, M. Harris, and R. Murphy, pp. 109–159. New York: Natural History Press.
   1968b *Yanomamö: the fierce people*. New York: Holt.
Codere, H.
   1950   *Fighting with property*. New York: J. J. Augustin.
Dalton, G.
   1969   Theoretical issues in economic anthropology. *Current Anthropology* **10**:63–102.
   1971a Traditional tribal and peasant economies: an introductory survey of economic anthropology. In *McCaleb modules in anthropology*. Reading, Massachusetts: Addison-Wesley.
   1971b Introduction: the subject of economic anthropology. In *Studies in economic anthropology*, edited by G. Dalton. Washington, D.C.: American Anthropological Association.
   1971c Introduction. In *Economic development and social change: the modernization of village communities*, edited by G. Dalton. New York: Natural History Press.
   1972   Peasantries in anthropology and history. *Current Anthropology* **13**:385–415.
   1975   Karl Polanyi's analysis of long-distance trade and his wider paradigm. In *Ancient civilization and trade*, edited by C. Lamberg-Karlovsky and J. Sabloff. Albuquerque, New Mexico: University of New Mexico Press.
   1978   The impact of colonization on aboriginal economies in stateless societies. In *Research in economic anthropology*, edited by G. Dalton. Greenwich Connecticut: JAI Pres.
Douglas, M.
   1958   Raffia cloth distribution in the Lele economy. *Africa* **28**:109–122.
   1962   Lele economy compared with the Bushong: a study of economic backwardness. In *Markets in Africa*, edited by P. Bohannan and G. Dalton. Evanston, Illinois: Northwestern University Press.
   1967   Primitive rationing: a study of controlled exchange. In *Themes in economic anthropology*, edited by R. Firth. London: Tavistock.
Drucker, P., and R. F. Heizer
   1967   *To make my name good*. Berkeley: University of California Press.
Duby, G.
   1974   *The early growth of the European economy: warriors and peasants from the seventh to the twelfth century*. London: Weidenfeld and Nicolson.
Einzig, P.
   1948   *Primitive money*. London: Eyre and Spotteswoode.
Evans-Pritchard, E. E.
   1954   Introduction. In *The gift*, by Marcel Mauss. London: Routledge and Kegan Paul.
Firth, R.
   1929   Currency, primitive. In *Encyclopedia Britannica*, 14th ed.

1936   *We, the Tikopia*. London: Allen & Unwin.
1940   *The work of the gods in Tikopia*. London: Percy Lund, Humphries.
Fortes, M.
1936   Ritual festivals and social cohesion in the hinterland of Gold Coast. *American Anthropologist* **38**:590–604.
1940   The political system of the Tallensi of the Northern Territories of the Gold Coast. In *African political systems*, edited by M. Fortes and E. E. Evans-Pritchard, pp. 283–271. London: Oxford University Press.
Hallpike, C. R.
1973   Functionalist interpretations of primitive warfare. *Man* **8**:451–470.
Harding, T. G.
1967   Money, kinship, and change in a New Guinea economy. *Southwestern Journal of Anthropology* **23**:209–233.
Heider, K.
1969   Visiting trade institutions. *American Anthropologist* **71**:462–471.
Mair, L.
1934   *An African people in the twentieth century*. London: Routledge and Kegan Paul.
Malinowski, B.
1920   War and weapons among the natives of the Trobriand Island. Man 35.
1921   The primitive economics of the Trobriand Islanders. *The Economic Journal* **31**:1–15.
1922   *Argonauts of the western Pacific*. London: Routledge and Kegan Paul.
1935   *Coral gardens and their magic*. New York: American Book Company.
Mauss, M.
1954   *The gift*. London: Routledge and Kegan Paul.
Middleton, J., and D. Tait
1958   *Tribes without rulers*. London: Routledge and Kegan Paul.
Myrdal, G.
1957   *Rich lands and poor*. New York: Harper.
Piddocke, S.
1965   The potlatch system of the southern Kwakiutl: a new perspective. *Southwestern Journal of Anthropology* **21**:244–264.
Polanyi, K.
1975   Traders and trade. In *Ancient civilization and trade*, edited by C. C. Lamberg-Karlovsky and J. A. Sabloff. Albuquerque, New Mexico: University of New Mexico Press.
Posnansky, M.
1972   The early development of trade in west Africa: some archaeological considerations. *Ghana Social Science Journal* **2**.
Powell, H. A.
1956   *An analysis of present-day social structure in the Trobriand Islands*. Ph.D. dissertation. University of London.
1960   Competitive leadership in Trobriand political organization. *Journal of the Royal Anthropological Institute* **90**:118–145.
Quiggin, A. H.
1949   *A survey of primitive money*. London: Methuen.
Rosman, A., and P. Rubel
1971   *Feasting with mine enemy*. New York: Columbia University Press.
Strathern, A.
1971   *The rope of Moka*. Cambridge: Cambridge University Press.
Swadesh, M.
1948   Motivations in Nootka warfare. *Southwestern Journal of Anthropology* **4**:76–93.
Swann, N.
1950   *Food and money in ancient China*. Princeton, New Jersey: Princeton University Press.

Uberoi, J. P. Singh
  1962   *Politics of the kula ring*. Manchester: The University Press.
Vaughan, A. T.
  1965   *New England frontier: puritans and Indians 1620–1675*. Boston: Little, Brown.
Vayda, A. P.
  1967   Pomo trade feasts. In *Tribal and peasant economies,* edited by G. Dalton, pp. 494–500. New York: Natural History Press.
Young, M.
  1971   *Fighting with food*. Cambridge: Cambridge University Press.

Chapter 12

A REAPPRAISAL OF REDISTRIBUTION: COMPLEX HAWAIIAN CHIEFDOMS

TIMOTHY K. EARLE

I. INTRODUCTION

Redistribution, a term familiar to most anthropologists, is still not well understood. Although it is commonly used in economic and evolutionary studies, its meaning remains imprecise. This chapter seeks to untangle the definition of redistribution and then to test selected propositions concerning its evolutionary significance. Two related issues are addressed: (1) redistribution as a typological category of primitive economies, and (2) redistribution as a causal factor in the evolution of social stratification.

Since Polanyi (1944, 1957) defined "redistribution," researchers have sought to characterize economic institutions or economies as "redistribu-

213

tional" and have sought an understanding of the functional and evolutionary importance of redistributional organization. The writings of Elman Service (1962, 1975) stand out as a principal interpretation of redistribution's import. In his evolutionary scheme, redistribution is postulated as a central factor in the development of chiefdoms. Service views chiefdoms as redistributional societies based on a permanent centralized agency for coordination. To paraphrase Service's evolutionary argument, this centralized agency (the redistributive hierarchy of chiefdoms) developed in response to ecologically determined specialization and its requirements for economic coordination. However, Service's proposition concerning redistribution is flawed by definitional and evidential problems. After examining the forms of redistribution and singling out mobilization as associated with chiefly redistributive hierarchies, this paper will test Service's hypothesis with data on the economic organization of the precontact Hawaiian chiefdoms.

II. REDISTRIBUTION: AN ANALYSIS OF INSTITUTIONAL FORMS

In his seminal article in *Trade and Markets in the Early Empires,* Karl Polanyi (1957) presented a three-part typology for the institutional forms of economic organization—"reciprocity," "redistribution," and market "exchange." His article was a reaction to what he saw as a trend in economic anthropology to apply inaccurately the "formal" concepts of Western economics to non-Western societies. Thus, his typology was aimed at recognizing the empirical forms of non-Western economic institutions and at showing their distinctiveness from Western economic modes.

According to Polanyi's definition, the primary defining characteristic of redistribution is its centrality of organization: "redistribution designates appropriational movements towards a center and out of it again . . ." (1957:250). To Polanyi (1957:254), redistribution describes a wide range of activities including the massive collecting and storage of goods in the archaic states of Egypt and Babylonia, the householding activities of a medieval manor and African *kraal,* and distribution of meat in a band society. Following Polanyi's lead, many authors have applied the term "redistribution" to everything from forceful seizures (Pospisil 1968 [1963]), to obligating marriage payments (Forde and Douglas 1967), to potlatching (Schneider 1974), to first-fruit ceremonies in chiefdoms (Sahlins 1958, 1972), to tribute/taxation in archaic and feudal states (Dalton 1967[1961]), to charity and progressive taxation in modern industrial societies (Smelser 1959). While all these activities are similar inasmuch as they involve the concentration and dispersal of goods, it can be asked legitimately whether any economic system does not involve this process in some way.

It is my belief that several separate institutional forms have been lumped together under the single cover term redistribution. Therefore, the goal of this paper is to isolate the separate organizational forms that have been called "redistribution" and to use this refined typology to examine the evolutionary significance of redistribution. The following four-part typology of redistributional institutions has been synthesized from the existing literature.

(1) *Leveling mechanisms* (Nash 1966:35,78–79; Schneider 1974:105,110): any cultural institution the effect of which is to counteract the concentration of wealth by individuals or groups. Examples: ceremonial obligations, potlatching, progressive taxation.

(2) *Householding* (Polanyi 1944, 1957): the pooling and general consumption of goods produced under the division of labor characteristic of a domestic unit. Example: The Domestic Mode of Production (Sahlins 1972).

(3) *Share-out:* the allocation of goods produced by cooperative labor to participants and the owners of the factors of production. Example: distribution of meat resulting from cooperative hunts.

(4) *Mobilization* (Smelser 1959): the recruitment of goods and services for the benefit of a group not coterminous with the contributing members. Examples: tribute, taxation, and corvée labor.

Among the four parts of this typology, two levels of distinguishing features are relevant (Figure 1). First, leveling mechanisms are distinguished from the three other types on structural criteria. A *leveling mechanism* has no single institutionalized structure; rather, it is distinguished by its *effect*—the counteraction of wealth concentration. In contrast, the other three are all specific social institutions characterized by centralized leadership that manages the production and distribution of goods within a group. Second, the three institutional forms of householding, share-out, and mobilization are distinguished by the *size* of groups that they organize. *Householding* organizes domestic production; *share-out,* interhousehold production usually within a single community; and *mobilization,* intercommunity production as

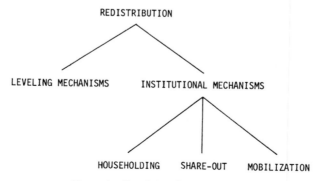

Figure 1 Typology of redistribution.

associated with "public economies." These typological distinctions imply that, since the organizational structures are diverse both in function and in size, explanations for the evolution of redistribution are equally varied.

Attempts to understand the evolution of redistribution have been limited by a failure to examine separately these diverse institutional forms. Therefore, many authors (cf. Polanyi 1957; Sahlins 1972) have concluded that redistributions (in the forms of leveling mechanisms, householding, and share-out) are widely represented at all levels of social complexity. This should not be surprising as these forms of redistribution execute general organizational functions found nearly universally in societies, and thus redistribution as a cover term has not been diacritical in the definition of evolutionary forms of social organization.

On the other hand, mobilization is more limited in its function and in its distribution. Redistribution in the form of mobilization is basic to ranked and stratified societies (cf. Service 1962; Sahlins 1972):

> . . . the channeling upwards [mobilization] of goods or services to socially determined allocative centers (usually king, chief, or priest), who then redistribute to either their subordinates at large by providing community services, or in specific allotments to individuals in accordance with their political, religious, or military status [Dalton 1967 [1961]:153].

In chiefdoms and primitive states, there is an elite stratum physically removed from most production such that these elites depend on goods and service mobilized from the commoner population to finance their public and private activities. The elites are both a hereditary aristocracy with an imposing life-style and a sociopolitical leadership group responsible for the general well-being of their dependents (cf. Goldman 1970). Elites are organized as a regionally centralized hierarchy, important for both mobilization and decision making. Goods are collected and orders are promulgated. As recognized by Service (1962), centralized hierarchical organization marks the evolution of chiefdoms, and this organization depends on mobilization for its existence.

III. SERVICE'S HYPOTHESIS

"Chiefdoms are *redistributional societies* with a permanent agency for coordination" (Service 1962:144). In line with Service's logic, this *redistributive hierarchy,* as I refer to it, evolved in response to economic specialization requiring central coordination. This specialization is a result of one or both of the following economic conditions: (1) "the pooling of individual skills in large-scale cooperative production," and (2) "the regional, or ecological, specialization of different local residential units" (Service 1962:145). In the first instance, the centralized organization of chiefdoms is seen as a consequence of the managerial requirements of cooperative labor activites (cf. Wittfogel 1957). Service believed, however, that the primary factor in the evolution of chiefdoms is the second condition, environmental diversity. His argument goes as follows: For a sedentary society, environmental diversity results in economic specialization; the centralized redistributive hierarchy of a chiefdom then evolves as an efficient means to distribute goods among the locally specialized communities.

> Most chiefdoms seem to have risen where important regional exchange and a consequent increase in local specialization came about because ecological differentiation was combined with considerable sedentariness [Service 1962:146].

In brief, this hypothesis seeks to explain the evolution of chiefdoms as the social consequence of developing Durkheimian "organic solidarity."

Despite the logical elegance of this ecological theory, it does *not* agree well with the ethnographic and ethnohistorical evidence of chiefly organization. Central to Service's argument is that the redistributive hierarchy acts to integrate locally specialized, community-based economies. As I will show for the specific case of Hawaiian chiefdoms, the local communities were organized as generalized subsistence units. The redistributive hierarchy functioned primarily in the special context of financing the elite stratum and its political activities.

IV. THE EVIDENCE FROM HAWAII: A COMPLEX CHIEFDOM

Perhaps nowhere in the world are chiefdoms so well represented and documented as they are in Polynesia (cf. Sahlins 1958; Goldman 1970). Within Polynesia, the Hawaiian Islands (Figure 2) offer an ideal opportunity to examine the relationship between environmental diversity and chiefly organization as postulated by Service. Initially, the islands are characterized by high environmental diversity. Within a single chiefdom's territory, the environment includes pelagic, coastal, riverine, upland, and mountain ecozones. The vegetation ranges from xerophytic communities receiving less than 500 mm rainfall a year to tropical forests receiving greater than 5000 mm a year. As would be predicted by Service's hypothesis, the social organization of the Hawaiian Islands was based aboriginally on a regional redistributive hierarchy involved in mobilization of goods and services from the commoner population. Hawaiian chiefs were a hereditary aristocracy removed from production activities but leaders in all economic, political, and religious affairs. The basic conditions of Service's argument are thus met—a regionally centralized chiefdom is found directly associated with high environmental diversity.

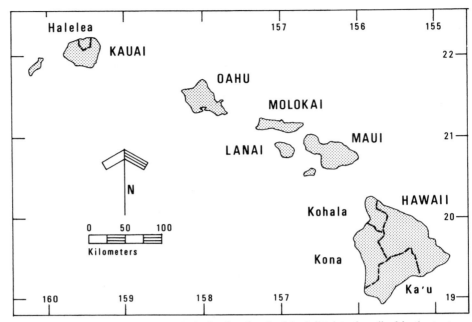

Figure 2   The Hawaiian Islands, indicating the aboriginal districts described in the text.

Although this association is evident, the exact nature of the relationship warrants closer scrutiny. Service suggests that the redistributive hierarchies of chiefdoms should be based on the centralized coordination of locally specialized communities. Such local specialization would correspond to environmentally diverse zones, and the resulting community economic interdependence would select for the evolution of a regional sociopolitical organization. However, in the following sections, the economy and social organization of the local Hawaiian community will be shown, in direct contradiction to Service's hypothesis, to have been economically generalized.

A. The Economy of the Hawaiian Community

Aboriginally, the local Hawaiian community was defined by its attachment to an administrative unit called the *ahupua'a.* In accordance with Service's hypothesis, it is this unit that should show economic specialization. The *ahupua'a* population was socially circumscribed by high endogamy and low emigration (Sahlins 1973). Economically, it formed the basis for many suprafamily cooperative labor activities like net-fishing and the construction of irrigation systems. *Ahupua'a* may be classified into two general types corresponding to contrasting geographic conditions. In geologically old areas, the local land division, called the *valley ahupua'a,* encompassed a full catchment area for a major stream; the agriculture of these valley *ahupua'a* was based on pondfield irrigation. This pattern, in which each major valley was a separate *ahupua'a,* was characteristic of Kaua'i, Oahu, Molokai, Maui, and parts of Hawaii. In contrast, in geologically young areas where major streams have not developed, the local land divisions, called *upland ahupua'a,* were arbitrary territorial strips that ran from the mountains to the sea. Because of the lack of a permanent water source, upland *ahupua'a* relied on rainfall agriculture. This upland pattern was typical of Hawaii and eastern Maui and the driest sections of the other islands. The relationship between resource ownership and the subsistence economy of the *ahupua'a* community is examined for the Halelea district, Kaua'i, typifying the valley *ahupua'a,* and the leeward districts of Hawaii, typifying the upland *ahupua'a* (Figures 2 and 3).

(1) *The Valley Ahupua'a of Halelea District, Kaua'i.* The economic organization of the valley *ahupua'a* is well illustrated by the land divisions of the Halelea district on the windward, northern coast of Kaua'i. The following description is a summary of an ethnohistoric and archaeological research project focused on the economic and social organization of a traditional district (Earle 1973, 1977). Nine *ahupua'a* have been identified for Halelea in 1850. Seven of these encompassed an entire drainage basin for each of the major streams, which have their headwaters in the high central mountains and flow to the Pacific. *Ahupua'a* boundaries ran along the dramatic knife-edge ridges dividing the valleys from each other; thus, each valley was a separate *ahupua'a.*

Aboriginally, the three major subsistence resource zones in Halelea (Figure 3) were the alluvial bottomlands, the shallow inshore waters, and the uplands. The alluvial bottomlands were intensively farmed by both irrigation and dry land agriculture. The primary crops included taro, sweet potato, and banana. The resources of the sea were of almost equal significance as fish provided the primary protein of the diet. Fishing in the shallow waters of the coral reefs and bays was most productive, and this zone was carefully divided among *ahupua'a* as "owned" territory. The less heavily utilized zone of the uplands and valley interiors was important for extensive hunting and collecting of feral and wild species such as pig, chicken, banana, and various fiber and wood producing plants. These resources were an important source of variety in the diet, of famine foods, and of numerous raw materials.

From Service's hypothesis, one might predict that these subsistence resource zones would have been subdivided such that communities would have tended to specialize in subsistence activities. However, the *ahupua'a* boundaries were laid out so as to include all necessary resources within a single *ahupua'a* territory, thus creating economically self-sufficient communities. By controlling a full valley catchment, an *ahupua'a* population was guaranteed areas of productive alluvial lands and, equally important, it held

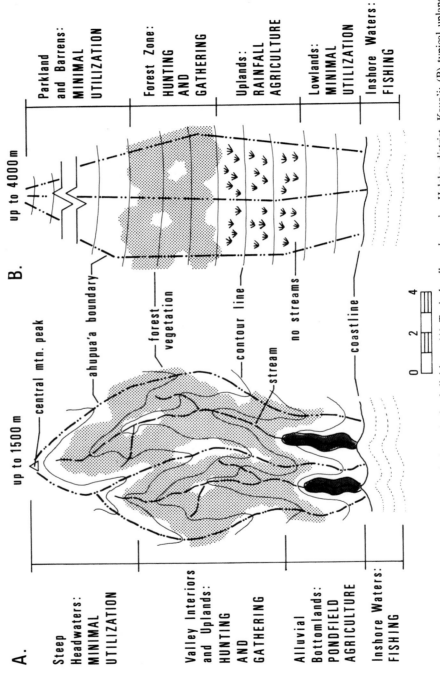

A.

up to 1500 m

central mtn. peak

Steep
Headwaters:
MINIMAL
UTILIZATION

Valley Interiors
and Uplands:
HUNTING
AND
GATHERING

Alluvial
Bottomlands:
PONDFIELD
AGRICULTURE

Inshore Waters:
FISHING

B.

up to 4000 m

Parkland
and Barrens:
MINIMAL
UTILIZATION

Forest Zone:
HUNTING
AND
GATHERING

Uplands:
RAINFALL
AGRICULTURE

Lowlands:
MINIMAL
UTILIZATION

Inshore Waters:
FISHING

ahupua'a boundary

forest
vegetation

contour line

stream

no streams

coastline

0   2   4

Figure 3 Schematic representation of *ahupua'a* land divisions. (A) Typical valley *ahupua'a*, Halelea district, Kaua'i; (B) typical upland *ahupua'a*, leeward districts, Hawaii. Scale approximate, in kilometers.

exclusive rights to the water necessary for irrigation. As already noted, boundary lines followed natural ridges, but near the sea these lines often deviated from the dominant or natural boundaries so as to divide critically productive sections between *ahupua'a*.

Each *ahupua'a* community maintained territorial control over substantial segments of each of the three subsistence resource zones. Although the sizes of these zones varied from one *ahupua'a* to the next, this variability corresponded closely to the population size of the *ahupua'a* (Earle 1973: Table 9). In other words, *ahupua'a* populations and their associated resource zones were distributed such that each community might be self-sufficient, based on a generalized subsistence economy. This organization of subsistence economies would have minimized interdependence between communities; from a subsistence standpoint, the local Halelean community was structured similarly to a segmental society.

(2) *The Upland Ahupua'a of Leeward Districts, Hawaii.* The economic organization of the upland *ahupua'a* is best illustrated by the leeward districts of Hawaii. On the island of Hawaii, there were traditionally three major leeward districts—Kohala, Kona, and Ka'u. Although a study, comparable to the Halelea project, is unavailable, the general pattern of the upland *ahupua'a* and its relationship to the primary subsistence resource zones have been documented by extensive archaeological and ethnohistorical research.

The environment of leeward Hawaii, in contrast to that of Halelea, is characteristic of a geologically recent region; the land surface slopes uniformly from the central volcanic mountains toward the sea. Vegetation zones correspond to the pattern of orographic rainfall determined by the combined effects of elevation and orientation to the trade winds (Carlquist 1970).

From Newman's (1970) summary monograph, three dominant resource zones may be recognized for the traditional subsistence economy of the leeward districts (Figure 3). First, since there were virtually no suitable water sources for irrigation, agriculture was restricted primarily to the intensive dry land farming of sweet potato and taro. The agricultural zone formed a band of upland soils limited largely by available rainfall (750–2000 mm annually). Second, fishing provided the necessary protein to complement the high caloric yields from root crop agriculture. This fishing was heavily concentrated in the shallow (less than 350 m) water zone immediately offshore (cf. Newman 1970: Map 15). Third, at an elevation immediately above the agricultural zone, there was a forest area used for extensive hunting and gathering and limited agriculture. Products procured in this zone were important for many uses including construction materials, variety foods, and medicines (cf. Handy and Handy 1972).

Evidently these subsistence resource zones were functionally equivalent to those described for Halelea, but their geomorphological location was quite distinct. Since the Halelean pattern was determined by the hydrology of the central stream, the three resources zones were spatially contiguous and all represented in a compact area near the sea. In contrast, the absence of major stream drainages on leeward Hawaii resulted in a vertical stratification of zones ringing the island at elevations determined by orographic rainfall (cf. Figure 3; Newman 1970:Map 15).

Each district was subdivided into territorial units, the *ahupua'a,* which formed the basis for the local community economy. The primary boundaries of each *ahupua'a* were constructed perpendicular to the slope contours so as to define an aribitrary strip of land running from the central mountains to the sea including sections of each economic zone (cf. Figure 3; Apple 1965: Figure 15). The most thorough archaeological data on an upland *ahupua'a* is available for Lapakahi *ahupua'a,* Kohala district, Hawaii (Newman 1970; Rosendahl 1971). Lapakahi is a narrow (approximately 1 km) territorial strip running about 7 km from the rolling uplands (maximum elevation about 600 m) to the sea. Along the coast, there are scattered archaeological features and one major village site. Moving inland for the next 3 km, the dry slopes above the sea were apparently unused, until, at about 240 m elevation, agricultural features are encountered (Newman 1970:Base Map). These agricultural features (low terraces, enclosures, mounds) extend to the rear of the *ahupua'a* and blanket virtually the entire inland section. This *ahupua'a* would, therefore, not have extended into the forest zone. Although Lapakahi did not control access to forest products, the territorial pattern is still one in which maximum resource diversity is included within the community boundaries.

On leeward Hawaii, the economic resource zones are geomorphically distinct from Halelea, but the traditional pattern of community territorial organization was functionally similar. The boundaries of each community were laid out to create units that were largely replications of each other. For the most part, because communities had access to all basic economic resources (especially farming and fishing areas), each could maintain generalized subsistence production.

B. Community Social Organization

A most provocative aspect of the economic organization of the *ahupua'a* was the apparent variability in household organization. As discussed at length elsewhere (Earle 1977), the social organization of Halelean commoners was founded on ostensive principles of household independence. Because of the compactness of resource zones in Halelea, households were able to establish themselves in locations proximate to the exploitative areas. There was, therefore, little need for household specialization, and evidence indicates that the household economy consisted of a balanced subsistence strategy including farming, fishing, and collecting.

In contrast, the economic zones of the upland *ahupua'a* on leeward Hawaii were spatially separate. In the wetter sections of Hawaii, the subsistence zones were compressed within a few kilometers of the sea. Whereas, in the drier areas like Kohala and Ka'u, the agricultural zone was at higher elevations, not contiguous to the fishing zone along the sea. At Lapakahi, the distance between zones is short enough that a population residing on the coast could farm the interior fields (cf. Rosendahl 1971). However, this was apparently not the case for Ka'u.

According to Handy and Pukui (1972[1958]), the spatial separation of subsistence resource zones in Ka'u resulted in economic specialization whereby inland households principally farmed and coastal households fished. This is clearly the type of situation that Service envisioned—environmental diversity causing economic specialization. In direct contradiction to Service's expectations, however, this economic specialization did not result in community specialization and political centrality. Rather, the response to specialization was an alteration of the local social organization such that the specialized households were integrated into a cognatic social unit, the *'ohana*, which crosscut the economic diversity. Arguing from informant data, Handy and Pukui (1972[1958]) described the *'ohana* as consisting of several related households *(hale)* exchanging specialized products. "Between households within the *'ohana* there was constant sharing and exchange of foods and of utilitarian articles and also of services . . ."(Handy and Pukui 1972[1958]:6). The striking conclusion is that, even in environmental conditions favoring specialization, the response is a change in local kinship organization rather than a political solution. The aim appears always to have been to *minimize* economic interdependence between community units.

C. Summary of Community Economy and Social Organization

For both the valley *ahupua'a* of Halelea and the upland *ahupua'a* of leeward Hawaii, the territorial boundaries of the local community were laid out to minimize differences in the resources available to *ahupua'a* populations. Even in the case where environmental diversity selected for economic specialization, the definition of the community territory and the internal organization of the community permitted a self-sufficient (generalized) community economy. In direct contradiction to Service's hypothesis regarding the integrative function of redistributive hierarchies, the subsistence economies of the Hawaiian chiefdoms were subdivided into repetitious community units. By minimizing the economic interdependence between communities, the structure of the local community largely eliminated the economic justification for a regional sociopolitical organization.

D. Economic Specialization between Districts

The island territory of a Hawaiian chiefdom was divided into major administrative units, the districts (*'okana* or *kalana*), each consisting of a large pie-shaped segment subdivided into *ahupua'a* (nine *ahupua'a* in Halelea district, 47 in Ka'u). As shown in the previous sections, *within* a district the *ahupua'a* were not specialized since territorial divisions were structured to create economically repetitive units. *Between* districts there were indeed marked environmental differences, but the local subsistence economies remained generalized and largely independent because alternative strategies were available.

The trade wind and orographic rainfall pattern creates a most pronounced environmental contrast between the leeward (dry) side of an island and the windward (wet) side. Although this is an environmental situation where economic specialization might be expected, there is little evidence for such a response. Aboriginally, the effects of this environmental variability were mitigated by two aspects of the subsistence economy: (1) irrigation practices, and (2) a variety of primary subsistence crops. First, taro was grown as the dominant crop on both the windward and leeward sides where water was available for irrigation. Although the permanent streams used for irrigation are most common to windward, runoff from the heavy mountain rainfall feeds many permanent streams to leeward as well. Some of the most extensive irrigation complexes were actually in leeward areas, such as Waimea, Kaua'i, and Waikiki, Oahu (cf. Handy 1940). Second, because taro and sweet potato were interchangeable staple crops in the Hawaiian diet, there was considerable flexibility in the dry land farming methods used in areas without permanent streams. The shorter growing season and reduced water requirements (minimum 750 mm) of sweet potato made it well suited to the restricted, seasonal rainfall of the leeward coasts. Whereas taro, with higher water requirements (minimum about 1500 mm), was ideal for the windward districts. Thus, farming was viable in both high and low rainfall areas because of both irrigation and a flexible dry land agriculture. Additionally, although there was some variability in fishing potential between districts (cf. Newman 1970), it is equally clear that fishing was practiced effectively in all areas. In sum, despite environmental contrasts, the districts were able to retain generalized economies based on a balance between agriculture and fishing, and this condition would have greatly reduced requirements for interdistrict trade. Again the expectations of Service's hypothesis are contrary to the minimal specialization observed in the Hawaiian case.

This is not to say that interdistrict trade did not exist. Specialized products such as tapa cloth and various woods were often localized and were exchanged between districts (Handy and Handy 1972:314–315). For example, Ellis (1963[1827]:229–230) described a traditional Hawaiian trade "fair" at which people from the southern districts of Puna and Ka'u exchanged dried fish, mats, and a particular tapa for pigs, dried taro, other tapas and mats, and tobacco from the northern district of Hamakua. The significant point of this exchange is not its simple presence; extensive intergroup exchange exists in all societies. Rather, this exchange was *not* channeled through the redistributive hierarchy. Exchange was direct barter between primary participants. Representatives of the chiefs were present, but they acted only as arbitrators and tax collectors.

In sum, the major environmental differences among the districts of a Hawaiian chiefdom were largely overcome by different options in the subsistence economies. The districts retained their primary self-sufficiency by stressing a balanced farming–fishing subsistence economy, and interdistrict trade was relatively rare. Exchange in specialized products that did take place between districts was handled by a direct barter system. As is shown in the following section, the channeling of goods through the redistributive hierarchy fulfilled a very different function from the integration of specialized economic units.

E. Economic Functions of the Redistributive Hierarchy

Redistribution in Hawaii involved the massive mobilization of goods at periodic ceremonial collections directed by the elite hierarchy. The most striking collections were associated with the annual *makahiki* ceremonies (cf. Malo 1951[1898]:141–159; Ii 1959: 70–77; Beckwith 1932). During this ceremonial period, the god Lono, represented as a stick figure, was sent on a tour around the islands. At each *ahupua'a,* the god would halt and receive the obligatory offerings from the local population. The size of this offering was carefully examined, and a niggardly *ahupua'a* was first asked to fulfill its total responsibility and then, if it failed to meet this obligation, it could be plundered. The goods collected during the *makahiki* were mainly raw materials and commodities used by the elites and their households; the perishable food collected was used to feed the chiefs and those directly involved in the collection (Malo 1951[1898]:143,145). The commodities (tapa clothing, fishing gear, etc.) and preservable food (hard *po'i* and dried fish) were then deposited in a central storehouse for the personal and political uses of the paramount chief (Ii 1959:121; Malo 1951[1898]:195).

Additional collections preceded the large feasts associated with special occasions, such as life-crisis ceremonies and temple constructions associated with the paramount chief. During these feasts, a significant portion of the amassed food, which was difficult to store in any case, was distributed directly to the commoner population. However, it seems highly unlikely that the *makahiki* or other regional collections could have served to integrate a regionally specialized economy. Economic specialization of local communities would have required a frequent and regular exchange between them. (Typically such exchanges take the form of a regional market or monthly fairs as in modern peasant economies.) Neither in Hawaii nor in the other Polynesian societies is there evidence for such regularity or predictability in the feasting. Sahlins (1958) lists only three general, chiefdom-wide collections a year; in reviewing the traditional histories (e.g., Malo 1952 [1898]; Ii 1959; Beckwith 1932), only two regular collections a year were noted and both of these took place in a single month. Additional feasts were probably irregular and relatively infrequent. In short, the evidence would strongly indicate that the collections and related feasts were not a viable means to organize locally specialized subsistence economies. A reexamination of mobilization associated with other chiefdoms would most probably yield similar conclusions. Redistribution is not adequate for the integrative economic function proposed by Service.

The questions remains as to what were the economic functions of redistributional mobilization in Hawaii? The three primary applications for goods mobilized during the collections were (1) support of the elite poulation; (2) establishment and maintenance of political relationships required by intensive intra- and intergroup competition; and (3) capital investment through the management of local economic strategies, like irrigation and aquaculture, used to maximize income flow to the elites (Earle 1977). The redistributive hierarchy of the Hawaiian chiefdom functioned to mobilize goods to support the operation of the political superstructure; in short, redistributional mobilization was a form of taxation.

This is not to gainsay the important benefits to the local subsistence economy. First, as is argued clearly by Gall and Saxe (Chapter 14), increased production intensity results in an increased economic insecurity. This was clearly the case for Hawaii where the irrigation systems were subjected to periodic destructions from stream flooding and tidal waves. Since such stochastic events occurred usually less than once every 20 years for a specific community, a purely local adaptation to such disasters was simply inefficient (Earle 1977). Rather, the Hawaiian elites were under obligations of generosity that required them to support a destitute population and aid in reconstruction. Second, capital investment in irrigation systems and fishponds appears to have significantly increased the efficiency of agricultural production in Hawaii. Irrigated taro was the strategy selected for wherever environmental conditions were favorable (Earle 1973:63–67). Such benefits are, however, hardly sufficient cause for the evolution of redistributive hierarchies. Indeed, arrangements like the regional reciprocal networks of acephalous societies (Dalton, Chapter 11) offer alternative mechanisms for both security and capital formation.

It seems plausible that an explanation for the development of redistributional mobilization is linked to a general explanation of social stratification. The increased "surplus" associated with mobilization is used to support an elite population removed from subsistence activities but performing various control functions. Elsewhere (Earle 1977), I have suggested that social stratification involves a shift from subsistence (minimizing) production strategy to a political (maximizing) strategy. The former is self-dampening and thus inherently stable. In contrast, the latter is self-amplifying as income/revenue is used partially to expand productive capacity. Such a positive feedback system is inherently developmental and will continue to expand until external factors (like island size in Polynesia) inhibit its growth. An explanation for redistributive hierarchies will require (1) an explication of the elaboration and institutionalization of the maximizing political economy and (2) an enumeration of the possible environmental and social conditions inhibiting its growth.

V. SUMMARY

This chapter has examined redistribution and offered a four-part typology (leveling mechanisms, householding, share-out, and mobilization) to characterize the very different economic institutions subsumed by the cover term. Within the typology, redistribution in the form of mobilization is seen as basic to chiefdoms and states.

Service (1962) has offered a hypothesis that would explain the evolution of chiefly redistributive hierarchies as a response to environmental variability. An examination of the aboriginal Hawaiian chiefdoms suggests that this hypothesis should be rejected for the following reasons:

(1) The definition of the community territory and the internal organization of the community population permitted a self-sufficient (generalized) economy.

(2) Major environmental diversity among districts was largely resolved by different options in the subsistence economy and not by extensive exchange.

(3) Exchange in specialized products was handled by kin obligations within a community and by direct barter between districts. Goods channeled through the redistributive hierarchy, in contrast, were used primarily to finance activities directed by the elites.

(4) The long-term periodicity and irregularity of mobilizations were inadequate to organize locally specialized subsistence economies.

This evidence suggests that redistributive mobilization should be interpreted as an essential mechanism used to finance the political and private activities of an elite population. In sum, an explanation of redistribution/mobilization is inextricably bound to the evolution of sociopolitical systems of stratification.

References

Apple, R. A.
   1965   Trails: from steppingstones to kerbstones. *Bernice P. Bishop Museum Special Publication* **53.**
Beckwith, M. W.
   1932   Kepelino's traditions of Hawaii. *Bernice P. Bishop Museum Bulletin* **95.**
Carlquist, S.
   1970   *Hawaii: a natural history.* New York: Natural History Press.
Dalton, G.
   1967   (1961) Economic theory and primitive society. In *Tribal and peasant economies,* edited by G. Dalton. New York: Natural History Press.
Earle, T. K.
   1973   *Control hierarchies in the traditional irrigation economy of Halelea district, Kaua'i, Hawaii.* Ann Arbor, Michigan: University Microfilms.
   1977   Economic and social organization of a complex chiefdom: the Halelea district, Kaua'i, Hawaii. *University of Michigan, Museum of Anthropology, Anthrolological Papers* **64** (in press).
Ellis, W.
   1963   (1827) *Journal of William Ellis.* Honolulu: Advertiser Publishing.
Forde, D., and M. Douglas
   1967   (1956) Primitive economics. In *Tribal and peasant economies,* edited by G. Dalton. New York: Natural History Press.
Goldman, I.
   1970   *Ancient polynesian society.* Chicago: University of Chicago Press.
Handy, E. S. C.
   1940   The Hawaiian planter: volume 1. *Bernice P. Bishop Museum Bulletin* **161.**
Handy, E. S. C., and E. G. Handy
   1972   Native planters in old Hawaii: their life, lore, and environment. *Bernice P. Bishop Museum Bulletin* **233.**
Handy, E. S. C., and M. K. Pukui
   1972   (1958) *The polynesian family system in Ka'u, Hawaii.* Rutland and Tokyo: Tuttle.
Ii, J. P.
   1959   *Fragments of Hawaiian history.* Honolulu: Bishop Museum Press.
Malo, D.
   1951   (1898) Hawaiian antiquities. *Bernice P. Bishop Museum Special Publication* **2,** 2nd edition.
Nash, M.
   1966   *Primitive and peasant economic systems.* San Francisco: Chandler.
Newman, T. S.
   1970   *Hawaiian fishing and farming on the island of Hawaii A.D. 1778.* Honolulu: Department of Land and Natural Resources.
Polanyi, K.
   1944   *The great transformation.* New York: Rinehart.
   1957   The economy as instituted process. In *Trade and market in the early empires,* edited by K. Polanyi, M. Arensberg, and H. Pearson. Glencoe, Illinois: Free Press.
Pospisil, L.
   1968   (1963) The Kapauku individualistic money economy. In *Economic anthropology,* edited by E. Le Clair and H. Schneider. New York: Holt.
Rosendahl, P.
   1971   Aboriginal agriculture and residence patterns in upland Lapakahi, Hawaii Island. Unpublished Ph. D. dissertation. Manoa: University of Hawaii.

Sahlins, M.
 1958 *Social stratification in Polynesia.* Seattle, Washington: University of Washington Press.
 1972 *Stone age economics.* Chicago: Aldine.
 1973 Historical anthropology of the Hawaiian Kingdom. Research proposal submitted to the National Science Foundation.
Schneider, H.
 1974 *Economic man.* New York: Free Press.
Service, E.
 1962 *Primitive social organization.* New York: Random House.
 1975 *Origins of the state and civilization: the process of cultural evolution.* New York: Norton.
Smelser, N.
 1959 A comparative view of exchange systems. *Economic Development* 7:173–182.
Wittfogel, K.
 1957 *Oriental despotism.* New Haven: Yale University Press.

Part V

Systemic Models of Exchange

Chapter 13

THE SIMULATION OF
A LINEAR EXCHANGE SYSTEM
UNDER EQUILIBRIUM CONDITIONS

HENRY WRIGHT AND MELINDA ZEDER

Variables related to exchange have figured in proposed explanations of the rise and diversification of egalitarian, ranked, and state-organized societies. Such propositions must remain incomplete and unsatisfactory without knowledge of how exchange networks actually operated and how this operation was related to other aspects of the participating cultural systems. One way to gain such knowledge is to construct models of the proposed exchange networks, to deduce from the operation of these the expected distributions of exported items in time and space, and to test these deductions with the archaeologically recovered evidence of such distributions. Computer simulation is a useful deductive tool in such an endeavor.

Even in a simple case, simulation can be viewed as having a succession of possible objectives. First, one can show that an established system will maintain a given equilibrium. Second, one can show that a system can organize itself and become larger or smaller, establishing new equilibria given different input conditions. Finally, one can vary the input variables and parameters of the operating system to generate testable implications. In this paper, we demonstrate merely that reciprocal systems as presently conceptualized by anthropologists could maintain a set equilibrium. The implications of our study for observed regularities in Late Archaic exchange systems in eastern North America, discussed at the end of this paper, came as a welcome surprise.

Our approach was inspired by R. A. Rappaport's suggestions regarding the regulation of linear or "chain-like" exchange arrangements among the Maring of east central New Guinea (1967:106–107). Rappaport states:

> Trade among the Maring is effected through direct exchange between individuals. It may be questioned whether a direct exchange apparatus that moves only two or three items critical to subsistence would be viable. If native salt and working axes were the only items moving

233

along a trade route, or were the only items freely exchangeable for each other, sufficient supplies of both might be jeopardized merely by inequities in production. Insufficiences would develop because the production of each of the two commodities would not be determined by the demand for that commodity, but by the demand for the commodity for which it was exchanged. That is, the production of native salt would not be limited by the demand for salt, but by the demand for axes. If all that the Simbai people could obtain for their salt were working axes they would be likely to suspend the manufacture of salt if they had a large supply of axes on hand, regardless of the state of the salt supply in the Jimi Valley. The converse might be the case if the ax manufacturers had large stockpiles of salt. . . .

The exchangeability of plumes, shells, and bridal axes with native-produced salt and working axes alters the relationship between these commodities. While the demands for salt and working axes were limited by the amounts required for specific processes of production, extraction, or metabolism, this is not the case with valuables. Plumes are perishable and there was, therefore, a constant demand for new ones. The size of bride prices is unspecified in advance, but a man is usually under pressure from his affines to pay well for his wife and is shamed if he is not able to do so. The unlimited demand for the valuables required to entice or pay for women, most importantly shells and "bridal axes," provided a mechanism for articulating the production of each of the two items critical to metabolism or subsistence to its own demand. As long as it was possible to exchange salt for shells or bridal axes, commodities for which the need for large but indefinite, salt would be produced. The production of salt would be suspended only with the suspension of the demand for it, and this demand presumably would reflect its status as a physiological necessity or near necessity. Conversely, as long as it was possible to obtain feathers for working axes, the latter would be produced. The demand for working axes, it may be assumed, would depend on the numbers of individuals gardening, the total area under production, and the kind of vegetation in which gardens were being cut [Rappaport 1967:106–107].

Rappaport's conjecture raised to us the interesting possibility that the extensive movement of "ritual" or "sociotechnic" artifacts, so often explained by archaeologists as the result of the spread of "cults," might serve to regulate exchange systems, among other possible purposes.

The assumption implicit in Rappaport's verbal model is that each community should be supplied with what it needs. The amassing of profits is a possible but usually self-defeating strategy in such networks. Changes in production result from the efforts of primitive traders to achieve the ideal of obtaining enough to satisfy the totality of their exchange partners rather than efforts to accumulate commodities. This is not to say that individual behavior is altruistic. The traders in the various communities of the network may be competitive; however, they are competing so that they can maximize alliances, not capital (Sahlins 1972; Dalton, Chapter 11). The regulation of vital flows of goods and assistance in such networks, where the various producers are at best dimly aware of each other's existence, must be accomplished by symbols that carry information about the changing demands of either the intermediate parties or the producer.

We attempted to construct three discrete simulations, the first two of which did not regulate themselves. However, these failures are instructive and worth brief discussion. The various input data and parameters of the three simulations were patterned on the basis of information on the Dani of west central New Guinea provided by Heider (1970), who in fact argued that Rappaport's proposition seemed applicable to his case. The input population data was constructed for eight communities with populations of about 200 people. Each community had between 2 and 12 births and 0 to 10 ordinary deaths per year. Every 5 to 13 years an epidemic would kill from 10 to 12 people. Every 14 to 55 years a major war would kill from 15 to 35 people. Deviation within the ranges implied by Heider in each year was selected with a random number table. This procedure generates more sudden variations than would one that selects normal variations around a mean, but this provides more of a challenge to the various equilibrating mechanisms. In addition to these generated population changes, two demographic disasters were built into the input variable. In year 22, the population of one of the producers is drastically cut. In years 51–52, the populations of both producers are drastically cut. The population changes for 60 years are appended. The community names are similar to those actually occurring in the Dani area, and the commodities are among those that are exchanged among Dani communities. The goods production and consumption rates are without specific foundation. Their absence from the otherwise exemplary Dani ethnography, as well as most other ethnographies, illustrates a weakness of a holistic or inductive approach. An explicit attempt to test almost any exchange model would force an ethnographer to record such rate data.

In our first attempt, which was intended only as a blocking out of storage and flow in the program, the system had the following features:

(1) There are eight component communities linearly arranged with production occurring only in the first and eighth villages. These two are assumed to have limitless resources. Exchange is possible only between adjacent communities. Communities exchange as units.

(2) Each producer makes only one commodity, which all communities require in fixed ratio to their populations.

(3) In each iterative "year" each community beginning with the producer takes what it needs of a commodity given its population and passes the rest on to the next farthest community from the producer.

(4) Each year the population of the component communities changes, so production and consumption will change. Each producing community attempts to regulate its production on the basis of whether it received too many or too few goods in the previous year. If too many, it cuts production. This forces the other producer, who receives too few goods, to increase production, and so on.

A vicious circle quickly leads to unacceptable deficits and surpluses, and the equitable distribution of goods ceases. We were unable to construct a regulator dependent solely on the information inherent in demographically dependent commodities, which could keep the system in equilibrium. While it may be that the fault is ours, we suspect that such is impossible, as Rappaport indeed argues in the above cited quote.

Our second attempt at simulating reciprocal exchange had a more complex means of regulation. It had the following features:

(1) As before, there are eight linearly arranged communities with production only at the ends.

(2) There are two classes of commodities: demographically dependent commodities that are used in fixed ratio to population and demographically nondependent commodities that are not. These are henceforth termed vital and symbolic commodities. Each producer makes one of each class of commodity in some ratio to its own population.

(3) In each iterative "year" in the model, each community first takes what it needs of the vital commodity and passes on the rest to the next community. Second, each takes a set fraction, the same for all communities, of the symbolic commodity and passes on the remainder.

(4) Each year the population of the component communities changes, so that the production of all commodities and the consumption of vital commodities will change. The model contains two hierarchically arranged regulatory mechanisms.

(a) The primary regulator corrects vital production on the basis of whether too many or too few vital goods were received the previous year, as in our first attempt.

(b) The secondary regulator operates in years when the producer fails to receive any vital commodities. The producer corrects its own vital production by changing it as a direct function of the increase or decrease in the received symbolic commodities over the amount received in the previous year.

The periodically operating secondary regulator works well under conditions of generally increasing population; however, it exacerbates system collapse in cases in which the population of one of the producers is declining. Such regulation is successful only because the purely population dependent secondary regulator periodically forces production up in times of increasing population, in spite of the depression of production created by the primary regulator, as noted in our discussion of the first attempt.

Our third and successful attempt at constructing a system capable of maintaining an equilibrium also involves two levels of regulation both dependent on the information carried by the symbolic commodities. It has the following features:

(1) As before there are eight communities in a linear arrangement with exchange only between adjacent communities and production only at the ends.

(2) As in the second attempt, the first and eighth communities each produce one vital commodity and one symbolic commodity in various ratios to their own populations.

(3) Also as in the second attempt, each community beginning with the producer takes what it needs of the vital commodity and a fixed proportion of the symbolic commodity and passes the remainder on to the next in line.

(4) Likewise, the model contains two hierarchically arranged regulatory devices, both of which depend on the flow of symbolic commodities to correct for the resulting deficits and surpluses in the vital commodities at either end of the line.

(a) Every year each producer corrects the production of its vital product by increasing or decreasing its production as a direct function of the increase or decrease in the received symbolic commodity over the amount received in the previous year divided by the local production of its own symbolic commodity. Since the difference in receipts is always small relative to local production, this is a very minimal correction.

(b) In years in which a producer fails to receive any vital commodities, he corrects the production of his own vital commodity by changing it as a direct function of the increase or decrease in the received symbolic commodity over the amount received in the previous year.

Even though this model approaches the logic of linear exchange suggested by Rappaport, we must emphasize that various aspects of it are simplified or highly speculative. First, most exchange involves many sets of partners rather than whole communities. Second, actual exchange also usually involves a number of commodities, and every point in a system would participate in the production of at least one of these commodities. Third, such commodities might range from largely demographically dependent to largely demographically independent rather than purely one or the other. Indeed, while there seem to be purely symbolic commodities in actual exchange systems, we do not know of any purely vital commodity of which each community took its needs and passed on the rest. There is provocative archaeological evidence that some commodities were passed on from community to community in fixed ratio (Renfrew et al. 1968). If needed finally, we do not know exactly how the knowledge of received goods actually affects local production. Hopefully our attempts to express such decision making as a transformation in our model will encourage ethnographers to investigate this as well as other points.

The program for the third attempt in the Fortran-related language WAT-FIV is appended. Graphical representation of the output of this third simulation, including the variation in amount of a commodity exported from a community each year and the variation in ratio of export to import at each step in a yearly interaction, is appended. From this we can see that the oscillating system can regulate itself under ordinary conditions and can handle the disaster of year 22, but the disasters of years 51 and 52 exceed the capacity of the regulators. Doubtless there are other such extreme conditions.

Beyond this, what good is this endeavor? In practical terms the utility of any simulation is enhanced to the extent to which it elucidates observed data. Several years ago, Howard Winters published a paper on what he called ''trade cycles'' in the Late Archaic communities of the Lower Tennessee Valley (Winters 1968). After arguing that items of copper and marine shell have a social value measurable in terms of the amount of each raw material included in each artifact, he studied the stratigraphic distribution of the relatively common marine shell artifacts. While local population, as indicated by burials, showed a relatively gradual rise and decline over several centuries, marine shell import exhibited sudden oscillations with an average periodicity of about one hundred years given Winters' dating scheme. He concludes by suggesting that there may have been three possible mechanisms for the movement of shell into the Lower Tennessee Valley. Briefly these are (1) that periodic visits were made to the coastal shell sources, (2) that a network of trading partners linked the coast to the interior, and (3) that an intermediate redistribution center existed, which interior peoples occasionally visited. Without debating the merits of the first and third mechanisms, let us focus on Winters' treatment of the second, which is basically the type of system we have formalized into a simulation model. He rejects this possibility because (1) such a reciprocal network would provide a steady flow of goods without supply fluctuations, and (2) there were few goods in the Lower Tennessee Valley that could be returned to the south, and the amount of copper received from the north was too small to be adequate for this purpose. Both objections can now be answered. In the case of the second, given our simulation, communities in the middle of the system need not contribute regulating symbolic commodities to the flow of goods, and the small amounts of copper moving against shell merely indicates that the Lower Tennessee Valley is much closer to the shell sources than the copper sources. In the case of the first objection, it is notable that the supply of commodities will fluctuate as a function of changes in the population of the producers. Such could arise from natural disasters in either the hurricane-ridden Gulf coast or the hydrologically unstable Great Lakes region, or such could arise as they do in our generated population figures as a result of occasional major raiding. Thus Winters' second mechanism need not be rejected and, in fact, should be further pursued both theoretically and empirically.

Even with the simple simulation at hand, areas of importance for empirical research are indicated. Take, for example, the Late Archaic network. First, efforts must be made to monitor Late Archaic populations in the copper- and shell-producing regions. Much work has been done on these communities, particularly in the Great Lakes region, but adequate surveys of the sort initiated by Winters in the Wabash Valley (Winters 1969) are nonexistent. Second, improved chronologies for the entire Late Archaic will be needed if one is to correlate such fluctuations in population in the north or the south with fluctuations in exchanged commodities in the central area.

The simulation must be considerably improved if it is to generate testable quantitative predictions about the distribution of exchanged goods. First, various intermediate communities must be allowed to produce goods for exchange. Without some possible production by all communities, a system has no way to grow in size and thus could never be built up link by link (Sahlins 1972:291–295). Second, it should be transformed into a network rather than a linear arrangement. Then we could see what kinds of linear and nonlinear arrangements would appear under different circumstances of population, production, etc. Third, the size of the program should be increased to handle more communities and more commodities.

In closing, we wish to emphasize what this exercise has and has not shown. It has not demonstrated that population changes determine exchange flows, nor that some commodities are symbols regulating production. We have written the program so that these variables would have these relations. However, the exercise has demonstrated that these things are possible given relatively parsimonious assumptions about exchange. We hope that archaeologists reading this paper in the future will keep these possibilities in mind and will strive to collect the data needed to test their implications.

(Note that Appendix A follows on p. 240.)

APPENDIX A. SIMULATION OF FOUR COMMODITIES PASSED THROUGH A LINEAR SYSTEM

```
      *JOB
C ***********************************************************************
C ** SIMULATION OF FOUR COMMODITIES PASSED THROUGH A LINEAR SYSTEM **
C ***********************************************************************
C ** VARIABLE DESCRIPTIONS **
C *************************
C   PCE(I,J)=POPULATION FOR EACH VILLAGE FOR EACH YEAR
C   VILL(J) = ARRAY CONTAINING NAMES OF VILLAGES IN THE SYSTEM
C   PERCENT OF POPULATION PRODUCING EACH COMMODITY IN VILLAGE OF ORIGIN
C     LABRAX=PERCENT OF POPULATION PRODUCING AXES (ABUNA)
C     LABRSA=PERCENT OF POPULATION PRODUCING SALT (WILIMAN)
C     LABRSH=PERCENT OF POPULATION PRODUCING SHELLS(ABUNA)
C     LABRFE=PERCENT OF POPULATION PRODUCING FEATHERS(WILIMAN)
C   QUANTITY OF EACH COMMODITY PRODUCED BY EACH PRODUCING MEMBER OF
C     VILLAGE OF ORIGIN PER YEAR
C     PRODAX(I)=UNITS OF AXES/PRODUCER/YEAR (ABUNA)
C     PRODSA(I)=UNITS OF SALT/PRODUCER/YEAR (WILIMAN)
C     PRODSH(I)=UNITS OF SHELLS/PRODUCER/YEAR (ABUNA)
C     PRODFE(I)=UNITS OF FEATHERS/PRODUCER/YEAR (WILIMAN)
C   QUANTITY OF EACH COMMODITY EXPORTED BY EACH VILLAGE
C     EXPAX(J)=AMOUNT OF AXES EXPORTED
C     EXPSA(J)=AMOUNT OF SALT EXPORTED
C     EXPSH(J)=AMOUNT OF SALT EXPORTED
C     EXPFE(J)=AMOUNT OF FEATHERS EXPORTED
C   NEED OF EACH VILLAGE FOR VITAL COMMODITIES
C     NEEDAX(J)=NEED OF EACH VILLAGE FOR AXES
C     NEEDSA(J)=NEED OF EACH VILLAGE FOR SALT
C   ACCESSMENT OF PRODUCING VILLAGES OF YEAR'S EXCHANGE
C     ACESAX=ACCESSMENT OF AXE PRODUCERS OF THE YEAR'S EXCHANGE
C     ACESSA=ACCESSMENT OF THE SALT PRODUCERS OF THE YEAR'S EXCHANGE
C   XCHNGE(L)=EXCHANGE RATIOS BETWEEN TWO VILLAGES:
C     AXES EXPORTED TO SALT RECEIVED
C ***************************
C ** DECLARATIONS **
C *****************
1         INTEGER  POP(60,8)
2         REAL PRODAX(61),PRODSA(61),PRODSH(61),PRODFE(61),EXPAX(60,8),
         1 EXPSA(60,8),EXPSH(61,8),EXPFE(61,8),NEEDAX(60,8),NEEDSA(60,8),
         2 XCHNGE(60,7),LABRAX,LABRSA,LABRSH,LABRFE,ACESAX(60),ACESSA(60)
3         CHARACTER*8 VILL(8)/'ABUNA','LOGATA','DLOKA','PALMATIK',
         1 'WANDUT','DOLOMAL','WILABUT','WILAMAN'/
4         COMMON PCINT
5         CHARACTER*10 POINT(60,8)
6         DIMENSION AXESL(5),SALTL(5),SHELLL(5),FEATHL(5)
7         DIMENSION POPULA(3),EXPORT(3),EXCHA(4),AXEXP(3),SALTE(3)
8         DATA POPULA/'POPU','LATI','ON  '/,EXPORT/' EXP','ORTS','    '/
9         DATA EXCHA/'EXCH','ANGE',' RAT','IOS '/
10        DATA AXEXP/'AXE ','EXPO','RTS '/,SALTE/'SALT',' EXP','ORTS'/
11        DATA AXESL/'A  ','X  ','E  ','S  ','   '/
12        DATA SALTL/'S  ','A  ','L  ','T  ','   '/
13        DATA SHELLL/'S  ','H  ','E  ','L  ','L  '/
14        DATA FEATHL/'F  ','E  ','A  ','T  ','H  '/
C **************************************
C ** READ INPUT AND INITIALIZE VARIABLES **
C **************************************
C ** READ FILE OF POPULATION
15        DO 2 I=1,60
16        PRODAX(I)=5.0
17        READ (5,1) (POP(I,J),J=1,8)
18    1   FORMAT (2X,8(2X,I3))
19    2   CONTINUE
C ** SET INITIAL PRODUCTION VALUES FOR ALL COMMODITIES
20        DO 3 I=1,61
21        PRODSA(I)=150.0
22        PRODSH(I)=20.0
23    3   PRODFE(I)=10.0
C ** SET INITIAL PRODUCTION PARTICIPANT PERCENTAGE
24        LABRAX=.09
25        LABRSA=.10
26        LABRSH=.15
27        LABRFE=.17
C ** INITIALIZE SHELL AND FEATHER ARRAYS FOR ALTERNATE ASSESSMENT
C ** INCLUDING REGULATORY GOODS RECIEVED  THE PREVIOUS YEAR
28        EXPSH(1,1)=(PRODSH(1)*(POP(1,1)*LABRSH))/2
29        EXPFE(1,8)=(PRODFE(1)*(POP(1,8)*LABRFE))/2
30        DO 4 J=2,8
31        EXPSH(1,J)=EXPSH(1,J-1)/2
32    4   EXPFE(1,9-J)=EXPFE(1,10-J)/2
C ****************************************
C ** RUN EXCHANGE CYCLE FOR 60 YEARS **
C ****************************************
33        DO 13 I=1,60
C ** COMPUTE CONSUMPTION VALUES OF AXES AND SALT FOR EACH TOWN
34        DO 5 J=1,8
35        NEEDAX(I,J)=POP(I,J)*.05
36    5   NEEDSA(I,J)=POP(I,J)*1.6
C ** COMPUTE EXPORT VALUES FOR COMMODITIES FOR VILLAGE OF ORIGIN
37        EXPAX(I,1)=PRODAX(I)*(POP(I,1)*LABRAX)-NEEDAX(I,1)
38        EXPSA(I,8)=PRODSA(I)*(POP(I,8)*LABRSA)-NEEDSA(I,8)
39        EXPSH(I+1,1)=(PRODSH(I)*(POP(I,1)*LABRSH))/2
40        EXPFE(I+1,8)=(PRODFE(I)*(POP(I,8)*LABRFE))/2
```

240

```
      C ** CCMPUTE EXPORT VALUES OF EACH COMMODITY FOR EACH VILLAGE
 41           DO 6 J=2,8
 42           EXPAX(I,J)=EXPAX(I,J-1)-NEEDAX(I,J)
 43           EXPSA(I,9-J)=EXPSA(I,10-J)-NEEDSA(I,9-J)
 44           EXPSH(I+1,J)=EXPSH((I+1),J-1)/2
 45     6     EXPFE(I+1,9-J)=EXPFE(I+1,10-J)/2
      C ** CCMPUTE EXCHANGE RATIOS
 46           DO 8 J=1,7
 47           IF (EXPSA(I,J+1).LE.0.0) GO TO 7
 48           XCHNGE(I,J)=EXPAX(I,J)/EXPSA(I,J+1)
 49           GO TO 8
 50     7     XCHNGE(I,J)=0.000000
 51     8     CONTINUE
      C ** CCMPUTE ASSESSMENT VALUES FOR AX PRODUCERS AND ADJUST PRODUCTION
 52           IF (EXPSA(I,2).LE.0.0) GO TO 9
 53           ACESAX(I)=1+((EXPFE(I+1,1)-EXPFE(I,1))/EXPSH(I,1))
 54           GO TO 10
      C ** CCMPUTE ALTERNATIVE ASSESSMENT VALUE IN CASE OF FAILURE OF SALT
      C ** PRODUCER TC PRODUCE ENOUGH SALT TO SUPPORT THE SYSTEM
 55     9     ACESAX(I)=EXPFE(I+1,1)/EXPFE(I,1)
 56     10    CONTINUE
 57           LABRAX=LABRAX*ACESAX(I)
      C ** CCMPUTE ASSESSMENT VALUE FOR SALT PRODUCERS AND ADJUST PRODUCTION
 58           IF (EXPAX(I,7).LE.0.0) GO TO 11
 59           ACESSA(I)=1+((EXPSH(I+1,8)-EXPSH(I,8))/EXPFE(I,8))
 60           GO TO 12
      C ** CCMPUTE ALTERNATIVE ASSESSMENT VALUE IN THE CASE OF FAILURE OF
      C ** AXE PRODUCERS TO PRODUCE ENOUGH AXES TO SUPPORT THE SYSTEM
 61     11    ACESSA(I)=EXPSH(I+1,8)/EXPSH(I,8)
 62     12    CONTINUE
 63           LABRSA=LABRSA*ACESSA(I)
 64     13    CONTINUE
      C ****************************************************************
      C ** CUTPUT RESULTS OF SIMULATED EXCHANGE FOR 60 YEARS **
      C ****************************************************************
      C ** PRINT TABLE OF VILLAGE POPULATIONS
 65           WRITE (6,29) POPULA
 66           WRITE (6,15)  (VILL(I),I=1,8)
 67           DO 14 I=1,60
 68     14    WRITE (6,16) I,(POP(I,J),J=1,8)
 69     15    FORMAT (13X,8(A8,2X))
 70     16    FORMAT ('0YEAR ',I2,8(6X,I4))
      C ** PRINT TABLE OF PRODUCTION, EXPORTS, AND ASSESSMENT
 71           WRITE (6,29) EXPORT
 72           DO 17 L=1,6
 73           WRITE (6,18)  (VILL(J),J=1,8)
 74           DO 17 K=1,10
 75           I=(L-1)*10+K
 76           WRITE (6,19)  I
 77           WRITE (6,20)  AXESL  ,LABRAX,(EXPAX(I,J),J=1,8),ACESAX(I)
 78           WRITE (6,20)  SALTL  ,LABRSA,(EXPSA(I,J),J=1,8),ACESSA(I)
 79           WRITE (6,21)  SHELLL ,LABRSH,(EXPSH(I+1,J),J=1,8)
 80     17    WRITE (6,21)  FEATHL ,LABRFE,(EXPFE(I+1,J),J=1,8)
 81     18    FORMAT (11X,'PRODUCE ',5X,8(A8,4X),1X,'ASSESSMENT')
 82     19    FORMAT ('0YEAR ',I2)
 83     20    FORMAT (3X,5A1,2X,F7.3,5X,8(F10.3,2X),2X,F10.4)
 84     21    FORMAT (3X,5A1,2X,F7.3,5X,8(F10.3,2X))
      C ** PRINT TABLE OF EXCHANGE RATIOS
 85           WRITE (6,29) EXCHA
 86           WRITE (6,24)  (VILL(I),I=1,7)
 87           WRITE (6,25)
 88           WRITE (6,24)  (VILL(I),I=2,8)
 89           DO 22 I=1,60
 90     22    WRITE (6,23) I,(XCHNGE(I,J),J=1,7)
 91     23    FORMAT ('0YEAR ',I2,3X,7 (3X,F10.3,3X))
 92     24    FORMAT ('0',9X,7(8X,A8))
 93     25    FORMAT ('+',9X,7(6X,'_____'))
      C ** CALL SUBROUTINE GRAPH TO GRAPH AXE PRODUCTION
 94           CALL GRAPH (EXPAX,60,8)
 95           WRITE (6,29) AXEXP
 96           WRITE (6,30)  (VILL(M),M=1,8)
 97           DO 26 I=1,60
 98     26    WRITE (6,31) I,(POINT(I,J),J=1,8)
 99           CALL GRAPH (EXPSA,60,8)
100           WRITE (6,29) SALTE
101           WRITE (6,30)  (VILL(M),M=1,8)
102           DO 27 I=1,60
103     27    WRITE (6,31) I,(POINT(I,J),J=1,8)
      C ** CALL SUBROUTINE GRAPH TO GRAPH EXCHANGE RATIOS
104           CALL GRAPH (XCHNGE,60,7)
105           WRITE (6,29) EXCHA
106           WRITE (6,32)  (VILL(I),I=1,7)
107           WRITE (6,33)
108           WRITE (6,32)  (VILL(I),I=2,8)
109           DO 28 I=1,60
110     28    WRITE (6,34) I,(POINT(I,J),J=1,7)
111     29    FORMAT ('1',53X,4A4)
112     30    FORMAT ('0',7X,3(6X,A8),4X,5(6X,A8))
113     31    FORMAT ('0YEAR ',I2,2X,8 (4X,A8))
114     32    FORMAT (8X,2(6X,A8),4X,5 (6X,A8))
115     33    FORMAT ('+',7X,2(4X,'_____'),4X,5(4X,'_____'))
116     34    FORMAT ('0YEAR',I2,2X,7(4X,A10))
117           STOP
118           END
```

241

```
119        SUBROUTINE GRAPH (X,L,M)
      C ***************************************************
      C ** SUBROUTINE TO CONVERT VALUES INTO AN INTEGER GRAPH**
      C ***************************************************
      C ** XMAX=MAXIMUM VALUE OF LINE TO BE GRAPHED
      C ** XMIN=MINIMUM VALUE OF LINE TO BE GRAPHED
      C ** RANGE=RANGE BETWEEN MINIMUM AND MAXIMUM VALUES
      C ** INTRVL=INTERVALS BETWEEN POINTS OF GRAPH ON A SCALE FROM 1 TO 10
      C ** TEMP=INTEGER VALUE OF POINT TO BE PLOTTED
      C ** CHAR=CHARACTER REPRESENTATION OF POINT
      C ** POINT=ARRAY OF CHARACTERS OF PLOT
      C ***************************************************
      C ** DECLARATIONS
120        REAL X(L,M), XMAX, XMIN, INTRVL
121        INTEGER TEMP(60,8)
122        CHARACTER*10 POINT(60,8)
123        CHARACTER*10 CHAR(11)/'*      ',' ',' *      ',' ',' *      ',' ',
          1'  *      ',' ',' *      ',' ',' *      ',
          2'  *      ',' ',' *,'      *,' ',' *,'      */
124        COMMON PCINT
      C ** FIND MINIMUM AND MAXIMUM VALUES OF LINE TO BE GRAPHED
125        DO 3 J=1,M
126        XMAX=X(1,J)
127        XMIN=X(1,J)
128        DO 2 I=2,L
129        IF (XMIN.LE.X(I,J)) GO TO 1
130        XMIN=X(I,J)
131        GO TO 2
132   1    CONTINUE
133        IF (XMAX.GE.X(I,J)) GO TO 2
134        XMAX=X(I,J)
135   2    CONTINUE
      C ** COMPUTE RANGE OF GRAPH
136        RANGE=XMAX-XMIN
      C ** COMPUTE INTERVALS OF POINTS ON GRAPH
137        INTRVL=RANGE/10
138        DO 3 I=1,L
      C ** COMPUTE INTEGER VALUE OF POINT
139        TEMP(I,J)=(X(I,J)-XMIN)/INTRVL
      C ** MAKE CHARACTER REPRESENTATION OF THE POINT
140        POINT(I,J)=CHAR(TEMP(I,J)+1)
141   3    CONTINUE
142        RETURN
143        END


      *RUN
```

					POPULATION			
	ABUNA	LOGATA	DLOKA	FALMATIK	WANDUT	DOLOMAL	WIDABUT	WILAMAN
YEAR 1	178	199	200	181	215	230	210	180
YEAR 2	181	203	199	184	212	231	215	171
YEAR 3	188	208	198	185	208	225	212	175
YEAR 4	165	210	194	180	210	229	210	170
YEAR 5	180	202	195	188	220	233	211	171
YEAR 6	182	202	195	164	221	213	209	177
YEAR 7	190	206	192	169	226	216	211	178
YEAR 8	190	204	172	177	207	218	211	177
YEAR 9	188	205	169	183	212	215	213	175
YEAR 10	187	214	172	188	220	223	220	184
YEAR 11	181	212	176	197	226	224	223	190
YEAR 12	178	221	185	203	225	227	221	195
YEAR 13	181	219	190	204	228	232	223	206
YEAR 14	184	212	190	200	228	231	221	201
YEAR 15	182	208	190	198	227	230	225	201
YEAR 16	184	208	195	200	232	231	229	201
YEAR 17	184	213	198	201	230	233	214	205
YEAR 18	193	219	197	200	231	234	218	202
YEAR 19	193	225	159	196	202	232	220	201
YEAR 20	200	225	205	195	208	190	226	202
YEAR 21	203	230	206	196	216	198	233	200
YEAR 22	163	233	207	197	221	196	235	202
YEAR 23	163	193	208	199	226	200	232	186
YEAR 24	162	201	208	205	226	199	235	19?

242

YEAR 25	171	206	207	215	230	200	234	188
YEAR 26	174	207	208	212	228	203	237	189
YEAR 27	181	216	205	214	230	214	241	195
YEAR 28	177	218	205	216	224	215	238	195
YEAR 29	170	225	204	221	224	214	235	195
YEAR 30	172	227	205	185	230	213	234	190
YEAR 31	174	227	205	189	233	212	239	184
YEAR 32	183	234	202	199	236	219	220	188
YEAR 33	188	235	205	205	219	213	226	190
YEAR 34	186	238	209	205	228	216	228	187
YEAR 35	187	239	210	208	237	215	228	192
YEAR 36	186	241	213	211	234	221	234	172
YEAR 37	180	243	213	214	236	225	237	178
YEAR 38	177	250	208	216	234	226	244	178
YEAR 39	172	254	208	205	235	229	250	176
YEAR 40	176	263	179	206	242	209	256	177
YEAR 41	174	261	183	211	246	213	249	182
YEAR 42	176	261	102	213	248	209	254	184
YEAR 43	174	267	184	212	245	204	249	190
YEAR 44	174	269	185	214	245	201	253	195
YEAR 45	183	275	188	219	229	213	251	194
YEAR 46	183	272	194	222	219	213	217	192
YEAR 47	188	270	199	215	214	220	215	199
YEAR 48	196	273	206	180	216	217	226	209
YEAR 49	205	275	216	126	219	220	225	209
YEAR 50	199	279	212	185	223	226	230	204
YEAR 51	200	282	207	186	217	230	230	205
YEAR 52	174	255	217	196	221	235	232	214
YEAR 53	178	257	224	196	219	237	232	170
YEAR 54	177	259	233	196	219	243	228	169
YEAR 55	178	261	230	198	221	244	234	170
YEAR 56	182	260	230	199	230	236	241	168
YEAR 57	191	264	238	199	232	233	244	172
YEAR 58	187	265	249	198	234	238	250	177
YEAR 59	194	268	249	202	241	241	250	179
YEAR 60	197	266	248	212	239	242	255	179

EXPORTS

	PRODUCE	ABUNA	LOGATA	DLOKA	FALMATIK	WANDUT	DOLOMAL	WIDABUT	WILAMAN	ASSESSMENT
YEAR 1										
AXES	0.091	71.200	61.250	51.250	42.200	31.450	19.950	9.450	0.450	1.0000
SALT	0.097	151.200	436.000	754.400	1074.400	1364.000	1708.000	2076.000	2412.000	1.0000
SHELL	0.150	267.000	133.500	66.750	33.375	16.687	8.344	4.172	2.086	
FEATH	0.170	1.195	2.391	4.781	9.562	19.125	38.250	76.500	153.000	
YEAR 2										
AXES	0.091	72.400	62.250	52.300	43.100	32.500	20.950	10.200	1.650	0.9998
SALT	0.097	11.399	300.999	625.799	944.199	1238.599	1577.799	1947.399	2291.399	1.0002
SHELL	0.150	271.500	135.750	67.875	33.937	16.969	8.484	4.242	2.121	
FEATH	0.170	1.136	2.271	4.542	9.084	18.169	36.337	72.675	145.350	
YEAR 3										
AXES	0.091	75.181	64.781	54.881	45.631	35.231	23.981	13.381	4.631	1.0001
SALT	0.097	67.199	368.000	700.800	1017.600	1313.600	1646.400	2006.400	2345.600	1.0006
SHELL	0.150	282.000	141.000	70.500	35.250	17.625	8.812	4.406	2.203	
FEATH	0.170	1.162	2.324	4.648	9.297	18.594	37.188	74.375	148.750	
YEAR 4										
AXES	0.091	73.989	63.489	53.789	44.789	34.289	22.839	12.339	3.839	0.9999
SALT	0.097	11.219	307.219	643.219	953.619	1241.619	1577.619	1944.019	2280.019	0.9998
SHELL	0.150	277.500	138.750	69.375	34.687	17.344	8.672	4.336	2.168	
FEATH	0.170	1.129	2.258	4.516	9.031	18.062	36.125	72.250	144.500	

243

		PRODUCE	ABUNA	LOGATA	DLOKA	PALMATIK	WANDUT	DOLOMAL	WIDABUT	WILAMAN	ASSESSMENT
YEAR 5											
AXES	0.091	71.980	61.880	52.130	42.730	31.730	20.080	9.530	0.980		1.0000
SALT	0.097	6.425	294.425	617.625	929.625	1230.425	1582.425	1955.225	2292.825		0.9996
SHELL	0.150	270.000	135.000	67.500	33.750	16.875	8.437	4.219	2.109		
FEATH	0.170	1.136	2.271	4.542	9.084	18.169	36.337	72.675	145.350		
YEAR 6											
AXES	0.091	72.782	62.682	52.932	44.732	33.682	23.032	12.582	3.732		1.0001
SALT	0.097	154.598	445.798	768.998	1080.998	1343.398	1696.998	2037.798	2372.198		1.0002
SHELL	0.150	273.000	136.500	68.250	34.125	17.062	8.531	4.266	2.133		
FEATH	0.170	1.175	2.351	4.702	9.403	18.806	37.612	75.225	150.450		
YEAR 7											
AXES	0.091	75.993	65.693	56.093	47.643	36.343	25.543	14.993	6.093		1.0000
SALT	0.097	130.030	434.030	763.629	1070.829	1341.229	1702.829	2048.429	2386.029		1.0006
SHELL	0.150	285.000	142.500	71.250	35.625	17.812	8.906	4.453	2.227		
FEATH	0.170	1.182	2.364	4.728	9.456	18.912	37.825	75.650	151.300		
YEAR 8											
AXES	0.091	75.995	65.795	57.195	48.345	37.995	27.095	16.545	7.695		1.0000
SALT	0.097	167.879	471.879	798.279	1073.479	1356.678	1687.878	2036.678	2374.278		1.0000
SHELL	0.150	285.000	142.500	71.250	35.625	17.812	8.906	4.453	2.227		
FEATH	0.170	1.175	2.351	4.702	9.403	18.806	37.612	75.225	150.450		
YEAR 9											
AXES	0.091	75.193	64.943	56.493	47.343	36.743	25.993	15.343	6.593		1.0000
SALT	0.097	131.449	432.249	760.249	1030.649	1323.449	1662.649	2006.649	2347.449		0.9998
SHELL	0.150	282.000	141.000	70.500	35.250	17.625	8.812	4.406	2.203		
FEATH	0.170	1.162	2.324	4.648	9.297	18.594	37.188	74.375	148.750		
YEAR 10											
AXES	0.091	74.790	64.090	55.490	46.090	35.090	23.940	12.940	3.740		1.0002
SALT	0.097	189.344	488.544	830.944	1106.144	1406.944	1758.944	2115.744	2467.744		0.9999
SHELL	0.150	280.500	140.250	70.125	35.062	17.531	8.766	4.383	2.191		
FEATH	0.170	1.222	2.444	4.887	9.775	19.550	39.100	78.200	156.400		
		PRODUCE	ABUNA	LOGATA	DLOKA	PALMATIK	WANDUT	DOLOMAL	WIDABUT	WILAMAN	ASSESSMENT
YEAR 11											
AXES	0.091	72.407	61.807	53.007	43.157	31.857	20.657	9.507	0.007		1.0001
SALT	0.097	245.589	535.189	874.389	1155.989	1471.189	1832.789	2191.189	2547.989		0.9996
SHELL	0.150	271.500	135.750	67.875	33.937	16.969	8.484	4.242	2.121		
FEATH	0.170	1.262	2.523	5.047	10.094	20.188	40.375	80.750	161.500		
YEAR 12											
AXES	0.091	71.218	60.168	50.918	40.768	29.518	18.168	7.118	-2.632		1.0001
SALT	0.097	277.726	562.526	916.125	1212.125	1536.926	1896.926	2260.125	2613.725		0.9998
SHELL	0.150	267.000	133.500	66.750	33.375	16.687	8.344	4.172	2.086		
FEATH	0.170	1.295	2.590	5.180	10.359	20.719	41.437	82.875	165.750		
YEAR 13											
AXES	0.091	72.428	61.478	51.978	41.778	30.378	18.778	7.628	-2.672		1.0003
SALT	0.097	397.293	686.893	1037.292	1341.292	1667.692	2032.492	2403.692	2760.492		1.0002
SHELL	0.150	271.500	135.750	67.875	33.937	16.969	8.484	4.242	2.121		
FEATH	0.170	1.368	2.736	5.472	10.944	21.887	43.775	87.550	175.100		
YEAR 14											
AXES	0.091	73.652	63.052	53.552	43.552	32.152	20.602	9.552	-0.498		0.9999
SALT	0.097	348.527	642.927	982.127	1286.127	1606.127	1970.927	2340.527	2694.126		1.0002
SHELL	0.150	276.000	138.000	69.000	34.500	17.250	8.625	4.312	2.156		
FEATH	0.170	1.335	2.670	5.339	10.678	21.356	42.712	85.425	170.850		
YEAR 15											
AXES	0.091	72.641	62.441	52.941	43.041	31.691	20.191	8.941	-1.109		1.0000
SALT	0.097	358.731	649.931	982.731	1286.731	1603.531	1966.731	2334.731	2694.731		0.9999
SHELL	0.150	273.000	136.500	68.250	34.125	17.062	8.531	4.266	2.133		
FEATH	0.170	1.335	2.670	5.339	10.678	21.356	42.712	85.425	170.850		
YEAR 16											
AXES	0.091	73.641	63.241	53.491	43.491	31.891	20.341	8.891	-1.159		1.0000
SALT	0.097	327.917	622.317	955.117	1267.117	1587.117	1958.317	2327.917	2694.316		1.0001
SHELL	0.150	276.000	138.000	69.000	34.500	17.250	8.625	4.312	2.156		
FEATH	0.170	1.335	2.670	5.339	10.678	21.356	42.712	85.425	170.850		
YEAR 17											
AXES	0.091	73.641	62.991	53.091	43.041	31.541	19.891	9.191	-1.059		1.0001
SALT	0.097	391.553	685.953	1026.753	1343.553	1665.153	2033.153	2405.953	2748.353		1.0000
SHELL	0.150	276.000	138.000	69.000	34.500	17.250	8.625	4.312	2.156		
FEATH	0.170	1.361	2.723	5.445	10.891	21.781	43.562	87.125	174.250		
YEAR 18											
AXES	0.091	77.252	66.302	56.452	46.452	34.902	23.202	12.302	2.202		0.9999
SALT	0.097	320.932	629.732	980.132	1295.332	1615.332	1984.932	2359.332	2708.132		1.0006
SHELL	0.150	289.500	144.750	72.375	36.187	18.094	9.047	4.523	2.262		
FEATH	0.170	1.341	2.683	5.366	10.731	21.462	42.925	85.850	171.700		
YEAR 19											
AXES	0.091	77.245	65.995	56.045	46.245	36.145	24.545	13.545	3.495		1.0000
SALT	0.097	349.348	658.148	1018.148	1336.548	1650.148	1973.348	2344.548	2696.548		1.0000
SHELL	0.150	289.500	144.750	72.375	36.187	18.094	9.047	4.523	2.262		
FEATH	0.170	1.335	2.670	5.339	10.678	21.356	42.712	85.425	170.850		

YEAR 20

	PRODUCE	ABUNA	LOGATA	DLOKA	FALMATIK	WANDUT	DOLOMAL	WIDABUT	WILAMAN	ASSESSMENT
AXES	0.091	80.045	68.795	58.545	48.795	38.395	28.895	17.595	7.495	1.0000
SALT	0.097	391.563	711.563	1071.563	1399.563	1711.563	2044.363	2348.363	2709.963	1.0005
SHELL	0.150	300.000	150.000	75.000	37.500	18.750	9.375	4.687	2.344	
FEATH	0.170	1.341	2.683	5.366	10.731	21.462	42.925	85.850	171.700	

YEAR 21

		ABUNA	LOGATA	DLOKA	FALMATIK	WANDUT	DOLOMAL	WIDABUT	WILAMAN	ASSESSMENT
AXES	0.091	81.248	69.748	59.448	49.648	38.848	28.948	17.298	7.298	1.0000
SALT	0.097	313.371	638.171	1006.171	1335.771	1649.371	1994.970	2311.771	2684.571	1.0002
SHELL	0.150	304.500	152.250	76.125	38.062	19.031	9.516	4.758	2.379	
FEATH	0.170	1.328	2.656	5.313	10.625	21.250	42.500	85.000	170.000	

YEAR 22

		ABUNA	LOGATA	DLOKA	FALMATIK	WANDUT	DOLOMAL	WIDABUT	WILAMAN	ASSESSMENT
AXES	0.091	65.235	53.585	43.235	33.385	22.335	12.535	0.785	-9.315	1.0000
SALT	0.097	388.837	649.637	1022.437	1353.637	1668.837	2022.437	2336.036	2712.036	0.9972
SHELL	0.150	244.500	122.250	61.125	30.562	15.281	7.641	3.820	1.910	
FEATH	0.170	1.341	2.683	5.366	10.731	21.462	42.925	85.850	171.700	

YEAR 23

		ABUNA	LOGATA	DLOKA	FALMATIK	WANDUT	DOLOMAL	WIDABUT	WILAMAN	ASSESSMENT
AXES	0.091	65.238	55.588	45.188	35.238	23.938	13.938	2.338	-6.962	0.9996
SALT	0.097	215.915	476.715	785.515	1118.315	1436.715	1798.315	2118.315	2489.515	1.0000
SHELL	0.150	244.500	122.250	61.125	30.562	15.281	7.641	3.820	1.910	
FEATH	0.170	1.235	2.470	4.941	9.881	19.762	39.525	79.050	158.100	

YEAR 24

		ABUNA	LOGATA	DLOKA	FALMATIK	WANDUT	DOLOMAL	WIDABUT	WILAMAN	ASSESSMENT
AXES	0.091	64.806	54.756	44.356	34.106	22.806	12.856	1.106	-8.144	1.0000
SALT	0.097	178.530	437.730	759.330	1092.130	1420.130	1781.730	2100.130	2476.130	0.9999
SHELL	0.150	243.000	121.500	60.750	30.375	15.187	7.594	3.797	1.898	
FEATH	0.170	1.229	2.457	4.914	9.828	19.656	39.312	78.625	157.250	

YEAR 25

		ABUNA	LOGATA	DLOKA	FALMATIK	WANDUT	DOLOMAL	WIDABUT	WILAMAN	ASSESSMENT
AXES	0.091	68.404	58.104	47.754	37.004	25.504	15.504	3.804	-5.596	1.0001
SALT	0.097	175.274	448.874	778.474	1109.674	1453.674	1821.674	2141.674	2516.074	1.0007
SHELL	0.150	256.500	128.250	64.125	32.062	16.031	8.016	4.008	2.004	
FEATH	0.170	1.248	2.497	4.994	9.987	19.975	39.950	79.900	159.800	

YEAR 26

		ABUNA	LOGATA	DLOKA	FALMATIK	WANDUT	DOLOMAL	WIDABUT	WILAMAN	ASSESSMENT
AXES	0.091	69.611	59.261	48.861	38.261	26.861	16.711	4.861	-4.589	1.0000
SALT	0.097	180.954	459.354	790.554	1123.354	1462.554	1827.354	2152.154	2531.354	1.0002
SHELL	0.150	261.000	130.500	65.250	32.625	16.312	8.156	4.078	2.039	
FEATH	0.170	1.255	2.510	5.020	10.041	20.081	40.162	80.325	160.650	

YEAR 27

		ABUNA	LOGATA	DLOKA	FALMATIK	WANDUT	DOLOMAL	WIDABUT	WILAMAN	ASSESSMENT
AXES	0.091	72.413	61.613	51.363	40.663	29.163	18.463	6.413	-3.337	1.0002
SALT	0.097	210.755	500.355	845.955	1173.955	1516.355	1884.355	2226.755	2612.354	1.0005
SHELL	0.150	271.500	135.750	67.875	33.937	16.969	8.484	4.242	2.121	
FEATH	0.170	1.295	2.590	5.180	10.359	20.719	41.437	82.875	165.750	

YEAR 28

		ABUNA	LOGATA	DLOKA	FALMATIK	WANDUT	DOLOMAL	WIDABUT	WILAMAN	ASSESSMENT
AXES	0.091	70.825	59.925	49.675	38.875	27.675	16.925	5.025	-4.725	1.0000
SALT	0.097	225.045	508.245	857.045	1185.045	1530.645	1889.044	2233.044	2613.844	0.9997
SHELL	0.150	265.500	132.750	66.375	33.187	16.594	8.297	4.148	2.074	
FEATH	0.170	1.295	2.590	5.180	10.359	20.719	41.437	82.875	165.750	

YEAR 29

		ABUNA	LOGATA	DLOKA	FALMATIK	WANDUT	DOLOMAL	WIDABUT	WILAMAN	ASSESSMENT
AXES	0.091	68.024	56.774	46.574	35.524	24.324	13.624	1.874	-7.876	1.0000
SALT	0.097	224.216	496.216	856.216	1182.616	1536.216	1894.616	2237.016	2613.016	0.9995
SHELL	0.150	255.000	127.500	63.750	31.875	15.937	7.969	3.984	1.992	
FEATH	0.170	1.295	2.590	5.180	10.359	20.719	41.437	82.875	165.750	

YEAR 30

	PRODUCE	ABUNA	LOGATA	DLOKA	FALMATIK	WANDUT	DOLOMAL	WIDABUT	WILAMAN	ASSESSMENT
AXES	0.091	68.825	57.475	47.225	37.975	26.475	15.825	4.125	-5.375	0.9999
SALT	0.097	199.004	474.204	837.404	1165.404	1461.404	1829.404	2170.204	2544.604	1.0001
SHELL	0.150	258.000	129.000	64.500	32.250	16.125	8.062	4.031	2.016	
FEATH	0.170	1.262	2.523	5.047	10.094	20.188	40.375	80.750	161.500	

YEAR 31

		ABUNA	LOGATA	DLOKA	FALMATIK	WANDUT	DOLOMAL	WIDABUT	WILAMAN	ASSESSMENT
AXES	0.091	69.615	58.265	48.015	38.565	26.915	16.315	4.365	-4.835	0.9998
SALT	0.097	98.238	376.638	739.838	1067.838	1370.238	1743.038	2082.238	2464.638	1.0001
SHELL	0.150	261.000	130.500	65.250	32.625	16.312	8.156	4.078	2.039	
FEATH	0.170	1.222	2.444	4.887	9.775	19.550	39.100	78.200	156.400	

YEAR 32

		ABUNA	LOGATA	DLOKA	FALMATIK	WANDUT	DOLOMAL	WIDABUT	WILAMAN	ASSESSMENT
AXES	0.091	73.203	61.503	51.402	41.452	29.652	18.702	7.702	-1.698	1.0001
SALT	0.097	129.824	422.624	797.024	1120.224	1438.624	1816.224	2166.624	2518.624	1.0007
SHELL	0.150	274.500	137.250	68.625	34.312	17.156	8.578	4.289	2.145	
FEATH	0.170	1.248	2.497	4.994	9.987	19.975	39.950	79.900	159.800	

YEAR 33

		ABUNA	LOGATA	DLOKA	FALMATIK	WANDUT	DOLOMAL	WIDABUT	WILAMAN	ASSESSMENT
AXES	0.091	75.211	63.461	53.211	42.961	32.011	21.361	10.061	0.561	1.0000
SALT	0.097	161.739	462.539	838.539	1166.539	1494.539	1844.939	2185.739	2547.339	1.0004
SHELL	0.150	282.000	141.000	70.500	35.250	17.625	8.812	4.406	2.203	
FEATH	0.170	1.262	2.523	5.047	10.094	20.188	40.375	80.750	161.500	

YEAR 34

		ABUNA	LOGATA	DLOKA	FALMATIK	WANDUT	DOLOMAL	WIDABUT	WILAMAN	ASSESSMENT
AXES	0.091	74.415	62.515	52.065	41.815	30.415	19.615	8.215	-1.135	0.9999
SALT	0.097	92.144	389.743	770.543	1104.943	1432.943	1797.743	2143.343	2508.143	0.9999
SHELL	0.150	279.000	139.500	69.750	34.875	17.437	8.719	4.359	2.180	
FEATH	0.170	1.242	2.484	4.967	9.934	19.869	39.737	79.475	158.950	

YEAR 35

		ABUNA	LOGATA	DLOKA	FALMATIK	WANDUT	DOLOMAL	WIDABUT	WILAMAN	ASSESSMENT
AXES	0.091	74.809	62.859	52.359	41.959	30.109	19.359	7.959	-1.641	1.0001
SALT	0.097	136.389	435.589	817.989	1153.989	1486.789	1865.989	2209.989	2574.789	1.0001
SHELL	0.150	280.500	140.250	70.125	35.062	17.531	8.766	4.383	2.191	
FEATH	0.170	1.275	2.550	5.100	10.200	20.400	40.800	81.600	163.200	

```
YEAR 36
  AXES    0.C91      74.419     62.369     51.719     41.169     29.469     18.419      6.719     -1.881     0.9995
  SALT    0.C97    -157.229    140.371    525.971    866.771   1204.371   1578.771   1932.370   2306.770     0.9999
  SHELL   0.150     279.000    139.500     69.750     34.875     17.437      8.719      4.359      2.180
  FEATH   0.170       1.142      2.284      4.569      9.137     18.275     36.550     73.100    146.200

YEAR 37
  AXES    0.C91      71.980     59.830     49.180     38.480     26.680     15.430      3.580     -5.320     1.0001
  SALT    0.C97     -89.755    198.245    587.045    927.845   1270.245   1647.845   2007.845   2387.045     0.9995
  SHELL   0.150     270.000    135.000     67.500     33.750     16.875      8.437      4.219      2.109
  FEATH   0.17C       1.182      2.364      4.728      9.456     18.912     37.825     75.650    151.300

YEAR 38
  AXES    0.C91      70.792     58.292     47.892     37.092     25.392     14.092      1.892     -7.008     1.0000
  SALT    0.C57    -102.241    180.959    580.959    913.759   1259.359   1633.759   1995.359   2385.759     0.9998
  SHELL   0.150     265.500    132.750     66.375     33.187     16.594      8.297      4.148      2.074
  FEATH   0.170       1.182      2.364      4.728      9.456     18.912     37.825     75.650    151.300

YEAR 39
  AXES    0.091      68.792     56.092     45.692     35.442     23.692     12.242     -0.258     -9.058     0.9999
  SALT    0.C97    -126.461    148.739    555.139    887.939   1215.939   1591.939   1958.339   2358.339     0.9718
  SHELL   0.150     258.000    129.000     64.500     32.250     16.125      8.062      4.031      2.016
  FEATH   0.170       1.169      2.337      4.675      9.350     18.700     37.400     74.800    149.600

YEAR 40
  AXES    0.C91      70.388     57.238     48.288     37.988     25.888     15.438      2.638     -6.212     1.0000
  SALT    0.C57    -152.860    128.740    549.540    835.940   1165.540   1552.740   1887.140   2296.740     1.0003
  SHELL   0.150     264.000    132.000     66.000     33.000     16.500      8.250      4.125      2.062
  FEATH   0.170       1.175      2.351      4.702      9.403     18.806     37.612     75.225    150.450
          PRODUCE    ABUNA      LOGATA     DLOKA      FALMATIK   WANDUT     DOLOMAL    WIDABUT    WILAMAN    ASSESSMENT

YEAR 41
  AXES    0.091      69.590     56.540     47.390     36.840     24.540     13.890      1.440     -7.660     1.0001
  SALT    0.C57     -96.753    181.647    599.247    892.047   1229.647   1623.247   1964.047   2362.447     0.9998
  SHELL   0.15C     261.000    130.500     65.250     32.625     16.312      8.156      4.078      2.039
  FEATH   0.170       1.209      2.417      4.834      9.669     19.337     38.675     77.350    154.700

YEAR 42
  AXES    0.C91      70.399     57.349     52.249     41.599     29.199     18.749      6.049     -3.151     1.0001
  SALT    0.C57      47.190    328.790    746.390    909.590   1250.390   1647.190   1981.590   2387.990     1.0002
  SHELL   0.150     264.000    132.000     66.000     33.000     16.500      8.250      4.125      2.062
  FEATH   0.170       1.222      2.444      4.887      9.775     19.550     39.100     78.200    156.400

YEAR 43
  AXES    0.091      69.603     56.253     47.053     36.453     24.203     14.003      1.553     -7.947     1.0002
  SALT    0.C97      10.276    288.676    715.876   1010.276   1349.476   1741.476   2067.876   2466.276     0.9999
  SHELL   0.150     261.000    130.500     65.250     32.625     16.312      8.156      4.078      2.039
  FEATH   0.170       1.262      2.523      5.047     10.094     20.188     40.375     80.750    161.500

YEAR 44
  AXES    0.C91      69.615     56.165     46.915     36.215     23.965     13.915      1.265     -8.485     1.0001
  SALT    0.C97      65.152    343.552    773.951   1069.951   1412.351   1804.351   2125.951   2530.751     1.0000
  SHELL   0.150     261.000    130.500     65.250     32.625     16.312      8.156      4.078      2.039
  FEATH   0.170       1.295      2.590      5.180     10.359     20.719     41.437     82.875    165.750

YEAR 45
  AXES    0.C91      73.226     59.476     50.076     39.126     27.676     17.026      4.476     -5.224     1.0000
  SALT    0.C97      24.974    317.774    757.774   1058.574   1408.974   1775.374   2116.174   2517.774     1.0006
  SHELL   0.150     274.500    137.250     68.625     34.312     17.156      8.578      4.289      2.145
  FEATH   0.170       1.288      2.577      5.153     10.306     20.612     41.225     82.450    164.900

YEAR 46
  AXES    0.C91      73.224     59.624     49.924     38.824     27.874     17.224      6.374     -3.226     1.0000
  SALT    0.C97      61.597    354.997    789.997   1099.997   1455.197   1805.597   2146.397   2493.597     1.0000
  SHELL   0.150     274.500    137.250     68.625     34.312     17.156      8.578      4.289      2.145
  FEATH   0.17C       1.275      2.550      5.100     10.200     20.400     40.800     81.600    163.200

YEAR 47
  AXES    0.091      75.221     61.721     51.771     41.021     30.321     19.321      8.571     -1.379     1.0002
  SALT    0.C57     150.908    451.708    883.708   1202.108   1546.108   1888.508   2240.508   2584.508     1.0004
  SHELL   0.150     282.000    141.000     70.500     35.250     17.625      8.812      4.406      2.203
  FEATH   0.170       1.321      2.643      5.286     10.572     21.144     42.287     84.575    169.150

YEAR 48
  AXES    0.C91      78.436     64.786     54.486     45.486     34.686     23.836     12.536      2.086     1.0002
  SALT    0.C97     293.079    606.678   1043.479   1373.078   1661.078   2006.678   2353.878   2715.478     1.0006
  SHELL   0.150     294.000    147.000     73.500     36.750     18.375      9.187      4.594      2.297
  FEATH   0.170       1.388      2.776      5.552     11.103     22.206     44.412     88.825    177.650

YEAR 49
  AXES    0.C91      82.060     68.310     57.510     51.210     40.260     29.260     18.010      7.560     1.0000
  SALT    0.C57     339.567    667.567   1107.567   1453.167   1654.767   2005.167   2357.167   2717.167     1.0006
  SHELL   0.150     307.500    153.750     76.875     38.437     19.219      9.609      4.805      2.402
  FEATH   0.17C       1.388      2.776      5.552     11.103     22.206     44.412     88.825    177.650

YEAR 50
  AXES    0.C91      79.658     65.708     55.108     45.858     34.708     23.408     11.908      1.708     0.9999
  SALT    0.C97     167.528    485.928    932.328   1271.528   1567.528   1924.328   2285.927   2653.927     0.9996
  SHELL   0.150     298.500    149.250     74.625     37.312     18.656      9.328      4.664      2.332
  FEATH   0.17C       1.355      2.709      5.419     10.837     21.675     43.350     86.700    173.400
          PRODUCE    ABUNA      LOGATA     DLOKA      FALMATIK   WANDUT     DOLOMAL    WIDABUT    WILAMAN    ASSESSMENT

YEAR 51
  AXES    0.C91      80.049     65.949     55.599     46.299     35.449     23.949     12.449      2.199     1.0000
  SALT    0.C57     182.552    502.552    953.752   1284.952   1582.552   1929.751   2297.751   2665.751     1.0001
  SHELL   0.150     300.000    150.000     75.000     37.500     18.750      9.375      4.687      2.344
  FEATH   0.170       1.361      2.723      5.445     10.891     21.781     43.562     87.125    174.250
```

```
YEAR 52
   AXES   0.051      69.644     56.894     46.044     36.244     25.194     13.444      1.844     -8.856     1.0002
   SALT   0.097     334.993    613.393   1021.393   1368.593   1682.193   2035.793   2411.793   2782.993     0.9983
   SHELL  0.150     261.000    130.500     65.250     32.625     16.312      8.156      4.078      2.039
   FEATH  0.170       1.421      2.842      5.684     11.369     22.737     45.475     90.950    181.900

YEAR 53
   AXES   0.091      71.261     58.411     47.211     37.411     26.461     14.611      3.011     -5.489     0.9989
   SALT   0.097    -262.353     22.447    433.647    792.047   1105.647   1456.047   1835.247   2206.447     1.0003
   SHELL  0.150     267.000    133.500     66.750     33.375     16.687      8.344      4.172      2.086
   FEATH  0.170       1.129      2.258      4.516      9.031     18.062     36.125     72.250    144.500

YEAR 54
   AXES   0.051      70.771     57.821     46.171     36.371     25.421     13.271      1.871     -6.579     0.9941
   SALT   0.057    -293.899    -10.699    403.701    776.501   1090.101   1440.501   1829.301   2194.101     0.9999
   SHELL  0.150     265.500    132.750     66.375     33.187     16.594      8.297      4.148      2.074
   FEATH  0.170       1.122      2.245      4.489      8.978     17.956     35.912     71.825    143.650

YEAR 55
   AXES   0.051      70.700     57.650     46.150     36.250     25.200     13.000      1.300     -7.200     1.0059
   SALT   0.057    -298.718    -13.918    403.682    771.682   1088.482   1442.082   1832.482   2206.882     1.0001
   SHELL  0.150     267.000    133.500     66.750     33.375     16.687      8.344      4.172      2.086
   FEATH  0.170       1.129      2.258      4.516      9.031     18.062     36.125     72.250    144.500

YEAR 56
   AXES   0.051      72.770     59.770     48.270     38.320     26.820     15.020      2.970     -5.430     0.9882
   SALT   0.097    -343.683    -52.483    363.517    731.517   1049.917   1417.917   1795.517   2181.117     1.0003
   SHELL  0.150     273.000    136.500     68.250     34.125     17.062      8.531      4.266      2.133
   FEATH  0.170       1.116      2.231      4.462      8.925     17.850     35.700     71.400    142.800

YEAR 57
   AXES   0.051      75.358     62.158     50.258     40.308     28.708     17.058      4.858     -3.742     1.0238
   SALT   0.097    -327.740    -22.140    400.260    781.060   1099.460   1470.660   1843.460   2233.860     1.0007
   SHELL  0.150     286.500    143.250     71.625     35.812     17.906      8.953      4.477      2.238
   FEATH  0.170       1.142      2.284      4.569      9.137     18.275     36.550     73.100    146.200

YEAR 58
   AXES   0.091      75.759     62.509     50.059     40.159     28.459     16.559      4.059     -4.791     1.0001
   SALT   0.097    -292.898      6.302    430.302    828.702   1145.502   1519.902   1900.702   2300.702     0.9997
   SHELL  0.150     280.500    140.250     70.125     35.062     17.531      8.766      4.383      2.191
   FEATH  0.170       1.175      2.351      4.702      9.403     18.806     37.612     75.225    150.450

YEAR 59
   AXES   0.091      78.605     65.205     52.755     42.655     30.605     18.555      6.055     -2.895     1.0000
   SALT   0.057    -306.139      4.261    433.061    831.461   1154.661   1540.260   1925.860   2325.860     1.0005
   SHELL  0.150     291.000    145.500     72.750     36.375     18.187      9.094      4.547      2.273
   FEATH  0.170       1.189      2.377      4.755      9.509     19.019     38.037     76.075    152.150

YEAR 60
   AXES   0.091      79.825     66.525     54.125     43.525     31.575     19.475      6.725     -2.225     1.0000
   SALT   0.097    -327.118    -11.918    413.682    810.482   1149.682   1532.082   1919.282   2327.282     1.0002
   SHELL  0.150     295.500    147.750     73.875     36.937     18.469      9.234      4.617      2.309
   FEATH  0.170       1.189      2.377      4.755      9.509     19.019     38.037     76.075    152.150
```

EXCHANGE RATIOS

	ABUNA	LOGATA	DLOKA	FALMATIK	WANDUT	DOLOMAL	WIDABUT
	LOGATA	DLOKA	FALMATIK	WANDUT	DOLOMAL	WIDABUT	WILAMAN
YEAR 1	0.163	0.081	0.048	0.031	0.018	0.010	0.004
YEAR 2	0.241	0.099	0.055	0.035	0.021	0.011	0.004
YEAR 3	0.204	0.092	0.054	0.035	0.021	0.012	0.006
YEAR 4	0.241	0.099	0.056	0.036	0.022	0.012	0.005
YEAR 5	0.244	0.100	0.056	0.035	0.020	0.010	0.004
YEAR 6	0.163	0.082	0.049	0.033	0.020	0.011	0.005
YEAR 7	0.175	0.086	0.052	0.036	0.021	0.012	0.006
YEAR 8	0.161	0.082	0.053	0.036	0.023	0.013	0.007
YEAR 9	0.174	0.085	0.055	0.036	0.022	0.013	0.007
YEAR 10	0.153	0.077	0.050	0.033	0.020	0.011	0.005
YEAR 11	0.135	0.071	0.046	0.029	0.017	0.009	0.004
YEAR 12	0.127	0.066	0.042	0.027	0.016	0.008	0.003
YEAR 13	0.105	0.059	0.039	0.025	0.015	0.008	0.003
YEAR 14	0.115	0.064	0.042	0.027	0.016	0.009	0.004
YEAR 15	0.112	0.064	0.041	0.027	0.016	0.009	0.003
YEAR 16	0.118	0.066	0.042	0.027	0.016	0.009	0.003
YEAR 17	0.107	0.061	0.040	0.026	0.016	0.008	0.003
YEAR 18	0.123	0.068	0.044	0.029	0.018	0.010	0.005
YEAR 19	0.117	0.065	0.042	0.028	0.018	0.010	0.005

YEAR 20	0.112	0.064	0.042	0.029	0.019	0.012	0.006
YEAR 21	0.127	0.069	0.045	0.030	0.019	0.013	0.006
YEAR 22	0.100	0.052	0.032	0.020	0.011	0.005	0.000
YEAR 23	0.137	0.071	0.040	0.025	0.013	0.007	0.001
YEAR 24	0.148	0.072	0.041	0.024	0.013	0.006	0.000
YEAR 25	0.152	0.075	0.043	0.025	0.014	0.007	0.002
YEAR 26	0.152	0.075	0.043	0.026	0.015	0.008	0.002
YEAR 27	0.145	0.073	0.044	0.027	0.015	0.008	0.002
YEAR 28	0.139	0.070	0.042	0.025	0.015	0.008	0.002
YEAR 29	0.137	0.066	0.039	0.023	0.013	0.006	0.001
YEAR 30	0.145	0.069	0.041	0.026	0.014	0.007	0.002
YEAR 31	0.185	0.079	0.045	0.028	0.015	0.008	0.002
YEAR 32	0.173	0.077	0.046	0.029	0.016	0.009	0.003
YEAR 33	0.163	0.076	0.046	0.029	0.017	0.010	0.004
YEAR 34	0.191	0.081	0.047	0.029	0.017	0.009	0.003
YEAR 35	0.172	0.077	0.045	0.028	0.016	0.009	0.003
YEAR 36	0.530	0.119	0.060	0.034	0.019	0.010	0.003
YEAR 37	0.363	0.102	0.053	0.030	0.016	0.008	0.001
YEAR 38	0.391	0.100	0.052	0.029	0.016	0.007	0.001
YEAR 39	0.462	0.101	0.051	0.029	0.015	0.006	-0.000
YEAR 40	0.547	0.104	0.058	0.033	0.017	0.008	0.001
YEAR 41	0.383	0.094	0.053	0.030	0.015	0.007	0.001
YEAR 42	0.214	0.077	0.057	0.033	0.018	0.009	0.003
YEAR 43	0.241	0.079	0.047	0.027	0.014	0.007	0.001
YEAR 44	0.203	0.073	0.044	0.026	0.013	0.007	0.000
YEAR 45	0.230	0.078	0.047	0.028	0.016	0.008	0.002
YEAR 46	0.207	0.076	0.045	0.027	0.015	0.008	0.003
YEAR 47	0.167	0.070	0.043	0.027	0.016	0.009	0.003
YEAR 48	0.129	0.062	0.040	0.027	0.017	0.010	0.005
YEAR 49	0.123	0.062	0.040	0.031	0.020	0.012	0.007
YEAR 50	0.164	0.070	0.043	0.029	0.018	0.010	0.004
YEAR 51	0.159	0.069	0.043	0.029	0.018	0.010	0.005
YEAR 52	0.114	0.056	0.034	0.022	0.012	0.006	0.001
YEAR 53	3.175	0.135	0.060	0.034	0.018	0.008	0.001
YEAR 54	0.000	0.143	0.059	0.033	0.018	0.007	0.001
YEAR 55	0.000	0.143	0.060	0.033	0.017	0.007	0.001
YEAR 56	0.000	0.164	0.066	0.036	0.019	0.008	0.001
YEAR 57	0.000	0.155	0.064	0.037	0.020	0.009	0.002
YEAR 58	12.021	0.145	0.060	0.035	0.019	0.009	0.002
YEAR 59	18.449	0.151	0.063	0.037	0.020	0.010	0.003
YEAR 60	0.000	0.161	0.067	0.038	0.021	0.010	0.003

AXE EXPORTS

	AEUNA	LOGATA	DLOKA	PALMATIK	WANDUT	DOLOMAL	WIDABUT	WILAMAN
YEAR 1	*	*	*	*	*	*	*	*
YEAR 2	*	*	*	*	*	*	*	*
YEAR 3	*	*	*	*	*	*	*	*
YEAR 4	*	*	*	*	*	*	*	*
YEAR 5	*	*	*	*	*	*	*	*
YEAR 6	*	*	*	*	*	*	*	*
YEAR 7	*	*	*	*	*	*	*	*

```
YEAR  8     *          *          *          *          *          *          *          *
YEAR  9     *          *          *          *          *          *          *          *
YEAR 10    *          *          *          *         *          *          *          *
YEAR 11   *          *          *         *         *          *          *         *
YEAR 12  *          *          *         *          *          *          *        *
YEAR 13   *          *          *         *          *          *          *        *
YEAR 14   *          *          *         *          *          *          *        *
YEAR 15   *          *          *         *          *          *          *        *
YEAR 16   *          *          *          *          *          *          *        *
YEAR 17   *          *          *          *          *          *          *         *
YEAR 18    *          *           *          *          *          *          *         *
YEAR 19    *          *           *          *          *          *           *         *
YEAR 20     *           *           *           *          *           *           *         *
YEAR 21      *           *           *           *          *           *           *         *
YEAR 22 *          *          *          *          *          *          *          *
YEAR 23 *          *          *          *          *          *          *          *
YEAR 24 *          *          *          *          *          *          *          *
YEAR 25  *          *          *          *          *          *          *          *
YEAR 26  *          *          *          *          *          *          *          *
YEAR 27   *          *          *          *          *          *          *          *
YEAR 28   *          *          *          *          *          *          *          *
YEAR 29 *          *          *          *          *          *          *          *
YEAR 30  *          *          *          *          *          *          *          *
YEAR 31  *          *          *          *          *          *          *          *
YEAR 32   *          *          *          *          *          *          *          *
YEAR 33    *          *          *          *          *          *          *          *
YEAR 34   *          *          *          *          *          *          *          *
YEAR 35   *          *          *          *          *          *          *          *
YEAR 36   *          *          *          *          *          *          *          *
YEAR 37   *          *          *          *          *          *          *          *
YEAR 38  *          *          *          *          *          *          *          *
YEAR 39 *          *          *          *          *          *          *          *
YEAR 40  *          *          *          *          *          *          *          *
YEAR 41 *          *          *          *          *          *          *          *
YEAR 42  *          *          *          *          *          *          *          *
YEAR 43 *          *          *          *          *          *          *          *
YEAR 44 *          *          *          *          *          *          *          *
YEAR 45  *          *          *          *          *          *          *          *
YEAR 46  *          *          *          *          *          *          *          *
YEAR 47   *          *          *          *          *          *          *          *
YEAR 48   *          *          *          *          *          *          *          *
YEAR 49    *           *           *           *          *           *           *          *
YEAR 50    *          *          *          *          *          *          *          *
YEAR 51    *          *          *          *          *          *          *          *
YEAR 52 *          *          *          *          *          *          *
YEAR 53  *          *          *          *          *          *          *
YEAR 54  *          *          *          *          *          *          *
YEAR 55   *          *          *          *          *          *          *
```

```
YEAR 56        *          *          *          *          *          *          *          *
YEAR 57          *          *          *          *          *          *          *  ,       *
YEAR 58          *          *          *          *          *          *          *          *
YEAR 59         *          *          *          *          *          *          *          *
YEAR 60          *          *          *          *          *          *          *          *
```

SALT EXPORTS

	AEUNA	LOGATA	DLOKA	FALMATIK	WANDUT	DOLOMAL	WIDABUT	WILAMAN
YEAR 1	*	*	*	*	*	*	*	*
YEAR 2	*	*	*	*	*	*	*	*
YEAR 3	*	*	*	*	*	*	*	*
YEAR 4	*	*	*	*	*	*	*	*
YEAR 5	*	*	*	*	*	*	*	*
YEAR 6	*	*	*	*	*	*	*	*
YEAR 7	*	*	*	*	*	*	*	*
YEAR 8	*	*	*	*	*	*	*	*
YEAR 9	*	*	*	*	*	*	*	*
YEAR 10	*	*	*	*	*	*	*	*
YEAR 11	*	*	*	*	*	*	*	*
YEAR 12	*	*	*	*	*	*	*	*
YEAR 13	*	*	*	*	*	*	*	*
YEAR 14	*	*	*	*	*	*	*	*
YEAR 15	*	*	*	*	*	*	*	*
YEAR 16	*	*	*	*	*	*	*	*
YEAR 17	*	*	*	*	*	*	*	*
YEAR 18	*	*	*	*	*	*	*	*
YEAR 19	*	*	*	*	*	*	*	*
YEAR 20	*	*	*	*	*	*	*	*
YEAR 21	*	*	*	*	*	*	*	*
YEAR 22	*	*	*	*	*	*	*	*
YEAR 23	*	*	*	*	*	*	*	*
YEAR 24	*	*	*	*	*	*	*	*
YEAR 25	*	*	*	*	*	*	*	*
YEAR 26	*	*	*	*	*	*	*	*
YEAR 27	*	*	*	*	*	*	*	*
YEAR 28	*	*	*	*	*	*	*	*
YEAR 29	*	*	*	*	*	*	*	*
YEAR 30	*	*	*	*	*	*	*	*
YEAR 31	*	*	*	*	*	*	*	*
YEAR 32	*	*	*	*	*	*	*	*
YEAR 33	*	*	*	*	*	*	*	*
YEAR 34	*	*	*	*	*	*	*	*
YEAR 35	*	*	*	*	*	*	*	*
YEAR 36	*	*	*	*	*	*	*	*
YEAR 37	*	*	*	*	*	*	*	*
YEAR 38	*	*	*	*	*	*	*	*
YEAR 39	*	*	*	*	*	*	*	*
YEAR 40	*	*	*	*	*	*	*	*
YEAR 41	*	*	*	*	*	*	*	*
YEAR 42	*	*	*	*	*	*	*	*

YEAR 43 * * * * * * * *
YEAR 44
YEAR 45
YEAR 46
YEAR 47
YEAR 48
YEAR 49
YEAR 50
YEAR 51
YEAR 52
YEAR 53
YEAR 54
YEAR 55
YEAR 56
YEAR 57
YEAR 58
YEAR 59
YEAR 60

EXCHANGE RATIOS

	BEUNA LOGATA	LOGATA DLOKA	DLOKA FALMATIK	FALMATIK WANDUT	WANDUT DOLOMAL	DOLOMAL WIDABUT	WIDABUT WILAMAN
YEAR 1	*	*	*	*	*	*	*
YEAR 2	*	*	*	*	*	*	*
YEAR 3	*	*	*	*	*	*	*
YEAR 4	*	*	*	*	*	*	*
YEAR 5	*	*	*	*	*	*	*
YEAR 6	*	*	*	*	*	*	*
YEAR 7	*	*	*	*	*	*	*
YEAR 8	*	*	*	*	*	*	*
YEAR 9	*	*	*	*	*	*	*
YEAR10	*	*	*	*	*	*	*
YEAR11	*	*	*	*	*	*	*
YEAR12	*	*	*	*	*	*	*
YEAR13	*	*	*	*	*	*	*
YEAR14	*	*	*	*	*	*	*
YEAR15	*	*	*	*	*	*	*
YEAR16	*	*	*	*	*	*	*
YEAR17	*	*	*	*	*	*	*
YEAR18	*	*	*	*	*	*	*
YEAR19	*	*	*	*	*	*	*
YEAR20	*	*	*	*	*	*	*
YEAR21	*	*	*	*	*	*	*
YEAR22	*	*	*	*	*	*	*
YEAR23	*	*	*	*	*	*	*
YEAR24	*	*	*	*	*	*	*
YEAR25	*	*	*	*	*	*	*
YEAR26	*	*	*	*	*	*	*
YEAR27	*	*	*	*	*	*	*
YEAR28	*	*	*	*	*	*	*

251

```
YEAR29    *          *          *          *          *          *          *
YEAR30    *          *          *          *          *          *          *
YEAR31    *          *          *          *          *          *          *
YEAR32    *          *          *          *          *          *          *
YEAR33    *          *          *          *          *          *          *
YEAR34    *          *          *          *          *          *          *
YEAR35    *          *          *          *          *          *          *
YEAR36    *             *          *          *          *          *
YEAR37    *            *          *          *          *          *
YEAR38    *            *          *          *          *          *
YEAR39    *            *          *          *          *          *
YEAR40    *            *          *          *          *          *
YEAR41    *           *           *          *          *          *
YEAR42    *           *           *          *          *          *
YEAR43    *           *          *          *          *          *
YEAR44    *          *          *          *          *          *
YEAR45    *          *          *          *          *          *
YEAR46    *          *          *          *          *          *
YEAR47    *          *          *          *          *           *
YEAR48    *          *          *          *          *           *
YEAR49    *          *          *          *          *           *
YEAR50    *          *          *          *          *          *
YEAR51    *          *          *          *          *          *
YEAR52    *          *          *          *          *          *
YEAR53      *           *          *          *          *          *
YEAR54    *           *          *          *          *          *
YEAR55    *           *          *          *          *          *
YEAR56    *           *          *          *          *          *
YEAR57    *           *          *          *          *          *
YEAR58      *           *          *          *          *          *
YEAR59       *           *          *          *          *          *
YEAR60    *           *          *          *          *          *
```

```
CORE USAGE      CBJECT CODE=    8600 BYTES,ARRAY AREA=   23678 BYTES,TOTAL AREA AVAILABLE=   32768  BYTES
DIAGNOSTICS     NUMBER OF ERRORS=    0, NUMBER OF WARNINGS=    0, NUMBER OF EXTENSIONS=    0
COMPILE TIME=   0.17 SEC,EXECUTION TIME=    1.21 SEC,  WATFIV - JUL 1973 V1L4    8.02.39   WEDNESDAY   10 MAR 76

        *WATFNI
```

Achnowledgments

The algorithm was devised by Wright and the actual programming was undertaken by Zeder. We are much appreciative of the comments of R. A. Rappaport, Bennett Bronson, William Marquardt, and our colleagues at the Museum of Anthropology. We are particularly indebted to Kieth Kintigh, who revised and condensed the program for publication.

References

Heider, K. G.
   1970   *The Dugum Dani*. Chicago: Aldine.
Rappaport, R. A.
   1967   *Pigs for the ancestors*. New Haven: Yale University Press.
Renfrew, C., J. Dixon, and D. Cann
   1968   Further analysis of Near Eastern obsidians. *Proceedings of the Prehistoric Society*
          34:319–331.
Sahlins, M.
   1972   *Stone age economics*. Chicago: Aldine.
Winters, H. D.
   1968   Value systems and trade cycles of the Late Archaic in the Midwest. In *New perspec-
          tives in archaeology*, edited by S. R. Binford and L. R. Binford. Chicago: Aldine.
   1969   The Riverton culture. *Illinois State Museum Report* No. 13.

Chapter 14

THE ECOLOGICAL EVOLUTION OF CULTURE: THE STATE AS PREDATOR IN SUCCESSION THEORY

PATRICIA L. GALL AND ARTHUR A. SAXE

I. INTRODUCTION

In a recent article, "The Cultural Evolution of Civilizations," Flannery (1972) reviews and synthesizes the available explanations for cultural evolution and classifies them into two categories: those that focus on "prime movers" (single category linear causation), and those that focus on multivariant "circular" causality. Flannery aligns himself with the latter and offers some insightful argument. Although his choice of words like "circular causation" and "devolution" are unfortunate, his paper, which dovetails nicely with the ideas presented here, is a strong plea for a general theory of systemic change considering human society as "one class of living system" (Flannery 1972:409). Flannery suggests that there are universal "processes" and "mechanisms" operating in the evolution of human society and other

255

complex living systems. The mechanisms, resulting in processual change, are selected for under specific "socio-environmental stresses" (conditions), which need not be universal. The six conditions listed as possible stresses are population growth, social circumscription, irrigation, warfare, trade, and symbiosis. When they occur, they either enhance or retard the two universal processes of segregation and centralization. In Flannery's usage, evolution is synonymous with increasing complexity. "Devolution" is the opposite. This results in two sets of "mechanisms," one evolutionary, one pathological. Since one system's gain is often at the expense of another (after all, extinction is ultimate simplification), we would be hard put to label "pathology" in evolutionary history without rooting for a particular species or system from the sidelines. Therefore, in this paper we shall speak of "increasing" or "decreasing" complexity and speak of them both as evolutionary, "evolution" being defined simply as systemic organizational change (Saxe n. d.).

Flannery concludes by generating rules which, with others, may some day simulate the rise of the state. We hope this paper will contribute to the fulfillment of this goal. In particular, we shall argue for the inclusion of two additional universal evolutionary mechanisms: succession and competition in the extrasystemic context of the ecosystem.

To do this we will apply some basic notions of succession in ecological theory as developed by Margalef (1968), Pianka (1974), and others. To paraphrase Margalef, the evolution of a specific species must be understood in the context of the ecosystem and particularly as the species articulates with the general ecosystemic process of succession—"evolution follows, encased in succession's frame" (1968:81). To restate Margalef (cf. 1968:80), the subject of this present chapter might best be described as *the ecological theatre and the evolutionary play*.

Flannery is justified in striking out at " 'cultural ecologists' who place such primary emphasis on the ways that civilized people get their food" (Flannery 1972:412). After all, simple layer cake models that underlie technological determinism may be systematic but are not systemic (Saxe n.d.). On the other hand, the case is overstated when Flannery asserts that "the most striking differences between states and simpler societies lie in the realm of decision-making and hierarchical organization, rather than in matter and energy exchanges" (Flannery 1972:412). It would be a strange system, indeed, that differed from another in organization but not in matter and energy exchanges. The issue appears to be a matter of emphasis, but as both aspects seem equally important, we shall attempt to reinstate the ecosystem among the universals that set the stage for the cultural evolutionary play entitled *The Rise and Spread of the State*. In so doing we shall also place the issue of matter and energy exchanges, the focal topic of this volume, in an evolutionary perspective.

II. STRATEGY FOR THE DEVELOPMENT OF EXPLANATORY MODELS OF COMPLEX SOCIOCULTURAL SYSTEMS

A. Ecology as a Context

One of the most important questions concerns the selective advantage of state sociocultural systems over that of other agriculturally based systems. Since early pristine state formations appear in the context of agriculture, it becomes important to explore the conditions under which a more hierarchical system, containing more specialization, might emerge and prosper at the expense of less complex systems. In other words, what new variables were activated under some conditions of agriculture that would confer a survival advantage to, and therefore "select for," systems that were increasingly hierarchical and more complex? In order to do this, the state sociocultural system must be treated as a whole unit—a system—the systemic behavior of which is being selected for as a whole.

B. Succession Defined

"Succession" is a descriptive term referring to the classification of ecological systems in terms of increasing complexity over time, the final condition of which is called "maturity." A word of caution, however, needs to be introduced. Since the taxonomy is concerned with trends of increasing complexity, we should not assume that this is the only trend in nature or that it is "progressive" in nature. To do so is to fall into the unilineal value-laden "progress" trap of the nineteenth century (Harris 1968). A taxonomy focusing on simplification would look very different and perhaps have very special utility in understanding unsuccessful cases. After all, success, given competition, does not occur without failure. Nor does this taxonomy substitute for an analysis of sociocultural processes. Rather it provides a frame for assessing what is there and what changes have taken place in the relationships between the variables as it developed and why.

Odum (1963:78) describes ecological succession as a directional, predictable, and orderly process of community development proceeding through alteration of the physical environment until a maximal stable ecological community is reached. Succession is characterized over time by increased complexity in the community as measured by the number and kinds of elements present and by emergence of new feeding levels (trophic levels) that result in increased hierarchical levels of organization. At the same time, the presence of more diversity and kinds of interaction tends to mean that the spatial extent of the system is greater. The net effect of these trends is such that the overall community is more stable in spite of the fact that the individual elements of it may not be. Later succession is characterized by increased amounts of energy in the system but slower energy turnover rates, because more energy is tied up in the biomass (structures, organization, standing crop, energy, and information).

Margalef views succession

> . . . as the occupation of an area by organisms involved in an incessant process of action and reaction which in time results in changes in both the environment and the community, both undergoing continous reciprocal influence and adjustment [Margalef 1968:27].

In this context the important question for the origin and spread of state sociocultural systems becomes one of dynamic interaction, in the context of energy flows, from the environment to the sociocultural system and back again.

Ignoring, for purposes of this paper, the origins of agriculturally based systems, we may note that only 5,000 or so years separated the beginnings of the neolithic from the appearance of agriculturally based states. What variation in those relationships created by the specific feeding behavior or energy extracting behavior of agricultural sociocultural systems would give a selective advantage to the state? Let us consider the consequences of agriculture, one of the major sources of energy for archaic states, in the context of succession.

C. Simplification and Insecurity

Agriculture depends on modifying the local ecosystem in a way that turns back the clock of succession, so to speak. Localized zones are modified so as to simplify the ecological arrangements in that zone. Certain characteristics of early succession can then be exploited by a local population.

Early phases of succession have critical systemic characteristics. One of the most important of these is, of course, high energy flux, or "turnover," which in turn allows a high level of energy tapoff. Further it is characterized by a rapid turnover of population (high productive rates, short life cycle). It is this set of general characteristics that mean rapid maturation rates and, therefore, an increase in the number of potential harvests for agriculturally based sociocultural systems. But, at the same time, early succession is also characterized by low diversity of types and by low complexity of organization and, when combined with the high rates of energy flux, is less stable than later succession stages (Margalef 1968:89).

Agriculture produces a condition of high energy yields, which supply a population with an additional mechanism for subsistence. As a consequence of obtaining high yields through simplified ecosystems, however, the sociocultural system becomes more vulnerable to fluctuations brought about by independent variations in rainfall, temperature, disease, and other non-sociocultural subsystems of the environment. Absolute security, in energy procurement, for agriculturally based sociocultural systems and, indeed, all living systems is a mirage.

It would appear that, other things being equal, sociocultural systems that have a managerial–redistributive network would have a selective advantage over systems that did not. Such a network would provide a mechanism whereby the perturbations of the local agricultural system could be buffered by the flow of energy from other local production zones through various exchange mechanisms. This would minimize the effect of serious crop failures, which are basically uncontrollable, at the local community level. Managerial–redistributive networks may well arise out of nonhierarchical or less hierarchical exchange structures (cf. Earle, Chapter 12; Flannery 1972). For a developed discussion of these networks, see Dalton, Chapter 11.

D. Demographic Insecurity

The onset of agriculture is correlated with some striking changes in population structure and size. The growth in population is not a smooth function of the degree of dependence on agriculture (Hassan 1973) but is interlocked with nutrition, new epidemiologies, and other variables. Nevertheless, there appears to be a general and positive relationship between agriculture and population growth in various parts of the world. Moreover that relationship continues and intensifies with the development of states (Harris 1974).

Agriculture allows the spatial range of the local sociocultural system to be reduced and, at the same time, allows the population density to increase. Thus more people become susceptible to more intensely localized perturbations of the agricultural system. Shifts from swidden companion-cropping toward monocropping only accelerate this density related phenomenon.

Further, as Hardesty (1975:71), in his discussion of the measurement of the niche width, points out, there is a positive correlation between population growth, intensification of land use, and a reduction in the number of extractive techniques, (i.e., more specialization). Such a reduction of activities certainly reduces potential competition with other groups, but it also increases the susceptibility of the local population to environmental perturbations, which increase as the localized simplification of the ecosystem increases. Thus, one response to competition (i.e., the avoidance of competition) can increase the adaptive value of managerial hierarchy.

E. Organization and Insecurity

What agriculture reduces (subsistence reliability), sociocultural organization can increase. Increased organizational complexity (Saxe 1970:79–100;

Service 1962), that is the inclusion of more specialized subsystems within one structurally differentiated system, can provide buffering against systems perturbations. For example, Flannery (1965:1247) suggest that animals that are fed agricultural surplus in good years may be cropped during regular periodic crop failures associated with dry farming in Khuzistan.

The continuance of hunting and gathering activities and other alternate food procurement systems is widespread among both living and archaeologically known agricultural populations and constitute another series of examples of buffering against environmental perturbations.

Generally speaking, in egalitarian sociocultural systems (band, tribe), the same personnel of the same organized social groupings must schedule their activities to incorporate alternative energy sources into their procurement system. Stratified sociocultural systems, both chiefdom and state organizations, are capable of utilizing different personnel of differently organized subsystems who act as specialized units for the purposes of incorporating alternate energy sources into the system. The redistributive hierarchy reduces their risks by actual or potential subsidy. Scheduling conflicts are thus eliminated and the effect of any one resource failing is reduced. Nevertheless, these more complex systems continue to face problems of subsistence reliability.

Overall state organization indeed buffers the local population against local systems perturbations by increasing the range and scale of exchanges under the state political umbrella. Due to continuing ecological simplification, however, state organized sociocultural systems ironically increase the *localized* population's susceptability to fluctuation. The state sociocultural system is, therefore, subject to continuing basic insecurities in energy production/consumption ratios as long as the process continues. Moreover, since specialization seems to be density dependent, insecurity represents a range of problems of potentially growing dimensions as populations grow. Ultimately, the preindustrial state that does not tap stored solar energy (coal-oil) is severely limited by the total input of solar energy in any one localized area from year to year and might be expected to be susceptible to fluctuations in solar energy. Thus, there is a limit on potential complexity (standing biomass) that can be reached within a particular region without input of energy from alternative locales (Margalef 1968:30–35; Odum 1971:251).

In addition, the more complex the stratified sociocultural system the more energy must be applied above and beyond its local buffering applications. Organization maintenance itself demands more and more energy.

F. Insecurity, Adaptive Strategies, and States

Relative to nonstate sociocultural systems, the state sociocultural system displays characteristics of greater maturity in an ecological succession.

Early succession, in general, evidences fewer subsystems that are more generalized in their adaptations to the environment and to each other. The pattern of dispersal tends to involve a widespread, more uniform dispersal of individuals and species and less interaction between them. Similarly, nonstate sociocultural organization tends to involve the replication of small localized units often through a "budding off" process (Chagnon 1968:40) and to be characterized by reciprocal horizontal energy exchanges and localized generalized feeding.

As the ecosystem matures and niches multiply, the distribution of subsystems takes a pattern of "organized dispersal," (Margalef 1968:31). Specialized adaptations emerge and are located where specialized feeding patterns are favored, as Barth (1956), Leach (1964), and Sahlins (1958) have so clearly demonstrated. A diverse set of narrower specialized niches is dependent on the presence of specialized superordinate regulator subsystems, which allows energy shunts among and between various parts. Since such a stratified organization itself requires energy for its maintenance, there is, therefore, a measurable increase in scale and complexity of the whole *beyond the sum of its parts*. In this context, "social stratification" implies superordinate interlocal networks linking specialized local units. To paraphrase Wright (n.d.), the state is defined as a sociocultural system in which there is specialized subsystem decision making that regulates varying exchanges between and among other subsystems and with other systems. Such a definition can be placed in the context of succession theory. Although Wright is defining an administrative bureaucracy (rather than the class stratified sociotype we call a state;, it implies, at a minimum, several trophic levels (feeding levels) and that the subsystems at the primary level of energy procurement tend to be diverse in niche and specialized.

The larger the number, more diverse and specialized the various subsystems, the more energy that must be tapped and stored by the superordinate system to be put into the exchange net. This is so for two reasons. The more specialized a part the more likely it is to experience failure given environmental perturbations noted above. Thus, more and more effective energy reserves must be available for buffering perturbations as needed by the parts of the system. The net effect of all this is that channels of exchange must increase in complexity and capacity to handle both the increased load and the number of pathways. As H. T. Odum has suggested, the loss of efficiency that comes with increased number of units in an organization (Parkinson's Law) may be the "natural cost of organizing for the accomplishment of work that cannot be done by individual parts . . . as a power tax in other words" (1971:213).

He continues,

To survive and maintain a competitive position, a system must draw the maximum power budget possible in a situation and process this budget in works that reinforce future survival and stability . . . As the number of compartments (populations, individuals, social groups, etc.) is increased, the number of possible pathways rises very rapidly . . . [Odum 1971:214].

The implication is clear. An arithmetic increase in size demands some kind of geometric increase in organizational energy requirements (i.e., organizational energy increases faster than the number of parts). How much will probably vary with the empirical situation.

These types of observations are summed up in succession theory under the name "standing crop" or "biomass," which is also related to complexity. As noted previously, in climax ecosystems the amount of energy incorporated, while quantitatively greater, is proportionally less available for exchanges. More of the energy is in storage in structure. In a tropical rainforest, for example, considerable energy is stored in the woody parts of slow growing trees. In this case of states, we may point to monumental architecture, "luxury" goods, permanent buildings, bureaucrats, and the exchange channels themselves as examples.

Thus, the movement toward increasing overall systemic complexity that buffers environmentally induced instability not only demands more specialization in its sources of energy, it also demands increases in number and amplitude of the pathways of the exchange networks and the hierarchical control mechanisms. Where there is a proliferation of parts and a limited energy budget so that not every part can connect with every other, hierarchical organization ("constrained randomness") is inevitable—if one is to stay within a finite energy budget.

Another structural demand for energy that results in increased "standing crop" is the extra buffering accorded the more crucial subsystems, particularly those in the managerial hierarchy.

Specialized primary energy and specialized "service" units close to the center (both geographically and strategically) will tend to be buffered more than units at the periphery so that they will be less unstable. A case in point would be the expansion of the middle class–working class as a buffered unit in the industrialized sector of a world economy at the "expense" (given finite energy supplies) of the same type of units elsewhere in the nonindustrialized world. In archaic states, the increasing ineffectiveness of state interaction with the periphery may represent a similar case of selective buffering either by decision or circumstance (Smith 1960:80–124).

Furthermore, as the hierarchy becomes more critical to the survival of the whole, then it too must be increasingly buffered. More energy is tapped off, leading to the observation that more of what goes up stays there (Earle, Chapter 12) at least until such time, if ever, as stress calls it out of storage. Thus, imbalanced redistribution and monopoly of force are two sides of the same coin in the development of the state (Saxe n.d.)

As we have already suggested, all this is supported by the increased specialization of localized units, which reverses the direction of succession in localized regions. The buffered "mature" core and the simplified producer subsystem are therefore two necessary parts of the same complex sociocultural system.

> . . . if there is a strong exploitation of the less mature subsystem by the more mature one, the line [of succession in the less mature subsystem] may not necessarily move. This is because the excess production, which the less mature ecosystem could use to increase its own maturity, is being transmitted to the other subsystem. Thus, the less mature subsystem is kept in a steady state of low maturity by the exploitation to which it is subjected [Margalef 1968:38; clarification added].

It is for this reason that colonies cannot be understood apart from their relation to the colonizer, since they are etically one sociocultural system. The relationship between intensive monocropping and poverty and population, in the colonial context, has already been noted. The "agricultural involution" of the Javanese plains is a case in point (Geertz 1963). Today, in Java, the limits of tolerable variation are being approached. Recent studies of the area indicate declining stature as well as the increased use of "famine" crops (root crops). Such crops have a high bulk yield but are low in nutrition and are being used more and more in the diet.

The incorporation of tribal sociocultural units into the internal structure of a state leads to decreased nutritional intake, restriction of available resources, and a reorganization of social units. The Temuan, a case in point, are moving from an egalitarian to a ranked system and some are adopting intensive agriculture. The aboriginal system, as it is destroyed, is reassembled as part of the Malaysian state. Systemic change is not simply additive, it is replacive (Gall 1976).

The first adaptive strategy of state systems, then, is to increase complexity, that is, to continue to diversify structurally, each part increasingly specialized to exploiting different sources of available energy or to administering, transforming, and/or transporting this energy among the parts.

The second set of adaptive strategies is implicit in our discussion of colonial incorporation. It involves a spatial expansion to the limits of the particular ecological zone(s) in which the dominant specializations can be practiced (i.e., the niches from which the largest energy returns can be drawn) (e.g., Lattimore 1940; Barth 1956). This expansionary trend may involve competition with other sociocultural systems if they are drawing on the same source of energy (Odum 1971:208).

One outcome of this competition may be to incorporate a competitor/prey within the state. Incorporation usually involves some structural simplification and reorganization of the prey as a functionally specialized and dependent part of the predator (Gall 1976). The territorial basis for monopoly of force (defining attributes of "states") and the fact that many states exhibit ethnic diversity (in contrast to most nonstates) reflect this fact.

Both states and nonstates are capable of mutualism and parasitism through trade and raid, or displacement of other groups as a result of competition. Only states are capable of incorporating and reorganizing large amounts of highly organized energy into their metabolism by means of predatory incorporation of other sociocultural systems. Sahlins (1961) characterizes the expansion of an egalitarian tribe into new territory as predation. Competition resulting in displacement of other ethnic groups is not predation in an ecological context. In the context of cultural evolution, the appearance of states is the analog of the appearance of heterotropes (carnivores) in biological evolution. It is probably this great negentropic ability that underlies the rapid spread of state organization in the world since their appearance some short 5,000 years ago.

Competition exists, as stated, when two systems draw on the same finite energy sources. Other things being equal, if allowed to go to saturation and if the systems do not readapt to avoid or lessen the competition, one system will eventually replace the other. This observation has been referred to as "competitive exclusion" (cf. Pianka 1974:141). Complete competitive exclusion is rare in nature. What determines the toleration limits of ecological overlap and the dynamics of the interactions must be determined for different sets of systemic interactions.

In general, when otherwise equivalent sociocultural systems are related as competitors, those systems that are able to incorporate more diverse kinds of energy sources (i.e., are capable of more effective feeding behavior) will expand at the expense of the less effective feeder. Generally speaking, the more complex the sociocultural system, the more generalized its overall feeding behavior, even while it exhibits many intensive local specializations. Sahlins (1958) found this was also true for Polynesian chiefdom organizations, although he lacked a mechanism, such as we are proposing, for explaining why.

The degree of specialization or generalization of one system is always relative to that of another system. It is a comparative judgment on an ordinal scale. It is determined by the number of available energy sources being utilized.

Even if a system is structurally capable of utilizing more sources of energy but it feeds on fewer sources than another system, we still say it is "more specialized" or "less generalized." The determinants of actual feeding behavior are often to be found in the extrasystemic environment (the community) of which the system in focus is a part. This is true of biological systems (Pianka 1974:209 and *passim*) as well as sociocultural systems (Saxe n.d.). These observations underlie the conclusion that evolution, through natural selection, is community controlled.

As stated, more complex sociocultural systems tend to be more generalized in their overall feeding behavior by virtue of their particular feeding specializations. This gives them a versatility when intersystem competition occurs. They can better exploit new energy sources, but also the complex sociocultural systems persevere because success in the long run goes to the specialist who can harness the greatest number of kilocalories. This is the juncture between cultural energetics and Service's "law of evolutionary potential" (Sahlins and Service 1960:93–121). Generalists tend toward specialists as they become dominants. They remain dominant until new energy sources appear or the old disappear.

Thus, the second adaptive strategy of states, spatial expansion, given intersystem competition, is most successfully accomplished by those systems that can put most energy resources into the zone of direct competition, develop specialized energy extraction techniques, and/or actively exclude the competitor so as to harness the greatest amount of energy. Other things being equal, then, the more complex sociocultural system tends to have an advantage over the simpler system and the state form over the nonstate form. In fact, increased organizational complexity in evolution may be seen as part of the adaptive strategies of populations in communities. Or, to vary the image, the emergence of increased organizational complexity may be seen as the result of natural selection.

G. Exchange, Buffering, and Cultural Evolution

The notion that sociocultrual systems must be seen as adaptive units has shown great utility in providing insights into understanding *why* systems are the way they are (Alkire 1965; Gall 1976; Neitschmann 1973; Rappaport 1968). Exchange systems linking units within a sociocultural system, but also linking them with units outside the system, become very important foci of attention when the role of energy exchange in succession and competition is considered. This context places questions of exchange systems in an evolutionary framework and thus part of the answer to the question, Why?

Alkire (1965) and Piddocke (1965) suggests that trade, on Lamotrek Atoll and the Northwest Coast respectively, functions as a buffer against unpredictable events in the localized ecosystems (Hardesty 1975). In the former case, it is typhoon activity, while in the latter, it is irregular anadromous fish migrations. Malinowski's kula trade not only makes utilitarian exchange more sociable but maintains ties that can be used to buffer local perturbations (Uberoi 1962). The "big-man" systems of Melanesia, which have been characterized as being transitional between egalitarian and ranked systems, provide buffers against perturbations. The yams that normally rot are survival food when the crops fail. Dalton (Chapter 11) notes such buffering action in his extended functional analysis of interlocal group exchange.

Any system has, as a consequence of its organization, a range of tolerance in the behavior of its variables. These are often the limits of its dynamic equilibrium. Since all systems are insecure with regard to some of their structural characteristics in relationship to environmental perturbation, once the parameters are exceeded the system must adapt or dissolve. The study of such structural insecurities, both at a universal and at the specific case study level, is critical. It is at the nexus of insecurity that natural selection is operative.

III. CONCLUSION

Classification (taxonomy) is a useful activity in the development of any science. We want to know what is there and in what forms. What we find has to be explained, however, and there are two steps or questions to be answered here. The first type of explanation answers the question of *how* the system works. What are the parts; how are they related? These questions and their answers together constitute what has been labeled as "functionalism" in social science or "physiology" in biology. The second set of explanations answers the question of *why* the system is the way it is. What accounts for its appearance and operation? These questions and their answers together constitute what has been labeled as evolutionism. It has been argued at length elsewhere that extrasystemic relations are always paramount in explaining systemic change (evolution) and therefore also stability (Saxe n.d.). Although functionalism and evolutionism are not mutually exclusive approaches, they are different. Evolutionary answers do presuppose answers to the functionalist questions, but not vice versa.

The understanding of exchange relations in different systems, the building of taxonomies, the understanding of systemic organizations, etc., are all vitally important forms of functional knowledge. If, however, we want to understand the evolution of these systems, we have to utilize a different strategy of theory building, one that utilizes functionalist knowledge but places it in an extrasystemic evoluntionary framework, so that we may grasp the larger processes that produced the systems we see operating. Some of these processes will be universal; some will be situation specific (cf. Flannery 1972:414).

A search for a general theory of evolution will concentrate on *exchanges* in matter and energy both intra- and intersystem. Because such exchanges are universal to all living systems, the properties of the exchanges offer a comparative basis to studies of both cultural and biological phenomena (Odum 1971:209). Necessary to an approach based on exchange interactions is the concept of the ecosystem, because, as Margalef emphasizes, "selection is controlled by the cybernetic mechanism at the level of the ecosystem" (1968:93). When we understand the processes universal to living systems, the particular socioenvironmental stresses that select for specific systems, such as the state, will be amenable to testing and prediction. Culture, notes the late Leslie White (1949), is man's extrasomatic means of adaptation.

Acknowledgments

We would like to acknowledge the encouragement of Lewis R. Binford and his senior graduate seminar at the University of New Mexico. We thank Susan Loughridge for her support and efforts on our behalf.

In spring, 1975, after presenting this paper in Dallas, Texas, we were happily surprised to find that John S. Athens (1975), a graduate student at the University of New Mexico, had independently arrived at a similar thesis.

References

Alkire, W. H.
1965   Lamotrek atoll and inter-island socio-economic ties. *Studies in anthropology.* Urbana, Illinois: University of Illinois Press.

Athens, J. S.
1975   Theory building and the study of evolutionary processes in complex societies. Mimeo. University of New Mexico.

Barth, F.
1956   Ecologic relationships of ethnic groups in Swat, North Pakistan. *American Anthropologist* **58**:1079–1086.

Chagnon, N. A.
1968   *Yanomamö: the fierce people.* New York: Holt.

Erlick, P. R.
1970   *Population, resources and environment.* New York: Freeman.

Flannery, K. V.
1965   The ecology of early food production in Mesopotamia. *Science* **147**:1247–1256.
1972   The cultural evolution of civilizations. *Annual of Ecology and Systematics* **3**:399–426.

Gall, P. L.
1976   Temuan socio-economic change: an ecological model. In *Anthropology of Southeast Asia Symposium,* edited by W. Wood. 1975 Annual Meeting, Mid West Conference of Asianists (in press).

Geertz, C.
1963   *Agricultural involution.* Berkeley: University of California Press.

Hardesty, D. L.
1975   The niche concept: suggestions for its use in human ecology. *Human Ecology* **3**:71–85.

Harris, M.
1968   *The rise of anthropological theory.* New York: Crowell.
1974   *Culture, people and nature.* New York: Crowell.

Hassan, F. A.
1973   On the mechanics of population growth during the Neolithic. *Current Anthropology* **14**.

Lattimore, O.
1940   *Inner Asian frontiers of China.* Boston: Beacon Press.

Leach, E. R.
1964   *Political systems of highland Burma.* London: Bell and Sons.

Margalef, R.
1968   *Perspectives in ecological theory.* Chicago: University of Chicago Press.

Nietschmann, B.
1973   *Between land and water.* New York: Academic Press.

Odum, E. P.
1959   *Fundamentals of ecology.* New York: Saunders.
1963   *Ecology.* New York: Holt.

Odum, H. T.

1971   *Environment, power and society.* New York: Wiley Interscience.

Pianka, E. R.

1974   *Evolutionary ecology.* New York: Harper and Row.

Piddocke, S.

1965   The potlatch system of the southern Kwakiutl: a new perspective. *Southwestern Journal of Anthropology* 21:244–246.

Rappaport, R.

1968   *Pigs for the ancestors.* New Haven: Yale University Press.

Sahlins, M. D.

1958   *Social stratification in Polynesia.* Seattle: University of Washington Press.

1961   The segmentary lineage: an organization of predatory expansion. *American Anthropologist* **63:**322–345.

Sahlins, M. D., and E. Service.

1960   *Evolution and culture.* Ann Arbor, Michigan: University of Michigan Press.

Saxe, A. A.

1970   Social dimensions of mortuary practices. Ann Arbor, Michigan: University Microfilms.

n.d.   On the origin of evolutionary processes: state formation in the Sandwich Islands, a systematic approach. In *Explanation of prehistoric organizational change,* edited by J. Hill (in preparation).

Service, E. R.

1962   *Primitive social organization.* New York: Random House.

Smith, M. G.

1960   *Government in Zazzau, 1800–1950.* London: Oxford University Press.

Uberoi, J. P. S.

1962   *Politics of the kula ring.* Manchester: University Press.

White, L. A.

1949   Energy and the evolution of culture. In *The science of culture.* New York: Grove Press.

Wright, H. T.

n.d.   Toward an explanation of the origin of the state. In *Explanation of prehistoric organizational change,* edited by J. Hill (in preparation).

Yengoyan, A. A.

1974   Deomographic aspects of poverty in the rural Phillippines. *Comparative Studies on Society and History* **16.**

INDEX